The
DILEMMA
of the
DEANSHIP

The

DILEMMA

Edited by

DANIEL E. GRIFFITHS

Dean, School of Education, Health,
* Nursing, and Arts Professions*
New York University

and

DONALD J. McCARTY

Professor of Educational Administration
School of Education
University of Wisconsin–Madison

of the

DEANSHIP

THE INTERSTATE
Printers & Publishers, Inc.

Danville, Illinois

Library of Congress Catalog Card No. 78-61237

ISBN 0-8134-2041-5

Foreword

While those who administer higher education are represented by a literature whose chief characteristic is poverty, the least among the poorest is the deanship. There has been so little theoretical, conceptual, or research literature published on the deanship as to constitute an embarrassment to both the practitioners and scholars of higher education. This book is an effort to lay the base for research and theoretical work which, in turn, will lead to a body of knowledge on which the deanship can rest. Culbertson, in the first chapter, details the steps which led, in January 1976, to a seminar sponsored by the School of Education, Health, Nursing, and the Arts Professions at New York University, where the seminar was held, and the University Council for Educational Administration. This book is a product of that seminar, at which most of the chapters were presented and critiqued. In order to cover the deanship more adequately than was possible at the seminar, additional papers were written by Doris W. Ryan, David D. Dill, and Joseph B. Giacquinta, and a final chapter was prepared by the co-editors.

There are always many people who labor to bring this type of a book to fruition, and in attempting to mention them some are inadvertently omitted. With apologies to those individuals, the authors would single out Jack Culbertson, the executive director of the University of Educational Administration, who encouraged and participated in the project from the beginning. The idea for the research program was conceived and developed by Paula Silver while she was an associate of UCEA, and it was through her enthusiasm and perseverance that the research design was developed, which subsequently formed the basis for the seminar and the book. Dean Arnold Spinner of New York University was largely responsible for planning and organizing the seminar. Rebecca Spicer deserves special mention for the art work for the figures in Chapters 1, 3, 7, and 11 and for managing

v

the flow of chapters from authors to editors to publishers, and the many other important elements of book publishing. All-in-all, this book represents the efforts of many dedicated people, and thanks are extended to all of them.

DANIEL E. GRIFFITHS
DONALD J. McCARTY

Contents

Part I

CHAPTER 1

Programmatic Research
on the Deanship:
Rationale and Strategy[1]

by

JACK CULBERTSON
University Council for Educational Administration

UCEA's plan for stimulating research on the deanship in higher education cannot be fully understood without some attention to history. One important and relatively recent event was UCEA's decision to broaden the meaning of "administration," as used in its mission statement, to encompass higher education as well as K-12 systems. This decision, which was made after considerable study and debate, was based upon two important assumptions, among others: first, leadership study and administrator preparation in higher education are sufficiently institutionalized to ensure their continued growth, development, and improvement; second, UCEA, given its experience and interests and the wide range of talent which comprise its networks, can contribute to the growth and development of administrator study and leadership preparation in higher education.

Another factor affecting UCEA's decision was the concern among professors about the rapid increase in the number of programs to prepare higher education leaders during the last decade at the same time that the growth in basic knowledge to undergird these programs has been very limited. Thus, Dressel and Mayhew, among others, have concluded that one of the major weaknesses in preparatory pro-

grams is the limited content currently available.[2] That this weakness
is recognized more generally is suggested by the fact that the creation
of new knowledge of higher education was assigned the highest priority among 12 developmental objectives by professors of higher education responding to a UCEA survey.[3] The papers in this volume represent one UCEA initiative directed at a widely perceived need.

Among the first activities initiated, following the UCEA decision
to expand its mission to encompass higher education administration,
was the convening of a task force of 11 deans of schools of education[4]
from differing UCEA institutions.[5] This meeting was stimulated in
part through informal communication with deans and in part by the
recognition that the UCEA central unit has its most direct links into
higher education administration through schools of education. There
were other more specific reasons for establishing links with leaders in
schools of education including the following:

1. The leadership and management of these schools constitute a
   very important part of the larger complex of educational leadership and administration in institutions of higher education.
2. Schools of education, as compared to medicine, law, and
   other professional schools, have been especially hard hit by
   declining enrollments.
3. Schools of education, as a general rule, are linked more integrally with both undergraduate and graduate education than
   are other professional schools.
4. Schools of education often have the largest student bodies of
   all the professional schools in institutions of higher education.

The generalizations just stated highlight the significance of
schools of education in the larger enterprise of higher education. It
was fitting, then, that at the first meeting of the task force, leadership
challenges before colleges of education and the need for new professional development opportunities for deans were the major topics discussed. A second meeting addressed the need for research on the
deanship, the significance of new research for professional development activities, and targets of research that might be addressed
through UCEA. Following the second meeting, Griffiths, Cyphert,
Gross, McCarty, Monahan, and other deans, along with Silver, formerly a director of the UCEA central staff, gave further attention to
research issues. From the various discussions there evolved the idea
that UCEA should seek to stimulate and facilitate a range of research

on the deanship. From this goal came the more specific idea of launching the effort through a research development seminar which was hosted by New York University. Such a seminar, it was concluded, would provide an initial opportunity to launch a stimulative research effort through UCEA which, if effective, would continue through this decade and into the next. An important underlying assumption was that programmatic and cumulative research could be stimulated and produced through UCEA using modes of inter-institutional cooperation and communication. A major purpose shaping this book, then, is the establishment of a base for a research program on the deanship in higher education.

RATIONALE FOR THE RESEARCH PROGRAM

A second influence shaping the conference and the projected research program to follow is more complex and abstract. It is based largely upon the work of Kuhn[6] and consists of concepts and generalizations about the growth and development of disciplines and fields of study generally. Since the concepts and generalizations inherent in the framework seek to pinpoint critical stages in the growth and development of fields of study, it can be used to analyze the capacities of the field of higher education administration to produce and use knowledge. Out of such analysis can come useful clues about how further development can be achieved and how research programs, such as the one projected in this volume, can facilitate development.

Simply stated, a field of study moves in its development, according to Kuhn, from a pre-paradigm to a paradigm state. This development typically is a very long and arduous one. After a discipline reaches a paradigm state, it can again undergo substantial change through paradigm shattering research and then enter a post-paradigm state. For a period of time in the post-paradigm state, the field may take on some, but not all, of the characteristics of the original pre-paradigm state. After an extended period of uncertainty and search a new paradigm can be achieved.

Kuhn's generalizations are derived from studies of the growth and development of more advanced scientific fields, particularly the physical sciences.[7] Even though professional fields are different from scientific disciplines, a case can be made that Kuhn's concepts and generalizations can fruitfully be used to examine inquiry in higher education. Thus, the heuristic value of the framework for analyzing knowledge production in higher education will be illustrated in this chapter. I should like to make clear at the outset, however, that the focus will not be upon tacit or clinical knowledge which is found in every professional field. Rather, attention will be directed to formally tested or "scientific" knowledge.[8]

In the Kuhnian framework, the concept of paradigm is central. For the purposes of this paper the following question is critical: What are the key indicators of paradigm achievement in a field? Kuhn has identified three important arenas in which indicators can be found: the scientific or scholarly community, the disciplinary matrix of a field, and shared scientific examples. Given these arenas, I shall now perform three tasks: define in more specific terms indicators of paradigm achievement and, by implication, indicators of pre-paradigm status; illustrate some applications of the indicators to higher education as a field of study; and suggest developmental objectives for advancing the study of higher education within the specific context of the deanship.

Although courses on higher education were initiated in the last century,[9] the study of higher education management and leadership in a more specialized sense had its origins in the 1950s.[10] It is understandable, then, that the field of higher education leadership and management, like educational leadership and management more generally, is in a pre-paradigm state. Before elaborating this thesis further, it will be necessary to clarify Kuhn's criteria with regard to "paradigm" state.

The first arena to study for indicators of paradigm achievement, as already noted, is within the scholarly community. In Kuhn's words,[11] "A paradigm governs, in the first instance, not a subject matter but a group of practitioners. Any study of paradigm-directed or paradigm-shattering research must begin by locating the responsible group or groups." Specific indicators of paradigm status within the scholarly community would be absorption by the community of the same technical literature, similar education and professional initiation, a cohesiveness that promotes relatively full communication and relatively unanimous professional judgments on scientific matters, and a shared set of goals, including the training of the community's successors.[12]

Difference rather than similarity and fragmentation rather than cohesion characterize higher education as a field of study. While one would expect greater differences in a professional field than in an academic discipline, given the former's commitment to social service ideas, diversity is a special feature of the higher education professoriate. I want to illustrate the point in only one area and then identify a few implications bearing upon knowledge production in the field.

The area chosen for discussion is the organizational units in which professors engaged in higher study and preparation reside. These units themselves are quite diverse. In some universities professors are located in centers of higher education; in others, departments of higher education; and, in still others, departments of educational administration. In some universities there is no formal organization in the sense that professors, who are usually few in number, are not affiliated with a unit having a higher education or administration label. Clearly, the differences in the units and the assumptions underlying their establishment and functioning make for special diversity in the higher education professoriate. Certain propositions bearing upon research production and types of organizational units can illuminate further the implications of diversity.

1. Professors of higher education located in centers and departments of higher education believe more strongly than those in departments of educational administration that higher education administration, as a field of study, has unique characteristics which distinctly separate it from K-12 administration. The case for establishing special centers or departments, in other words, must be made on the basis of distinctiveness, and their functioning reinforces distinctiveness.

2. Professors concerned with higher education leadership in departments of educational administration, with greater frequency than those in centers and departments of higher education administration, define specialized content more in terms of the administration *qua* administration literature and less in terms of the general and wide-ranging literature on higher education. There are, in other words, greater tendencies in departments of education administration for professors of higher education to integrate their work with general administration since they work directly with professors in this area. Typically, the staffs in these departments are also smaller than those in centers and departments of higher education, and they have greater difficulty achieving specialized knowledge in the various areas of study related to higher education.

3. Graduate students studying higher education in departments of educational administration are more likely to experience core courses with students studying K-12 administration than are

graduate students in centers or departments of higher education. Curriculum planning and course development for these two classes of students are likely, in other words, to achieve more integration in departments of educati nal administration.

4. Professors of higher education in centers of higher education are more strongly committed to the performance of research than are professors located in other organizational units. In addition, centers of higher education generally have a greater proportion of professors with advanced training in social science disciplines, and these professors make greater use of concepts and modes of inquiry from these disciplines than do professors in other units.

Other clues about diversity in the higher education community could be identified by analyzing differences within organizational units. For example, in the same units, in many institutions, there are professors of community college administration, professors focusing on four-year institutions, professors who are practicing administrators of higher education, and professors without higher education administration experience. Suffice it to say, at this point, that there is great diversity of perspective about research in the higher education professoriate.

Diverse groups of professors and their attend: it differences in perspective make for "Incommensurable ways of viewing the world," to use a phrase from Kuhn. This incommensurability stems primarily from differing definitions of leadership and administration. Some believe that higher education administration and leadership as a field of study is a sub-specialty in the higher education field while others equate it with the general study of higher education. Some see the study of higher education administration as closely related to the study of administration in other organizations while others see it as a relatively distinctive effort. From the differences in definitions flow other differences affecting research. Immediate results are difficulties in achieving full communication, marked differences in professional judgments, varied definitions of relevant literature, and variation in the design and content of training programs. The field exhibits, in other words, indicators of a pre-paradigm state of development.

A second arena for indicators of a paradigmatic state is the disciplinary matrix which guides inquiry in a field.[13] Kuhn chose the term *disciplinary matrix* rather than the concept of theory as a general indicator because he considered the latter to be more limiting for his pur-

poses and more subject to confusion in meaning. He sees a "disciplinary matrix" as made up of several components which serve as
criteria or indicators of a paradigmatic state. These criteria or indicators are reflected in the following questions:

First, does a field possess "symbolic generalizations" which
function "in part as laws but also as definitions for a field"? Second,
does the scientific community share a belief in particular models, including relatively heuristic ones, which provide it "preferred or per-
missible analogies and metaphors"? Finally, is there widespread
commitment in a field to the scientific values needed to assess the
adequacy of theories as well as values needed to evaluate predictions?

In using the concept of a disciplinary matrix to think about higher
education management and leadership as a field of study, one recognizes that such a matrix and its sub-components are not in use. Francis and Hobbs,[14] for example, have presented data in support of the
view that professors in the higher education community are generally
isolated from such disciplines as economics and sociology in which
some matrix components are present. They reported a study which
identified 92 articles on higher education appearing in such
discipline-based journals as the *American Economic Review* and the
American Political Science Review during the 1965-69 period. These
authors also studied articles appearing in the *Educational Record,* the
Journal of Higher Education, and *Change* magazine for the 1969-71
period and found that no reference was made to any of the
discipline-based articles on higher education. From such data Francis
and Hobbs concluded that professors of higher education are cut off
from disciplines. They argued, further, that this state of affairs is
clearly preferred by many professors, including leaders in the field.
They quoted Mayhew, a leading higher education scholar, concerning
his comments on the work of a young scholar as follows:[15] "If (he)
will move from his present firm grounding in theory and some kinds
of data to a firmer grounding in clinical experience and broader ranges
of data, he should become a first-rate scholar." They took issue with
Mayhew's position as follows:[16] "On the contrary, in our view that
emphasis is precisely what will stultify both that young scholar and
higher education as a field of study." In this interchange is reflected
not only a difference in view but also a basic question in the field
about the role of theory and the use of discipline-based approaches to
research.[17]

A study of the content presented in the proceedings of annual
meetings of the Association of Higher Education would provide addi-

tional evidence on the accuracy of the Francis and Hobbs view about the isolation of higher educationists as would a study of textual materials written by higher education professors and leaders. Scholars of higher education and higher management, in other words, are currently much more oriented toward the thoughtful analyses of problems and issues than toward scientific approaches. There is value to this type of scholarship in a professional field. However, a concentration on this type of scholarship, to the exclusion of basic inquiry, does not make for the cumulative research necessary for a field to move toward a paradigm state.

Values for judging prediction and theory, another part of the "disciplinary matrix" used by Kuhn, are perhaps less operational in higher education than laws and models, an understandable situation, for how can values be used for judging theories if the idea of theory does not have widespread acceptance in the field and if it is not used to guide research? Before the values central to scientific study can be applied, there must be pertinent conceptualizations and research to which to apply them.

Based upon the brief analysis undertaken here, we can conclude that in higher education, including higher education management and leadership, there is very limited use of laws, models, and scientific values. There is also evidence that the perceived values of these elements of a disciplinary matrix are not widely accepted within the higher education professoriate.

The third indicator of paradigm status is whether or not there are shared scientific examples within a field, which Kuhn defined as "Concrete problem solutions that students encounter from the start of their scientific education." As Kuhn says:[18]

> Viewed as solutions to scientific puzzles, shared examples are learned by doing science rather than by acquiring rules for doing it. Through experiences with problem-solving, the laws and theories students learn take on empirical meaning.

Since shared examples in the form of solutions to scientific problems are possible only after a community of scholars has developed shared components of a disciplinary matrix and has typically used these components intensively, it follows again that the field of higher education study, like other fields in education, has not reached this stage. The attainment of "shared examples" is the most difficult test of paradigm achievement and of theories used in such achievement. Consequently, this component constitutes the final hurdle for a field of study as it moves from a pre-paradigm to a paradigm stage of development. Much groundwork, including intensive and extensive research, must be achieved before shared examples can be realized.

In sum, then, higher education management and leadership is a relatively young field of study. Even though considerable progress has been achieved in a relatively short time, like other fields in education, it is in a pre-paradigm stage of development. Those pursuing studies in the field are very diverse individuals, and their differing organizational units in universities reinforce and promote diversity. Shared commitments to the use of disciplinary-based concepts and modes of inquiry and to theory-oriented research are limited. Shared examples reflecting concrete solutions to scientific problems are lacking. Consequently, there is a lack of cumulative research effort in the field and much diversity in communication perspectives.

As noted earlier, by applying Kuhn's concepts to the higher education field, clues about desirable future directions can be identified. Based upon an acceptance of Kuhn's concepts and the brief analyses undertaken, certain long-range outcomes judged desirable for higher education as a field of study can be projected, among which are the following:

1. A greater consensus in the professoriate on what the parameters are of higher education and higher education management and leadership as fields of study.
2. National structures of communication which provide opportunities for exchange across differing groups.[19]
3. Greater use of concepts and modes of inquiry from social science disciplines.
4. A reduction over time in the diversity of research perspectives in the higher education professoriate.
5. Acceptance among scholars of the importance of scientific generalizations, models, and values.
6. More theory-based research which moves in the direction of "shared examples."

Now that some introductory generalizations about the current state of higher education as a field of study have been set forth and some desirable longer-range developmental outcomes have been articulated, the framework used in planning the content for this volume can be elaborated.

THE GOALS AND STRATEGY OF THE RESEARCH PROGRAM

The six long-range outcomes enumerated above might be regarded as the guiding objectives toward which a program of research
should be directed. They do not offer much guidance, however, for
decisions about how such a research program might be structured and
organized. During initial discussions, those concerned with designing
the projected research program considered several alternative organizing frameworks, including: a research problem approach, in
which significant research questions would be identified in advance as
bases for research programs; a discipline approach, in which each
academic discipline would represent a program of research; a
methodology approach, in which such data-gathering methods as case
studies, observations, surveys, experiments, and taxonomy-based instruments would each yield programs of research; and a practical
problem approach, in which key issues would serve as bases for research programs. Since there were some apparent problems associated with each of those approaches, especially in relation to the
desired long-range outcomes, it was decided that the program design
should be as comprehensive and flexible as possible; that is, it should
potentially encompass a wide range of research interests and
methodologies relevant to the deanship in higher education.

Such a plan was conceptualized as a series of "domains of inquiry" differentiated from each other by the degree of globalness of
perspective each domain represents. The range of perspectives is dia-
grammed in Figure 1.1, which can be explained as follows: The inter-
connected circles represent different units of analysis, different foci of
attention, or different domains of inquiry and include individuals, the
individual-organization interface, organizations as such, and the
organization-environment interface. Both the "Baseline Data" and
the "Organizational Change" domains are intended to be cross-
sections of the other domains, since they might encompass several or
all of the other perspectives.

The six domains, which are based upon ideas elaborated at the
second task force meeting of deans and upon other sources, may be
briefly illustrated as follows:[20]

1. *Baseline Data About the Deanship*—who deans are; their
   background, professional experiences, and career patterns;
   the settings in which they work; some key differences between
   schools of education and other professional schools (i.e., basic
   survey research).

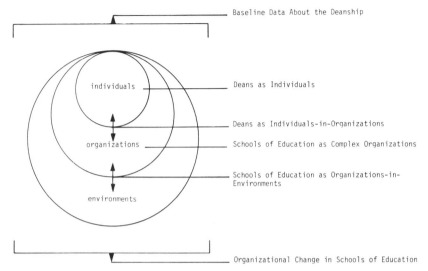

Figure 1.1. Conceptual framework for the research program: the domain structure.

2. *Deans as Individuals*—personality characteristics, including personality profiles, needs, value orientations, motivations, and conceptual styles of deans; their personal histories; others' perceptions of their personalities (i.e., research based on psychological frameworks).

3. *Deans as Individuals-in-Organizations*—the role of the dean, including what deans do and are expected to do, their role orientations; leader behavior; small group interaction patterns (i.e., task and function analyses; research based on role, leadership, and small-group frameworks).

4. *Colleges of Education as Complex Organizations*—structural characteristics of colleges of education, including governance and decision-making structures, communication patterns, and organizational complexity; bureaucratization, policy implementation (i.e., research based on organization, communication, and decision frameworks).

5. *Colleges of Education as Organizations-in-Environments*—typologies of environments; the organizational suprastructure; policy and policy making; boundary-spanning mechanisms; system openness/closedness; influential external groups; social forces (i.e., research based upon organization-environment transaction frameworks).

6. *Organizational Change and the Deanship*—diffusion of innovations in higher education; research, development, and diffusion structures in higher education; the dean as change agent;
strategies and tactics for change; planning mechanisms; the
implementation of innovations within colleges (i.e., research
based upon organization change frameworks).

Figure 1.2 summarizes in another way the various domains for
study. Among the observations which can be made about the domains
in order to clarify further desired outcomes of the projected programs
of research are the following:

Figure 1.2. Domain descriptors.

The emergent program is directed immediately toward deans of
schools of education in the United States and Canada. However, it is
hoped that research activities, over the long range, can be extended to
include deans of business, medical, law, nursing, and other schools. It
is assumed that methods and concepts developed for the study of one
deanship can be efficiently adapted for use in others and that comparative studies will be illuminating.

The projections clearly reflect a visible emphasis upon theory-
oriented research. An underlying assumption is that work to stimulate
theory-oriented research can, if successful, have longer-range impact
on the study of higher education that transcends given problems and
time periods. As such work accumulates, the long journey from pre-
paradigm to paradigm status can begin.

At the same time another operating assumption is that non-theory-based research will be required in the projected-research program. The domain concerned with baseline data, especially, will feature inductive research approaches. Such research is clearly necessary in the pre-paradigm stages of a field's development and, if carefully done, can lead to significant generalizations and useful taxonomies. If such work is not carefully done, of course, there is the danger of acquiring masses of facts which are without meaning or which have very limited meaning or cumulative effect.

The schema also reflects a judgment that there are concepts and frameworks from social science fields which can usefully advance research in higher education. In these fields the components of a "disciplinary matrix," to borrow Kuhn's phrase again, are more developed. The concepts and modes of inquiry in the social sciences, while having their limitations, have been used to study a wide variety of problems in different professional fields, including various species of administration and leadership. Because of their varied and extensive use, they offer concepts, generalizations, models, and scientific values associated with a "disciplinary mix" to a degree greater than the literature on administration.

There are certain risks in initiating a program directed at greater uses of the social sciences in higher education study. There is the well-known tendency, for example, for underdeveloped fields to reach for concepts and modes of inquiry in more developed fields for status rather than for effective-use purposes. New fields are especially susceptible to this tendency. For this and for other reasons there is the risk that theories acquired may never effectively be tested through careful research and systematic acquisition of facts. If those pursuing studies without a theory base are susceptible to the gathering of too many facts or to gathering them indiscriminately, those enamored with theory are susceptible to the gathering of too few facts. Put differently, there is a tendency not to test theories and concepts taken from one field for general use in another. Clearly, the general field of educational administration during the last 20 years has had shortcomings in this latter area. Without cumulative research there cannot be movement toward a paradigm state.

Even with the risks inherent in borrowing social science concepts and modes of inquiry for use in research, the potential benefits would seem to outweigh the risks. Therefore, a part of any long-range strategy for stimulating research should be that of encouraging greater numbers of social scientists to study higher education administration.

Research talent in all fields is scarce and, as Peterson has noted, any marked increase in higher education staffs will be difficult to achieve in the foreseeable future.[21] Greater involvement of social scientists will, among other things, require the creation of new communication channels which link more effectively higher education scholars, higher education leaders, and social scientists nationally and regionally. Also needed will be systematic efforts to recruit more social scientists into higher education professorships (as several of the centers for the study of higher education have done) and to facilitate their research efforts.[22]

As more social scientists become involved in the study of higher education, the benefits can be twofold. First, inquiry processes and products in the higher education field can be strengthened and better bases for cumulative research can be acquired. Second, concepts and modes of inquiry in social science disciplines can be further tested and refined.

Figure 1.3 illustrates stages in the production of research on the deanship. The treatment is related to the domain on "Deans as Individuals-in-Organizations." Several observations about the conceptualization of the proposed research program can usefully be added.

Illustrative activities related to "Deans as Individuals-in-Organizations" suggest there are many research options that might be pursued through UCEA. These options are increased proportionally when all the potential domains of inquiry are considered. Since there is a relative lack of research on the deanship and there are diverse interests and talents within UCEA, there is reason in this approach. However, the approach does not ensure that all the domains will be addressed or that those which are chosen for research will be addressed to the same degree or with the same quality of effort.

Figure 1.3 suggests that the important starting point on research is with concepts and theories generally originating in the social science and related literature. While this is an accurate reflection of the intended emphasis of the effort, it may oversimplify the situation. The movement from concepts to practice and vice versa is seldom, in other words, a one-way process. An important assumption, in fact, is that it is highly desirable for scholars to move back and forth between concepts and practice in the making of decisions about the most relevant and useful theories to guide research.

Figure 1.3 implies certain stages in the research program. The first stage has to do with the identification and selection of relevant

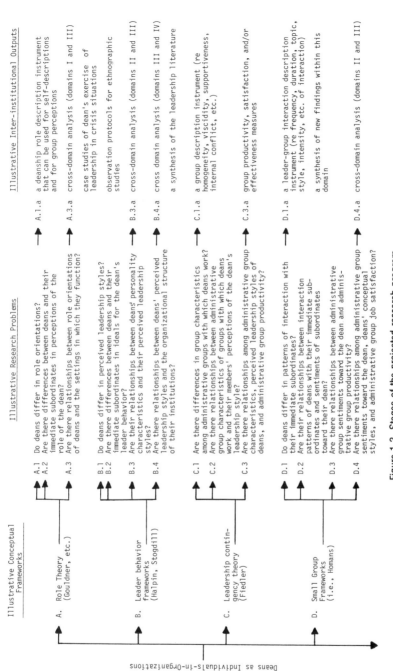

Figure 1.3. Stages of the projected research program.

theories to guide research in given domains. Important activities supportive of future research would be analyses and syntheses of concepts, theories, and research findings pertinent to the various domains. It is anticipated that this volume will make important initial contributions to synthesis of relevant conceptualizations in the domains and that there will be opportunities for additional syntheses. Such syntheses can aid professors and graduate students interested in undertaking research in given domains.

Studies to be undertaken during the design process, then, will draw upon identified concepts and theories judged relevant to questions or problems in given domains. Over time some researchers will focus upon aspects of the deanships in given units (e.g., medical schools), and others will focus upon more than one deanship across professional schools. As studies emerge, there can be additional opportunities for a second stage of synthesis. It is hoped, in other words, that over time sufficient knowledge will emerge to justify new syntheses in given domains, syntheses across domains, and syntheses across professional schools. The results, in turn, should provide bases for refinements or changes in the concepts or theories originally chosen.

Figure 1.3 also contains illustrative outcomes which can be achieved through inter-institutional efforts. Such efforts, if effectively conceived and coordinated, can be advantageous. Selected individuals, for example, can produce syntheses which are of value to various scholars and graduate students interested in research. A few individuals, to take another example, can produce instruments designed to measure variables in given domains which, in turn, can provide bases for broader-based cooperative efforts. Similar arrangements can be effected concerning other research-related functions.

Associated with studies of the deanship are, of course, potential problems as well as opportunities. One problem is that of saturation or the making of unreasonable demands on already heavily burdened leaders. Another problem is the possible stimulation of ill-conceived or low-quality research. UCEA and its member leaders will need to give special attention to these and other problems as the effort unfolds.

SUMMARY

Higher education management and leadership represents a relatively new field of study. Although its growth as a field of preparation has been rapid to this point and its continued growth seems assured, it is, to use Kuhn's concepts, in a pre-paradigm stage of development as far as study is concerned. This stage of development is recognized widely among the higher education professoriate as is the need for knowledge production in the field.

UCEA has recently broadened its effort to encompass management and leadership in higher education as well as in K-12 systems. One major research program sponsored by the organization will focus upon the deanship in higher education. Its goal will be greater knowledge about the deanship and its environment. Six domains have been selected as potential foci for research activities, and a general plan for stimulating research through UCEA has been projected. The first stage of this plan is the set of papers presented in this volume. These papers, and the research which they hopefully will stimulate, should provide very important building blocks for the future.

NOTES

1. Appreciation is expressed to Nicholas Nash, UCEA Associate Director, and to Paula Silver, a former Associate Director, who provided helpful reactions to earlier drafts of this chapter.
2. Dressel and Mayhew recently noted: "The major weakness of higher education curricula center (sic) on course content." See Paul Dressel and Lewis Mayhew, *Higher Education as a Field of Study* (San Francisco: Jossey-Bass, 1974), p. 111.
3. Jack Newell, "A Report on the Higher Education Survey," *UCEA Newsletter* (Vol. 14, No. 3, January 1973), pp. 12-16.
4. In this paper, "schools of education" will be used as a synonym for colleges of education, departments of education, and similar units.
5. Attending one or both of these meetings were: Joan Dee, Daniel Griffiths, Myer Horowitz, William Monahan, Donald McCarty, David Clark, Donald Anderson, Robert Woods, Robert Gilberts, Bert Sharp, and Frederick Cyphert.
6. Thomas S. Kuhn, *The Structure of Scientific Revolutions*, 2nd ed. (Chicago: University of Chicago Press, 1974), pp. 12-16.
7. Given Kuhn's orientation to disciplines, his concepts apply much more to basic or conclusion-oriented research than to policy research. Since the projected UCEA research program on the deanship is directed much more at basic research, Kuhn's concepts are relevant to the development of a rationale for the program.
8. For a treatment of differing types of knowledge and their development in higher education, see Fred Harcleroad (ed.), *Higher Education: A Developing Field of Study* (Iowa City: The Association of Higher Education, 1974), pp. 3-17. For a more general treatment, see Jack Culbertson, "Linking Agents and the Sources and Uses of Knowledge" in Nicholas Nash and Jack Culbertson (eds.), *Linking Processes and the Improvement of Education* (Columbus, Ohio: UCEA, 1977).
9. Collins Burnett, "Higher Education as a Specialized Field of Study," *Journal of Research and Development in Higher Education* (Vol. 6, No. 2, Winter 1973), p. 7.

10. Marvin Peterson, "Form, Functions, and Strategic Issues in the Study of Higher Education," *Journal of Research and Development in Higher Education* (Vol. 6, No. 2, Winter 1973), p. 22.

11. Kuhn, *op. cit.*, p. 180.

12. *Ibid.*, p. 15.

13. *Ibid.*, p. 182.

14. Bruce Francis and Walter Hobbs, "The Isolation of Higher Educationists." Paper presented at the annual meeting of the Association of Professors of Higher Education, March 1973.

15. Lewis Mayhew, *The Literature of Higher Education* (San Francisco: Jossey-Bass, 1972), pp. 6-7.

16. Francis and Hobbs, *op. cit.*, p. 3.

17. For additional information on higher education context see Collins Burnett, "Higher Education as a Specialized Field of Study," *Journal of Research and Development in Education* (Vol. 6, No. 2, Winter 1973), pp. 4-15; also see Samuel Kellams, "Higher Education as a Potential Profession," *Journal of Research and Development in Higher Education* (Vol. 6, No. 2, Winter 1973), pp. 30-41.

18. Kuhn, *op. cit.*, pp. 187-188.

19. For an insightful discussion of professional communication, see Robert Silverman, "Communication as the Basis for Disciplinary and Professional Development in Higher Education," *Journal for Research and Development in Education* (Vol. 6, No. 2, Winter 1973), pp. 67-79.

20. See Paula Silver, "The Deanship in Schools of Education: A Long-Range Research Strategy." Paper prepared for the Deans' Task Force meeting of May 1975, The University Council for Educational Administration, Columbus, Ohio, May 1975 (mimeographed).

21. Marvin Peterson, "Form, Functions and Strategic Issues in the Study of Higher Education," *Journal of Research and Development in Higher Education* (Vol. 6, No. 2, Winter 1973), pp. 16-29.

22. For a summary of how social scientists and other groups and agencies have been involved in the study of higher education, see Peterson, *Ibid.*, pp. 17-24.

CHAPTER 2

Research and Theory in the Administration of Higher Education[1]

by
DANIEL E. GRIFFITHS
New York University

It is the purpose of this paper to explore theory and research in the study and practice of higher education administration. This paper is, however, not restricted to a review of the literature; rather it is an examination of certain fundamental assumptions regarding theoretical work in administration. Further, as is the case in other chapters in this book, suggestions will be made to guide the further direction of intellectual aspects of administration in higher education.

First, a few brief comments on the basic terms in this paper: *theory, research,* and *higher education administration.* There is a strong inclination on my part to use a narrow definition of theory: I would prefer to restrict the use of *theory* to those instances in which there is a set of assumptions from which empirical laws or principles can be derived.[2] If I did this, however, the paper would be remarkably brief. Therefore, I use theory in a loose sense and will accept work which approximates my desired definition. By *research*, I mean all organized, systematic, and intentional efforts to know more about the nature of administration in higher education. *Higher education* is used to mean post-secondary, but I have the university in mind most of the time. When using the term *administration* I am interested in the organizationally related behavior of presidents, deans, department chairmen, and others who do administration.

THE PRESENT SCENE

Talcott Parsons made a useful distinction when he contended that organizations devoted primarily to offering professional services have both "administrative" and "operative" systems.[3] In a university, the administrative system is concerned with the organization as a whole: recruitment and admission of students, operation and maintenance of buildings, purchasing equipment and materials, public relations, faculty benefits, and the like. On the other hand, the operative system is concerned with teaching students and doing research. While it is useful to make the distinction one should not assume that the two systems are autonomous. Rather, they interact frequently and often conflict.

Administrative System

This paper is concerned primarily with the operative system, but it should be noted that the administrative system appears to utilize theoretic concepts and scientific methods to a greater extent than the operative system does. Rourke and Brooks, for instance, were able to write a book in 1966 entitled *The Managerial Revolution in Higher Education*.[4] They documented the growing use of computers, program budgeting, and improved information in decision-making. They noted in their last paragraph the need for a revolution on the academic side to match the revolution on the management side of higher education.[5]

An article entitled "New Tools and Techniques in University Administration" summarized management advances as program budgeting, management information systems, modeling, management by objectives, and organizational development.[6]

Perhaps more to the point is the development of sophisticated models for planning and budgeting. While this is proceeding at a number of universities, I am most familiar with what is happening at Stanford. An academic planning office has been established, charged with doing a wide range of studies designed to improve both the administrative and operative sides of the university. The titles of a few studies indicate their range and depth:

Numerical Models for Faculty Planning

A Dynamic Equilibrium Model for University Budgeting

Planning Models for Top Administrators in Colleges
and Universities

A Model for Planning the Transition to Equilibrium
of a University Budget

In addition, there is *Constrained Maximization of a University Preference Function*, a modeling approach that combines subjective estimates of preference for outcomes in terms of academic criteria with available financial data.[7] In this study there is a definite mingling of the administrative and the operative.

These studies are efforts to use operations research, economic theory, and marketing in the solution of the financial and administrative problems of the university. They are indicative of the inclination toward the use of scientific methods in the administrative system.

Operative System

The operative system shows no such inclination. Sanford opened *The American College* with the statement, "Practice in higher education, as in politics, remains largely untouched by the facts and principles of science."[8] He then went on to demonstrate the validity of his point by producing a thousand-page book without a single chapter on management science or administration. Three years later, Doi observed:

> College and university administrators still remain untouchable as objects for systematic research on role perception and conflict, personality characteristics, value orientation, status-seeking behavior, and identification with institution. Published works about administrators, of which there is no dearth, are mainly anecdotal or advisory.[9]

Since Doi was able to mention only seven works, it would seem that he was overly generous in his appraisal.

The situation, as Doi described it, appears to be changed very little. The books generally used by classes in higher education are chatty, lightweight volumes, usually well written from a grammatical perspective, but lacking in references to the general administration literature or to the few research studies reported in such journals as the *Administrative Science Quarterly*.[10] They are filled with personal opinions; broad, often unverified generalizations; testimonials; observations; and, occasionally, genuine wisdom. The literature of higher education administration appears to be very similar to the literature of educational administration prior to 1954, except that it is better written. The fact that some professors of higher education either are now sending their students to courses in general administration or are themselves introducing their students to the general administration literature indicates that they feel the need for a change. What appears to be happening is that professors know their literature is not useful, and they are unthinkingly turning to what seems to be the only alternative, general administration. There is another alternative and that is to study the administration of higher education as a field in its own right and to apply scientific methods to that study. It could be that new theories might emerge from such an approach.

Lessons from the Past

Should higher education move toward theory as did lower education in the 1950s, there are several lessons that can be learned. Early in what has now come to be known as the "theory movement," the first University Council for Educational Administration seminar was held at the University of Chicago in 1957. Andrew Halpin gave the first paper, and he warned against expecting too much from theory and of the intellectual pitfalls into which those who loved their models could fall:[11]

> We must guard against castigating the practitioner as "purely empirical."[12]

> Administrators and social scientists alike must guard against personal motives that are less than lofty.[13]

> Neither a particular theory nor the *idea of theory* are things to be sold, to be marketed as an advertiser might market a new breakfast cereal.[14]

> These premises lead to a preoccupation with theory for the sake of theory, a form of intellectual masturbation.[15]

> This should teach all of us concerned with theory development some sense of humility, . . .[16]

> But if we view various theories of administration in the spirit of Bohr's principle of complementarity rather than construe these theories as *competing* explanations of the truth, our progress will be healthier. The attitude may also alleviate some of the

obnoxious symptoms of young investigators freshly pregnant with theory.[17]

None of Halpin's warnings was taken seriously by professors of educational administration, with the result that all the predicted pitfalls were encountered.[18] In addition, there was an effort to develop highly abstract and formally elaborate theories that went beyond the lines of research that spawned them. While it was good fun at the time, it was not particularly helpful and, in fact, might even have been harmful. This book should not have the effect of stimulating another similar round of theory production. Rather, we should pay attention to Trow's review of *Administrative Theory in Education*, in which he said:

> What is conspicuously absent from most of these papers is any evidence of theoretically guided research in educational administration actually being done; substantive problems being defined and empirically studied; uniformities being discovered, related to each other, and accounted for; or any other form of theorizing actually going on in and through research.[19]

Higher education should not fall into the same trap as did educational administration. It should start now to do the research on administration in colleges and universities that will lay the groundwork for formal theories that can well come later.

TOWARD A NEW PARADIGM

The administration of higher education (operative) is at a very interesting point in its development. While Culbertson contends that the field is, to use Kuhn's concept, at the pre-paradigm stage, there is not general agreement with the argument.[20] Some professors, as noted above, are now moving the study of higher education administration toward educational administration, a field that is dominated by general administration, which has as its fundamental assumption the idea that the administration of all institutions is basically the same. It makes no difference, it is argued, whether one administers a school, an army, a church, an industry, or a governmental agency, the same theories hold true, the same research is applicable, and the same wisdom is useful. To one who holds this assumption, universities are included with all other institutions. Since general administration is at the paradigm stage (there exists a scholarly community, a discipline matrix, and concrete problem solutions), to include higher education administration would mean that it too is at the paradigm, not pre-paradigm, stage.

There are many who think that the paradigm presently employed in general administration is less than useful and that marked changes are needed. This point of view is examined below.

Then there are many professors of higher education administration content to stay in the old mode, teaching by testimonials. Needless to say, this position finds no support in this book.

Critique of General Administration

Kuhn points out that paradigms are ". . . universally recognized scientific achievements that for a time provide model problems and solutions to a community of practitioners."[21] While the paradigms in administrative research are not as well-established as those in astronomy, physics, chemistry, and biology, they are in existence, and they do dominate the research that is done. It seems to me that they are not appropriate or particularly useful because they are based on assumptions about administration and organization that are no longer valid. It is assumed that organizations have goals that the members strive to attain, that there are roles, sets of expectations for the members which are agreed upon (the nomothetic dimension), that behavior is more or less governed by a set of rules (bureaucratic structure), that decision-making is a systematic process, that only legitimate power is employed, and that merit is superior to politics. Administration, organizations, and organizational behavior are viewed in our theories as essentially orderly and rational. It is unlikely that anyone but a committed researcher would consider such a description to typify a modern university. Indeed, there are those who believe the description does not apply to any modern organization.

Theories of modern administration must start with the people in the organizations administered: how they feel and think about administrators, what they consider to be important, what they expect from their administrators, how they view their organizations, and how they perceive the world in which they live.

Lord Morris of Grasmere, an English philosopher and university administrator, has described clearly, concisely, and with remarkable brevity an emerging concept of the administrator in the modern world.[22] The significant element, he said, is, "The peoples do not want to be governed, and clearly they do not believe that there is any real and final necessity to be governed."[23] Further, "Yet governments must clearly go on trying to govern. And it is against this background that administrators will have to live and work."[24] In terms of governmental leadership, he thinks, "The most that is likely to emerge is a leader who is a genius at forecasting what is practical in government, which means fundamentally, and perhaps exclusively, what is 'acceptable.'"[25]

We are, apparently, living with a new kind of politics, and this has repercussions on all who would aspire to govern and to administer. As Lord Morris puts it, "The new Machiavelli can no longer make up his mind what he wants to do and then bring the people round to putting up with it. His primary problem, almost it seems his whole problem, is to find some act of government, or any act of government, which is acceptable."[26]

Men are saying much the same thing in our country. Commager was correct when he said: "There is no consensus. There is less harmony in our society, to my mind, than at any time since, say Reconstruction. Perhaps the '60's and '70's are a great divide—the divide of disillusionment."[27]

What are the reasons for the collapse of consensus? Nisbet has given considerable thought to the problem and has expressed it this way:

> There is every reason for concluding that we are living in one of history's twilight periods; in our time a twilight of politics. It is the fate of all civilizations to outgrow the system of power that binds them. This, quite clearly, is happening in the West today, not least in the United States. I believe the waning of the political order is a fact of highest significance, and far too little noted.[28]

> Currents of localism and regionalism, as well as of ethnic, religious, communal, and other particularlist values, all generated in such large degree by the repugnance for the national state and its processes of power will surely sweep up educational institutions along with other signal features of our society.[29]

It is very difficult to be an administrator in these circumstances. Government policies (including those of boards of trustees and even university senates) will be apt to be very changeable, and the circumstances that affect statesmanship will affect administration. The administrator will, for instance, have to see that his methods are "acceptable" and he will have to make everything that he does "comprehensible" to the various publics. Further, it is the traditional role of the administrator to propose solutions to the problems confronting his institution. This role will continue unchanged; however, it must function within the new context. As Lord Morris said, "But the professional administrator must research the facts and devise an operable scheme. And by the same token it is his task to present an acceptable scheme; for today only acceptable schemes are operable."[30]

It is my opinion that we are now at the stage described by Lord Morris in practice, but not in our theory. It is clear to me that faculties of universities really do not want presidents and deans, but that these administrators are necessary if the institutions are going to operate. Deans do not have clearly defined jobs because of the power of faculties, senates or other bodies, and unions, and because of the nature of the university.

The administrator in higher education faces a challenge that approaches uniqueness. (It is also found in some research organizations and among medical doctors in hospitals.) The challenge is to obtain organizational goals in an environment that prizes and rewards idiographic behavior. In most higher education institutions, control of the reward system has passed from the hands of the administrator to the faculty or a union. Promotions, tenure, and often salary increments are controlled by faculty committees. The highest rewards, those of national or international recognition for scholarship, reside outside the university, and the administrator has only an indirect connection to this recognition. (The administrator might make time and facilities available to the professor to do his research and thus contribute to the professor's success.) The administrator in higher education is attempting to meet organizational goals while having little or no control over the reward system and while the members have little or no interest in organizational goals. Conventional theories of administration do not speak to these considerations in higher education.

The Philosophy of Self-interest

It seems to me that in order to understand the way members view the organizations in which they work and live, it is useful to examine a philosophical position that is now very popular in Western Europe and that is gaining supporters in this country, namely, phenomenology. Greenfield raised this point at the International Intervisitation Programme in 1974, when he recommended that: "Research into organizational problems should consider and begin to use the phenomenological perspective."[31]

In discussing, but not defining phenomenology, he says it is

". . . That view which sees organizations as the perceived social reality within which individuals make decisions and take actions which seem right and proper to them."[32] This leads Greenfield to define theory as "Sets of meanings which people use to make sense of their world and behavior within it."[33] In short, in this definition he equates theory with common sense, and this, I believe, we should reject.

At this point I should, logically, offer a definition of phenomenology, but it is more difficult than one would assume. It seems that phenomenologists have not agreed on a definition, and I suppose this is to be expected. In responding to the question, "What is phenomenology?" Thevanaz says, "The question is as irritating for the layman who hearing the word would like to know at least roughly what it means, as it is for the historian of philosophy or the philosophical specialist who has the feeling of pursuing an elusive doctrine, never clearly defined during the fifty years of its rich evolution. . . ."[34]

I think, though, that English's definition, which is probably not satisfactory to phenomenologists, does shed some light on the word:

> Phenomenology: a theoretical point of view that advocates the study of phenomena or direct experience taken naively or at face value; the view that behavior is determined by the phenomena of experience rather than by external, objective, physically described reality.[35]

As a way of elaborating, English uses the illustration,

> Cows, busses, a threatening voice, a delightful aroma, a remembered event of long ago, are to be studied just as they are for the experiencer, not as modified by any observational rules.[36]

There are a number of ideas in phenomenology that are of value to us as theoreticians who are attempting to understand the behavior of individuals in higher education. I believe, for instance, that the real world is much more as it is seen by the phenomenologists than it is as viewed by Weber or by Getzels and Guba. And while a theory does not need to correspond to reality to be useful, when given two theories of reality it is more heuristic to choose the one that does correspond more closely. To get back to the point, it seems to me that Weber sees organizations as essentially goal-directed with the members committed to achieving the goals, rule-oriented, relatively stable, fulfilling legitimate (that is, publicly sanctioned) purposes, and existing in a world in which there is a high degree of consensus on values

and ends. The phenomenologists view organizations as "invented social reality,"[37] as having no goals of their own, but serving as vehicles
for the achievement of the goals of their members. Because so many
faculty members appear to operate on this assumption, I see the
theoretical ideas of Cohen, March, and Olsen as more useful than
role, decision, or systems theory in explaining behavior in educational
organizations. While I do not believe that Cohen, March, and Olsen
are phenomenologists, they appear to assume that faculties and
academic administrators behave in accordance with the philosophy of
phenomenology.[38]

Two other comments on phenomenology before moving on.
While it would be useful to study organizations using some of the
orientation of the phenomenologists, I would warn against developing
phenomenological theories of administration. Phenomenology is essentially a method of inquiry, at best a philosophy.[39] The use of
phenomenology should be restricted to methods of research and as
variables in theoretical statements. In fact, it is very difficult to
understand how there could be a phenomenological theory of administration since the theory would have to contain generalizations about
reality, and these by definition deny the basic tenets of phenomenology.

Concepts

Present efforts at theorizing in educational administration employ
concepts that are stated in sociological, psychological, economic, or
anthropological language, and these are abstractions. For instance,
we talk of a person as occupying a role. Role is a sociological abstraction. The phenomenologist would prefer to speak of the person as a
basic fact. As Vandenberg puts it for education, "The task of educational theory is the restoration of the wholeness of educational
phenomena as they appear within the educating perspective."[40]
Whether this is something more than what many of us mean when we
ask for "flat" descriptions of administrative situations I do not know,
but, at any rate, it is good advice.

Let us take two of the basic concepts through which the administrative theorists view the world. Probably the most common is *role*.
This concept was invented by Linton, who found it useful in describing primitive cultures. (I might say that the people he wrote about
could not read, so we do not know whether they consider Linton's
roles to be descriptive of their culture.) He used role to mean the

expectations held by members for the positions in a given society. When Gross attempted to use role theory in his superintendency study (the first empirical test of role theory), he found that different people held different expectations for the superintendent, and the superintendent occupied many different roles—superintendent, father, husband, Rotarian, vestryman, etc. He thereupon invented the concept of multiple roles. Shades of Ptolemy! I submit that the concept of role as the set of expectations held for a position has little value in today's complex organizations. We would be better off if we described behaviors and perceptions and dropped the role spectacles. In calling for dropping abstraction in describing people in organizations, I believe the phenomenologists to be correct.

Much of the same sort of thing has happened to the concept *bureaucracy*. When in what are called the Aston Studies the concept of bureaucracy was put to an empirical test, it was found necessary to develop six different types: full bureaucracy, nascent full bureaucracy, workflow bureaucracy, nascent workflow bureaucracy, pre-workflow bureaucracy, and personnel bureaucracy. The study indicated that the concept of a single bureaucratic type is no longer useful, because bureaucracy takes different forms in different settings.[41]

It appears that when the abstractions of administrative theorists are subjected to rigorous, empirical testing, they are found to be less than useful. It is necessary to modify the concepts making them less abstract and, therefore, less general. As research continues it is probable that the refinement of concepts will continue to the point that the original concept will bear little relationship to the concept that finally emerges. Needless to say, the theories built with these concepts will be refined and they, too, will be quite different from the originals.

What I have been trying to say in this section is that present theories do not permit us to view administration and organizations as they really are, and certainly they do not hold for the operative side of universities. New theories are needed to describe adequately, explain, and predict behavior in organizations. These theories should start with flat descriptions of behavior, aspects of behavior should be related to other aspects, and explanations of the relationships should be attempted. This is the essence of theorizing.

ISSUES IN THEORY DEVELOPMENT AND RESEARCH

At this point let us turn to the issues that must be confronted and

resolved in the process of theory building and research in the administration of higher education. There appear to be four issues that could
be discussed with profit. There is considerable controversy over the
issue of whether present theories of administration are general or particular. Then there is the issue of whether what has become known as
the scientific method, such as is used in the physical sciences, is
appropriate for theorizing in administration. A related issue of
methodology is the place of models and modeling in administrative
theory. And, last, what should be the substance of research and
theory in this field. There are, no doubt, other issues, but these will
suffice for this chapter.

General or Particular

The issue of whether administrative theory should be general or
particular is of tremendous importance because most students of administrative theory believe that administration is administration regardless of where it takes place and that organizations differ only in
degree. With this as a basic assumption theories developed in one
context are used in others, and research done in one setting is applied
in all others. It must be remembered that all of the theories and most
of the research findings taught in educational administration are from
business, industry, and government studies. The prevailing attitude in
educational administration is summarized by Lipham: "Heavy re-
liance must be placed upon transfer of learning—to the dismay of
some who express fear that inappropriate transfer will be made."[42]
Crane and Walker assert:

> In the present state of both organizational and administrative
> studies, it could be said that a theory can be dependable without
> its having been rigorously tested in educational organizations.[43]

It must be pointed out, however, that there has been opposition
to this point of view in higher education administration. Millet published *The Academic Community: An Essay on Organization* in 1962,
in which he developed this thesis:

> *I believe ideas drawn from business and public administration
> have only a very limited applicability to colleges and univer-
> sities.* [Millet's italics.] More than this, the essential ideas about
> business and public administration, such as they are, may actu-
> ally promote a widespread and unfortunate misunderstanding of
> the nature of the college and university in our society.[44]

While Millet's thesis received little support—in fact, the literature of administration developed in the opposite direction—the occasional studies done in higher education and critiques tend to verify his point. Hill and French, in a study on "Perceptions of the Power of Department Chairmen by Professors," concluded, "The findings reported here tend to confirm the impression of a number of students that colleges are unique kinds of organizations."[45] In the only comprehensive bibliographical analysis that I could find, Olive offers the hypothesis that existing theories of organizational behavior and administration may not be applicable to present-day universities. In support of her hypothesis she says:

> Governmental agencies and business corporations have an internal organization which is unlike that of the university. Among the differences mentioned are these: the goals of the university are not specific and clearly defined; the product or service produced is not tangible; the customer (student) exerts limited influence; the employees (faculty) are dedicated to their specialized fields, not to the employing institutions; and the decision-making process is diffused in a way not typical of other forms of organization. Such differences suggest the inadequacy of present theories on problems of university administration and the incontestable and urgent need for new thinking and new approaches to research in this field.[46]

There are few empirical tests of the relevance of theoretical work in one field to another field. One such study, which did attempt to use a theoretical frame developed in industry and government to categorize New York City school personnel, found serious differences.[47] These were summarized as follows:

> A significant distinction between Presthus' and our studies, however, occurs in the fact that some two-thirds of all teachers were found to be either pupil-oriented or intellectuals. Presthus has no categories even remotely resembling these, leading us to question the wholesale and indiscriminate application of studies of business, industry, the military, and the federal government to education.[48]

Blau's study, *The Organization of Academic Work*, offers the opposite conclusion. He attempted to determine whether academic institutions and government bureaus and private firms were homologous, that is, whether they exhibited empirical regularities in size, differentiation of structure, and administrative structure. He concluded, "The administrative structure of academic institutions exhibits a remarkable homology with that of other institutions.''[49] It may be that if one compares universities and colleges with other organizations on purely structural grounds, without studying how the structures work, they will appear to be similar. Further, as will be elaborated below, the use of a particular model, in this case bureaucracy, biases the results the researcher gets.

The only theories developed exclusively from studies of educational institutions (11 studies of universities) known to me bear no resemblance to any of the theories now in use in educational administration. I would feel more comfortable with the Cohen, March, and Olsen formulation if I could see some clear relationship between their research and the resulting theory; nonetheless, the theory appears to explain certain aspects of university governance. Their theoretical framework can be summarized as follows:[50] While most organizations can be so-named some of the time, public, educational, and illegitimate ones consistently display the characteristics of organized anarchies. They operate on the basis of inconsistent and ill-defined preferences—fuzzy goals, if you will; unclear technology, that is, their own processes are not understood by their members; and fluid participation, that is, the members change frequently and devote varying amounts of time and energy to decision-making and, further, the audiences and decision-makers change capriciously. Decision-making in such organizations is described by the authors as the "Garbage Can Model," for obvious reasons.

It would certainly seem that there is no clear evidence to support the contention that administrative theories can automatically be considered to be general or universal. Further, it would appear that the theorist in higher education administration must give very serious thought to the idea that colleges and universities are unique institutions.

While I have been making the argument that administrative theories might well be more particularistic than general, I do not go to the extreme position of Mayntz, who says:

> Propositions which hold for such diverse phenomena as an army, a trade union, and a university . . . must necessarily be either trivial or so abstract as to tell hardly anything of interest about concrete reality.[51]

One who holds such a position must believe that every organization is unique and that it is impossible to generalize at all. Rather, it would seem that borrowing theories or research studies should be done with great care. Lichtman and Hunt reviewed a large number of theories of organization and concluded, "The extreme variability found within and among organizations renders one-sided normative theories less useful in understanding organizational behavior than models that recognize situational contingencies."[52] Whether one may safely borrow research or theory done in a particular type of organization to use in other situations is dependent on whether there is a reasonable degree of isomorphism with the situation in which the theory or research is to be applied. This might be ascertained by applying a set of criteria developed by Katzell.[53] These are, in summary:

- Size
- Degree of interaction and interdependence
- Personalities of organizational members
- Degree of congruence between organizational goals and goals and needs of members
- Who has ability and motivation to take action to further organization's objectives

These criteria are sufficiently detailed to act as a brake on persons who are prone to use theories and studies from other organizations in a thoughtless manner.

In summary, it appears that one should not assume that administrative theories have universal application, but rather that any theory should be used only after that theory has been tested for validity by the use of the above criteria.

Appropriateness of Scientific Method

When, as described above, the social context in which people live tends to put emphasis on the individual as the central factor, all of the more or less accepted ways of thinking are challenged. This is happening now. What is often called "scientific method" or "scientific theory-building" is challenged as being "narrow and rigid."[54] It is now suggested by many that we rely instead on "wisdom" or knowledge developed person-by-person on a case-to-case basis.

Suppes' position on this is very close to mine:

> It is often thought and said that what we most need in education
> is wisdom and broad understanding of the issues that confront

us. Not at all, I say. What we need are deeply structured theories in education that drastically reduce, if not eliminate, the need for wisdom. I do not want wise men to design or build the airplane I fly in, but rather technical men who understand the theory of aerodynamics and the structural properties of metal.

And so it is with education. Wisdom we need, I will admit, but good theories we need even more. I want to see a new generation of trained theorists and an equally competent band of experimentalists to surround them, and I look for the day when they will show that the theories I now cherish were mainly humble way stations on the road to the theoretical palaces they have constructed.[55]

The traditional argument against the scientific method is that everything significant cannot be observed and measured. To some extent this is a fallacious argument in that many "facts" which were at one time not observable or measurable become observable and measurable as new technology developed. So this argument is not against scientific methodology in principle, only in its application. It is an argument based on an inadequate technology rather than on an inadequate methodology. On the other hand, there still remain many unobservables, particularly in the social sciences.

It would seem that the solution is for the administrative researcher to use the approaches of science in building the knowledge base of higher education administration, but in its application the administrator will often have to rely on his experience and good sense—what is often called wisdom. Certainly, the theoretical base we now have is not sufficient to allow anyone to operate on that exclusively. Whether there will ever be such a complete base is highly dubious, but certainly a theoretical base much better than the one we now have is entirely possible.

Models and Modeling

If professors of higher education administration are going to make progress in developing theories of administration, they must make some decisions as to whether they will employ models and, if so, which models they will use to guide their work. I am using the term *model* in a rather old-fashioned way and prefer Tyler's definition:

When an area about which we already know a good deal is used to suggest laws for an area about which little is known, then the familiar area providing the form of the laws may be called a model for the new area.[56]

The problem in model selection is that the researcher must be certain that the theory he is using as a model is isomorphic to the area about which he wishes to theorize. In fact, it may be that so much must be known that the model serves no useful function. In other words, if one wishes to develop a theory of university governance, he should know a great deal about university governance, so much that he might be able to develop a theory without a model.[57] In fact, it might be easier to do theory-building in higher education administration directly, that is, from description to explanation to prediction rather than indirectly through the use of models.

I think that Baldridge, for example, would have been better off had he proceeded in this way. In his study of New York University, he reviewed three theories—bureaucratic, collegial, and political—and concluded, "There simply was no available model in organizational theory that could analyze these activities."[58] However, he obviously felt compelled to have a "model" and constructed what he called a political model, which was in reality a number of questions that he wanted to raise. It is quite clear that what he ended up with was no model at all; but this did not stop him from being seduced by the word, for after recognizing that he had no model he entered upon a discussion of New York University as a political "system."[59] He never did establish that the university was a system, another word with strong model implications. In fact, he then said, "The sophisticated social observer knows, however, that official structure and official documents hide a wild, informal, and dynamic set of processes that can be understood only by participation, observation, and depth interviews."[60] This is certainly true of New York University, and it is too bad that Baldridge did not do his study in such a way as to reveal what was hidden. What I am saying is that a commitment to modeling can often be an obstruction to understanding the situation.

The Hawthorne studies are another example of persistence in using an established model. Here the behavior of young women who assembled electrical relays and men who worked in a wiring bank room was studied and considered to be irrational because the workers apparently behaved in ways contrary to the model. The researchers had a theory of small groups and "explained" the behavior. If they had looked beyond their small-group bias they would have found several other reasons for the behavior.[61]

There are times when modeling is useful. Dubin and Beisse's study "The Assistant: Academic Subaltern" is an example of such a case.[62] They analyzed the teaching assistant as a person in role conflict: a student serving as apprentice teacher. The model was useful because the researchers established an isomorphism and then followed research leads suggested by the model. The model led to a modest study in that it concerned a single position, not an entire university. It is the kind of study that eventually leads to the development of useful theories.

Substance of Research

Finally, I am concerned about the substance of research in the administration of higher education. Little of the research is done on what administrators actually *do*. I believe that administration should be considered as something that people do. In this sense it is similar to other things that people do: medicine, dentistry, mathematics, teaching, and baseball. If administration is something people do, research must be done on the actual practice of administration.

By way of getting started, let us review a few days in the life of a university dean:

9:15 A.M. – Chaired meeting of committee convened by the president to prepare a long-range policy for the university's participation in intercollegiate athletics. The committee was comprised of three professors chosen by the faculty council, two students chosen by the student council, and two deans, one chosen by the president and the other by the chairman. The agenda included review of plans for new sports center, examination of intramural athletics, and review of statement on the value of intercollegiate athletics.

10:30 A.M. – Met with deans' group. A weekly meeting of the five deans of the School of Education, Health, Nursing, and Arts Professions. The meeting lasted through a sandwich lunch. The agenda included final recommendations on tenure and promotion; discussion of a number of problems relating to the transfer of a research and training center into the school; and a report on expanding the school's activity in research in special education.

2:00 P.M. – Attended a meeting of the Organizational Committee of the Study of the Common Undergraduate Program. The committee was chaired by the vice-president for academic affairs and was comprised of the deans of the five undergraduate colleges, the five chairpersons of curriculum committees, and two students. The meeting was concerned with final plans for getting the study underway.

3:30 P.M. – Met with the Director of Research and Training Center Program of the Rehabilitation Services Administration to discuss problems emanating from a site visit of the school's Deafness Research and Training Center.

4:30 P.M. – Met with the board of trustees of the school's Para-Educator Center. The discussion was focused on raising money.

5:30 P.M. – Attended a dinner with the National Advisory Board of the school's Deafness Research and Training Center. Meeting of the board followed the dinner and lasted until 10:00 P.M.

Items in the day's mail included a request from a student to have his grades raised so he could enter graduate school and a copy of a letter from an ophthalmologist to the president demanding that the school be investigated because the dean did not pull a TV tape of a "Sunrise Semester" session which included an optometrist on a panel of four specialists in learning disabilities.

Quite a different day was this:

10:00 A.M. – Chaired faculty meeting. The agenda included a report on the university study of undergraduate education; report of the faculty welfare committee, which dealt with faculty loads, retirement benefits, faculty performance ratings, and the IRS action on tuition remission; report from the university senate dealing with a uniform time module for classes, affirmative action, and some activities of the board of trustees; report by the dean on retention and attrition in doctoral programs. The meeting lasted until 12 noon.

1:00 P.M. – Met with the assistant dean for administration on a problem dealing with moving a research institute.

2:00 P.M. – Participated in a doctoral oral as a reader.

A more typical day was this:

8:30 A.M. – Met with president and central administration to discuss off-campus programs on Long Island.

9:30 A.M. – Met with the New York State Commissioner's Task Force on Teacher Education and Certification, of which he is a member. This meeting lasted until 1:30 P.M.

2:00 P.M. – Met with members of the department of music and music education to talk about themselves, plans for the future, problems such as plans to lessen doctoral attrition, review of economic indicators, and new programs. The meeting lasted until 4:00 P.M.

4:15 P.M. – Met with chairman of Faculty Welfare Committee to discuss problems in two programs.

5:45 P.M. – Attended a dinner and welcome of audience to the Peter Agnew Memorial Lecture. This event was over at 9:00 P.M.

After such a recitation, several sets of research questions surface. The answers to those questions would help us to understand administrator behavior and would serve as a basis for improved theory.

The first observation is that the dean was constantly involved with other people. Solitary activity was rare and took place before 10:00 A.M. and on the train, while he was commuting. While with a group, the dean was often, but not always, the chairman. The group activity was sometimes policymaking, sometimes problem-solving, sometimes information-receiving, and the dean's work varied with the group. What kind of behavior on the part of the dean would have been most appropriate? Appropriate to what? What skills should he develop? What personality predispositions should be dampened or reinforced? How would the dean know when he was effective?

Every administrator is concerned about how he uses his time. While the days described above do not constitute a scientific sample, they are not atypical in higher education administration. Were these activities the best use of the dean's time? Could he have spent his time more effectively doing other things? What are the criteria for use of time? There are few guides to this set of concerns; there is little knowledge for administrators to use.

There are many questions concerning the authority of the administrator in education. The fact that he is constantly in interaction with people in his organization means that there is the need to talk things out, to negotiate, to bargain, and to do it on a face-to-face basis. What is known and what should be known of the authority position of the administrator in higher education? How does the authority of the university administrator differ from the authority of elementary or secondary school administrators?

One last set of questions. Even the brief overview of a few days which we are considering in the life of a dean raises inquiries concerning the physical health and stamina of administrators. Are there people who are less vigorous and are just as effective? Just what part does physical health play in the success of an administrator? Similar questions can be raised about mental health.

In this section I have expressed concern about the level of our knowledge about administrators as individuals. I have raised many old questions, most notable that of the criteria of effectiveness. I have stressed the need to study actual behavior by observation and have deplored the abstractness that is now the vogue.

SUMMARY

This chapter is an effort to review critically the literature on theory and research in the administration of higher education. It would appear that there is more activity in the administrative system than in the operative system. In fact, it can be said that the administrative system of many universities is far advanced in its use of management science, but that the operative is conspicuous for the lack of utilization of theory and research.

It was acknowledged that there is a tendency on the part of those who teach the administration of higher education to move in the direction of general administration; however, a critical analysis of general administration revealed many weaknesses in this approach. It was pointed out that the assumptions on which the present paradigm are based do not adequately describe organization behavior, largely because of changes in society and in individuals. In addition, it appears that the weight of evidence is on the side of those who contend that the university is a unique institution and that general administration is of little value in helping to understand it. A set of criteria for transfer of knowledge to the university setting was offered.

The usefulness of the scientific method and the problems of modeling were explored. The chapter concluded with the argument that research and theorizing in the administration of higher education should begin with an intensive study of the behavior of administrators.

NOTES

1. This is to acknowledge the help of Professors Deane Bornheimer, Richard Lonsdale, and Paul Cullinan of New York University, and Professor David Clark of Indiana University, both for their advice and for their information and materials. The author is most appreciative to these professors who have been diligent, if not always successful, in their efforts to educate deans.

2. A more precise form of this definition is that of Herbert Fiegl, "Principles and Problems of Theory Construction in Psychology," in *Current Trends in Psychological Theory* (Pittsburgh: University of Pittsburgh Press, 1951), p. 182.

3. Talcott Parsons, "The Mental Hospital as a Type of Organization," in Milton Greenblatt *et al.* (eds.), *The Patient and the Mental Hospital* (Glencoe, Ill.: Free Press, 1957), pp. 109-129, as referred to in Roberta Lynn Satow, "Value-Rational Authority and Professional Organizations: Weber's Missing Type," *Administrative Science Quarterly* (Vol. 20, No. 4, December 1974), p. 527.

4. Francis E. Rourke and Glenn E. Brooks, *The Managerial Revolution in Higher Education* (Baltimore: Johns Hopkins University Press, 1966).

5. *Ibid.*, p. 129.

6. Daniel H. Perlman, "New Tools and Techniques in University Administration," *Educational Record* (Vol. 55, No. 1, Winter 1974), pp. 34-42.

7. These publications may be obtained from the Academic Planning Office, Office of the Vice-President and Provost, Stanford University, Stanford, Calif. 94305.

8. Nevitt Sanford, *The American College* (New York: John Wiley, 1962), p. 1.

9. James I. Doi, "Organization and Administration, Finance and Facilities," *Review of Educational Research* (Vol. 35, No. 4, October 1965), p. 352.

10. An ERIC search and discussions with professors of higher education lead the author to believe that the following are the most widely used general texts: Asa S. Knowles, *Handbook of College and University Administration* (New York: McGraw-Hill, 1970); Algo D. and Jean Glidden Henderson, *Higher Education in America* (San Francisco: Jossey-Bass, 1974); Arthur J. Dibden (ed.), *The Academic Deanship in American Colleges and Universities* (Carbondale: Southern Illinois University Press, 1968); J. Douglas Brown, *The Liberal University* (New York: McGraw-Hill, 1969); Eugene C. Lee and Frank M. Bowen, *The Multi-campus University* (New York: McGraw-Hill, 1971).

11. Andrew Halpin, "The Development of Theory in Educational Administration," in Andrew Halpin (ed.), *Administrative Theory in Education* (Midwest Administration Center, University of Chicago, 1958).

12. *Ibid.*, p. 11.

13. *Ibid.*, p. 13.

14. *Ibid.*, p. 15.

15. *Ibid.*

16. *Ibid.*, p. 17.

17. *Ibid.*, p. 18.

18. Daniel E. Griffiths, "Some Thoughts About Theory in Educational Administration, 1975," *UCEA Review* (Vol. 17, No. 1, 1975), pp. 12-28.

19. Martin Trow, Review in *Administrative Science Quarterly* (Vol. 4, No. 1, June 1959), p. 125.

20. Jack Culbertson, "Programmatic Research on the Deanship: Rationale and Strategy," this volume, chapter 1.

21. Thomas S. Kuhn, *The Structure of Scientific Revolutions* (Chicago: University of Chicago Press, 1970), p. 8.

22. Lord Morris, "Acceptability: The New Emphasis in Educational Administration" in Meredydd Hughes *Administering Education: International Challenge* (London: Athlone Press, 1975), pp. 13-19.

23. *Ibid.*, p. 14.

24. *Ibid.*, p. 15.

25. *Ibid.*

26. *Ibid.*, p. 14.
27. *Time* (July 15, 1974), p. 23.
28. Robert Nisbet, "The Decline of Academic Nationalism," *Change* (Summer 1974), p. 26.
29. *Ibid.*, p. 31.
30. Lord Morris, *op. cit.*, p. 6.
31. T. Barr Greenfield, "Theory About Organizations: A New Perspective and Its Implications for Schools" in Hughes, *op. cit.*, p. 92.
32. *Ibid.*, p. 79.
33. *Ibid.*, p. 77.
34. Pierre Thevanaz, *What Is Phenomenology* (Chicago: Quadrangle Books, 1962), p. 37.
35. Horace B. and Ava Champney English, *A Comprehensive Dictionary of Psychological and Psychoanalytical Terms* (New York: Longmans, Green, 1958), p. 387.
36. *Ibid.*
37. T. Barr Greenfield, "Organizations as Social Inventions: Rethinking Assumptions About Change," *Applied Behavioral Science* (Vol. 9, No. 5, 1973), pp. 551-574.
38. Michael D. Cohen, James G. Marsh, and Johan P. Olsen, "A Garbage Can Model of Organizational Choice," *Administrative Science Quarterly* (March 1972), pp. 1-25.
39. James M. Edie (ed.), "Introduction," in Thevanaz, *op. cit.*
40. D. Vandenberg, "Phenomenology and Educational Research," in D. E. Denton (ed.), *Existentialism and Phenomenology in Education* (New York: Teachers College Press, 1974), p. 189.
41. D. S. Pugh *et al.*, "Dimensions of Organizational Structure," *Administrative Science Quarterly* (Vol. 13, No. 1, June 1968), pp. 65-105.
42. James M. Lipham, "Content Selection in Organizational Theory and Behavior in Education," in Jack Culbertson *et al.* (eds.), *Social Science Content for Preparing Educational Leaders* (Columbus: Charles E. Merrill, 1973), p. 311.
43. A. R. Crane and W. G. Walker, "The Theory-Based Perspective," in Culbertson, *et al.*, *op. cit.*, p. 403.
44. John D. Millet, *The Academic Community: An Essay on Organization* (New York: McGraw-Hill, 1962), p. 4.
45. Winston W. Hill and Wendell L. French, "Perceptions of the Power of Department Chairmen by Professors," *Administrative Science Quarterly* (Vol. 2, No. 4, March 1967), p. 572.
46. Betsy Ann Olive, "The Administration of Higher Education: A Bibliographical Survey," *Administrative Science Quarterly* (Vol. 2, No. 4, March 1967), p. 677.
47. Daniel E. Griffiths, Samuel Goldman, and Wayne J. McFarland, "Teacher Mobility in New York City," *Educational Administration Quarterly* (Vol. 1, No. 1, 1965), pp. 15-31.
48. *Ibid.*, p. 30.
49. Peter M. Blau, *The Organization of Academic Work* (New York: John Wiley, 1973), p. 13.
50. Cohen *et al.*, *op. cit.*
51. Renate Mayntz, "The Study of Organizations," *Current Sociology* (Vol. 13, No. 3, 1964), pp. 95-155, as quoted in T. Barr Greenfield, "Theory in the Study of Organizations and Administrative Structures: A New Perspective," in Hughes, *op. cit.*
52. Cary M. Lichtman and Raymond G. Hunt, "Personality and Organization Theory:

A Review of Some Conceptual Literature," *Psychological Bulletin* (Vol. 76, No. 4), pp. 283-285.

53. Raymond Katzell, "Contrasting Systems of Work Organization," *American Psychologist* (Vol. 17, 1962), pp. 102-108, as summarized in Lichtman and Hunt, *ibid.*

54. Richard Kendall and David R. Byrne, "Thinking About the Greenfield-Griffiths Debate," *UCEA Review* (Vol. 19, No. 1, October 1977), p. 8.

55. Patrick Suppes, "The Place of Theory in Educational Research," *Educational Researcher* (Vol. 3, No. 6, June 1974), p. 9.

56. Ralph W. Tyler, "The Contributions of the Behavioral Sciences to Educational Research," in Frank W. Banghart (ed.), *First Annual Phi Delta Kappa Symposium on Educational Research* (Bloomington, Ind.: Phi Delta Kappa, 1960).

57. This idea became clear to the author in a discussion with May Brodbeck.

58. J. Victor Baldridge, *Power and Conflict in the University* (New York: John Wiley, 1971), p. 21.

59. *Ibid.*, p. 27.

60. *Ibid.*, p. 32.

61. Bertram Gross, "The Scientific Approach to Administration" in Daniel E. Griffiths (ed.), *Behavioral Science and Educational Administration*, NSSE Yearbook, 1964, pp. 50-56.

62. Robert Dubin and Frederic Beisse, "The Assistant: Academic Subaltern," *Administrative Science Quarterly* (Vol. 2, No. 4, March 1967), pp. 521-547.

CHAPTER 3

Strategies for Implementing Inter-institutional Research Programs[1]

by
PAULA F. SILVER
The University of Tulsa

INTRODUCTION

The Research Development Seminar is a particularly exciting event for me, since it is the public birth of a project that has occupied much UCEA staff interest and attention for almost two years. The gestation period has been a long one and, to stretch the metaphor too far, I hope it has much well-nurtured growth and successful development to maturity.

The project to which I refer is a long-range multi-dimensional program of research about higher education administration with particular emphasis on the deanship in schools of education. The conceptual structure of this research program, as described by Jack Culbertson earlier, was further elaborated by the conceptual papers and research reports presented and discussed throughout the conference. Challenging research questions were raised, and it is clear that much interest in participating in the research program was stimulated.

As a former UCEA staff member, I have been especially concerned with ways and means of bringing this project to fruition, of motivating and facilitating basic research on the deanship in an environment of constraint. This paper reflects that concern. Its focus is on alternative strategies for implementing the research program described and elaborated in the preceding papers.[2]

Before examining some specific strategies for implementing the long-range program, I would find it helpful to review the goals of the program and some major challenges to be confronted in achieving these goals. The first part of this paper, therefore, pertains to the general background of the project—its goals and expected outcomes and some constraints. The second part is an exploration of alternative strategies and structures for overcoming or circumventing the constraints so as to achieve the objectives.

SOME BACKGROUND CONSIDERATIONS

As Culbertson described earlier, the ultimate goal of this project is increased knowledge production in the field of higher education administration, with particular emphasis on the deanship in schools of education. Several intermediate objectives can be specified which relate to the goal and which are predicated on the assumption that Kuhn's[3] analysis is sound and that basic knowledge is best derived from particular models in which the scientific community believes. The intermediate objectives, as listed below, are viewed as contributing to the generation of one or more theoretical framework(s) from which knowledge can be "found" through inquiry. These objectives, or expected outcomes, are:

1. A range of theory-based studies of the deanship[4] within each domain of inquiry.[5]
2. A body of "baseline data" or "flat descriptions" of the deanship.[6]
3. A number of syntheses of studies founded upon similar or related theoretical frameworks.
4. Some syntheses encompassing research findings in an entire domain of inquiry and directed toward the generation of theories of higher education administration.
5. Syntheses of research and theory generation based upon cross-domain analyses.

Of the two types of objectives, research productivity and theory generation, the latter represents the greater risk and requires further clarification.

It might be assumed at the outset that the creative genius of the theorist can certainly not be programmed but might be expected to emerge when problems are intensively studied or when circumstances are conducive to such inventiveness. The research program projected here is expected to have impact upon *the circumstances surrounding conceptual creativity* in three respects: (1) the generation of cumulative data from the perspective of each of several theories borrowed from other fields might render the adaptation of those theories to the higher education phenomenon feasible: in other words, theories borrowed from other disciplines, upon being tested through research on the deanship, might be altered, modified, or refined so as to "fit" the higher education experience more usefully; (2) unexpected interrelationships might be discerned by culling and cross-analyzing data derived from different related perspectives; and (3) the various opportunities for interpersonal interaction among scholars with related interests might increase the likelihood of mutual stimulation and creative dialogue.

Since the initial conception of this research program, an assumption has been that the research will be undertaken through inter-institutional cooperative efforts. One reason for this assumption is that UCEA's mission is the improvement of preparation programs by means of such cooperative efforts. Another reason, as Culbertson,[7] Haller,[8] and others have noted, is the necessity for addressing contemporary problems in the field of education through large-scale research and development programs. In addition, it is apparent that no single institution has or can spare the resources of money, time, expertise, interest, and creative imagination to maximize the expected outcomes of the projected research program. Finally, the interests expressed by many geographically dispersed leaders encourage a multi-institutional approach, one with which UCEA has had extensive experience.

Early in the preliminary discussions it was also decided that a logical basis for organizing participation and responsibility would be the use of a domain structure. That is, for each domain of inquiry an individual institution or group of institutions would assume responsibility for goal attainment. Thus, each domain might be regarded as a separate research program with its own objectives of research productivity, synthesis, and theory generation. Inter-domain coordination and analysis can be regarded as a distinct program to address a different type of problem.

Potential Problem Areas

The research program here is an ambitious, if not grandiose, undertaking. It represents a novel approach to knowledge production in the field of higher education. The difficulties to be encountered in implementing the program need to be recognized and might finally prove insurmountable. While some of these difficulties will emerge as the research efforts evolve, others are apparent at the outset and should be addressed. Four interrelated problem areas have been identified for review in this paper: financial constraints, competition for resources, the perceived theory-practice dichotomy, and interpersonal conflict. They are presented here in the context of the challenge they represent to design strategies which will enable the minimization or circumvention of impediments to successful goal attainment.

1. Financial constraints

That most institutions of higher learning are suffering severe financial duress hardly needs to be elaborated here. The combined impact of declining enrollment faced by many institutions, rising costs, and scant federal or foundation support for basic research[9] places stringent limits on the resources available for travel, conferences, research assistants, instrumentation, and the other concomitants of large-scale research. In the face of these financial constraints, those interested in the projected research program are challenged to build upon the "cooperative ethic" that has so long characterized UCEA,[10] to incorporate dissertation research as much as possible into the comprehensive plan, and to generate external resources to support either the total plan or the segments of the program.

2. Competition for resources

Culbertson alluded earlier to some of the political problems of a field in the pre-paradigmatic stage of development.[11] Similar problems were cited by Ravetz,[12] who also described the relative insecurity of professionals within a field during its early stages of development, an insecurity born of the awareness of the limited knowledge base upon which one's status and prestige rest. One result, as Ravetz described, is a sort of "voluntary conspiracy" of professors and students wherein students who want to succeed refrain from raising challenging questions and wherein prospective students who seem likely to raise such questions are excluded.

These problems—of discrete and sometimes competing reference groups in the field of higher education itself, of interdisciplinary research groups, and of limited controversial dialogue—can be regarded as political problems insofar as they imply competition for scarce resources. Apart from financial costs, the garnering and allocation of such resources as time, knowledge, skill, authority, and prestige are important in the projected research program. Indicative of the necessity of attracting the needed combination of knowledge and skills is a list provided by Worthen of 25 tasks necessary in the conduct of educational research and some 80 competencies required for those tasks.[13] Problems associated with the allocation of intangible resources might be illustrated by the hypothetical case of a student participant working with a professor from one institution who is challenged by a professor from another institution. The student might face a threat to job prospects, to status or recognition at the home institution, and even to completion of the dissertation, while both professors in the controversy might encounter similar threats to their status.

Political considerations such as these represent a challenge to those implementing the projected program to encompass as much diversity, flexibility, and individuality as possible in the context of a coordinated effort. The challenge, more specifically, is to design a program which offers a broad range of rewards to participants in the form of opportunities for leadership, supportive and stimulating dialogue, the acquisition of knowledge and skill, publication, and other recognition.

3. The perceived theory-practice dichotomy

Historically, there has always been a perceived dichotomy between theory and practice that is especially acute in the applied fields, including higher education administration. In such fields there is urgent demand for solutions to practical problems and for the development of useful technologies as well as impatience, especially on the part of many prospective and incumbent practitioners, with any theory or research that is not directly related to practice.

Of the many outcomes of this dichotomy noted by Ravetz,[14] two are particularly relevant to the projected research program. One outcome is that scholars become drawn into a consultant or practitioner role, which reduces their time for and interest in research and which provides an alternative reward structure to that of research and publication. It seems that this outcome is exacerbated in a tight economy, when consultation fees are coveted and when high student enrollments are needed. This trend can be illustrated by the findings of a study conducted by Seldin and Wakin.[15] In their 1973 replication of an earlier study (1966) of how deans evaluate professors, the authors found that:

> A twofold trend is evident: more emphasis is placed on what professors are doing on-campus rather than off-campus; and information gathering in evaluating teaching performance is less haphazard, more structured, more concerned with student views. . . . What differs significantly is the decline in attention paid to research, publication, public service, and activity in professional societies—the traditional benchmarks of academic success.[16]

Another outcome of the perceived theory-practice dichotomy in applied fields is that facile, *apparent* solutions are frequently invented for highly complicated, multi-faceted problems. As Ravetz stated,

> When an immature field takes on the task of expanding its research effort for the solution of some urgent practical problem, there will be a tendency for the outcome of its labours to be a weighty argument establishing the conclusions that its sponsors and its public wanted all along. . . .[17]

This tendency can be observed frequently in education despite documentation that many of the most significant technological advances have been outgrowths of theoretical scientific work.[18]

The potentially negative impact of the perceived rift between theory and practice on the proposed research program is quite obvious. In addition to the drawing of professors' attention from basic research and the provision of an alternative reward structure, this rift represents divergent value orientations of professors (and consequently students) within departments of higher education administration themselves; it represents further fragmentation of the reference groups or "significant others" within the field. The challenge of this historically prevalent perceived dichotomy to sponsors of the proposed research program is to design ways of attracting a broad range of participants, including those who seek solutions to practical problems, those with highly developed technical skills, and those already committed to theory and basic research.

4. Interpersonal conflict

The financial, political, and historical problem areas are, of course, integrally related to the social problems that might arise during the personal interactions of participants. Inter-institutional endeavors tend to be hampered by the fact that the participating institutions are distinct social systems with their own traditions, reward structures, and socialization processes. This social separateness can be particularly detrimental to a research effort, for which intensive interpersonal interaction across department and institution boundaries would be desirable. Because the need for success within one's own milieu is great, especially for students and participants with a relatively local orientation, the potential for emotional stress, interpersonal conflict, and competition is high in an inter-institutional program.

A related factor is the traditional requirement of "private ownership" of research problems, designs, and findings, a requirement that might tend to limit collaboration.[19] On the other hand, a programmatic research effort which allowed for independent studies could at the same time stimulate additional independent and joint studies as well as create opportunities for publication. The challenge to program sponsors, of course, is to minimize personal dissatisfaction while optimizing the cross-fertilization of ideas in a stimulating and supportive atmosphere of scholarship.

That these problem areas are intricately interrelated and that they have far-reaching direct and indirect consequences for the conduct of inquiry are quite apparent. If, for example, the few federal and foundation dollars are earmarked for mission-oriented research, as opposed to basic or theory-oriented research, then leaders in financially pressed institutions will encourage professors to focus their energies in that direction and reward those who get money. These professors, in turn, will engage their doctoral students in mission-oriented research and will become "significant others" in the socialization of those students to the profession, so that the students' participation in a theory-oriented research project is either unlikely or a source of interpersonal conflict. Similarly, if a professor is faced with job insecurity, he might concentrate major energy on designing popular courses and winning student approval (rarely accomplished through tough-minded theory and research courses) and on securing other job possibilities, to the exclusion of ill-rewarded basic research. Such a professor might seek visibility through an inter-institutional program, but would not be likely to risk alienating others in a research-related dialogue.

In sum, the many interrelated problems represent a profound challenge to those interested in implementing the proposed research program. The problems also represent a unique opportunity, though—an opportunity to create novel and inventive strategies for achieving increased knowledge production.

ALTERNATIVE COORDINATION STRATEGIES

As noted earlier, the research program projected at this seminar has been conceptualized as an inter-institutional cooperative effort based upon a set of domains of inquiry. This type of allocation of responsibility implies two levels of coordination, the within-domain level and the inter-domain (overall coordination) level. The first focus in this paper will be on the within-domain level so that factors affecting overall coordination might be illuminated.

For *each* domain of inquiry, the expected outcomes involve the production and synthesis of a body of research. Attainment of these objectives would entail a variety of tasks, which would likely vary from one domain to another, depending, to some extent, upon the communication and decision-making pattern adopted for each domain. The tasks and activities appropriate for all the domains can be considered to be of three types—support, inquiry, and dissemination—which can be described and illustrated as follows:

Support activities are those which enable and facilitate the conduct of inquiry. Illustrative activities of this type would be planning and coordinating the domain-specific program, designing ways of pooling and allocating existing funds, generating additional funds, stimulating research, sharing such information as bibliographies and instruments, and coordinating research efforts.

Although *inquiry* itself would often be accomplished by means of individual or small-group studies, some aspects of the actual research might be regarded as appropriate for a domain as a whole. Examples of such activities would be: instrument development, including pilot testing and refinement; research proposal reviews and constructive criticism; mutual assistance for data collection; and the sharing of data analysis expertise.

Dissemination of information, in the context of this program, would imply more than simply making the new information available by writing for publication. It would encompass, for example: analyses of related research findings; syntheses of research related to a particular theory, to the domain in general, or to other domains; and theory refinement or theory development.

Since there is a wide range of tasks and activities related to goal attainment within each domain, extensive interpersonal interaction and a degree of coordination are quite obviously needed. How this coordination is accomplished can be expected to affect both the choice of activities within each domain and the effectiveness with which the objectives are achieved. The range of possible coordination strategies is, of course, practically limitless, and the factors influencing decisions about which strategy to adopt can be expected to vary from one institution to another. However, for illustration and analysis of some advantages and disadvantages of particular types of organization patterns, four prototypic coordination strategies have been identified. These four patterns, conceived as ranging along a continuum from *highly centralized* to *highly decentralized*, depending upon the locus of decision-making and the flow of communication, are depicted in Figure 3.1. They are related, but not identical, to four patterns

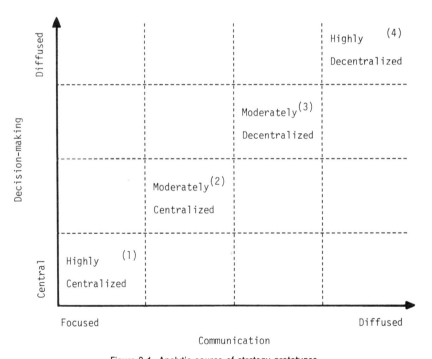

Figure 3.1. Analytic source of strategy prototypes.

described by Culbertson[20] and three described by Barbaresi[21] for the administration of programmatic research. None of the strategies is likely to be utilized in "pure" form; however, an overview of each might help both to generate ideas about implementation and to guide assessments of the relative feasibility and effectiveness of the alternatives. For each strategy, a representative diagram with a description is presented along with a discussion of some advantages and disadvantages.

Pattern 1. High Centralization

The distinguishing feature of a highly centralized coordination strategy would be an individual or small group within one institution that assumes responsibility for planning, coordinating, and overseeing the entire domain of activity and that serves as the focal point of communication within that domain. Whatever activities directed to-

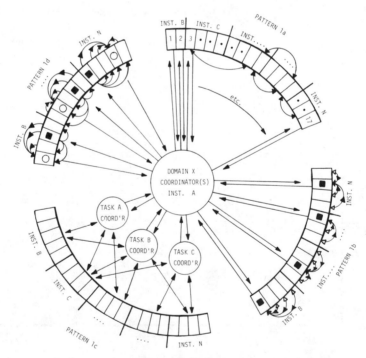

Figure 3.2. High centralization strategy: alternative communication patterns within a domain.[22]

ward support, inquiry, and dissemination are generated within that domain would be originated and/or directed by the central group, and all communication with participants from other institutions would flow to and from that central coordinating body.

This pattern, as represented in Figure 3.2, would be a rather efficient style of implementation, since the leaders would be relatively few in number and located conveniently close to each other. It also has the potential for enabling a comprehensive plan that could be actualized and coordinated relatively quickly. Since this strategy would likely encompass a limited range of activities, it is potentially the least financially demanding implementation pattern. It has the disadvantages, however, of placing the burden of greatest investment of time, energy, and money on one institution and of delimiting to one institution the range of expertise, creativity, and leadership talent that might otherwise be brought to bear on the problem of implementation.

Pattern 2. Moderate Centralization

As in the strategy just described, this pattern would require an individual or group of coordinators in one institution to assume general monitoring and control. However, the coordinator(s) would

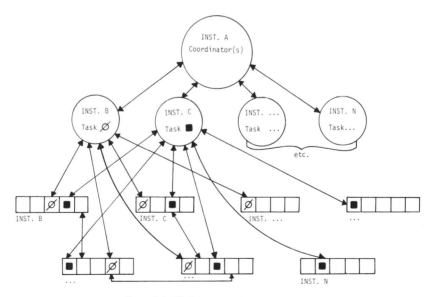

Figure 3.3. Moderate centralization strategy.

designate persons in *other* universities for leadership in the implementation of particular activities. For example, whereas a team in institution A would design a comprehensive domain-specific plan, the team would delegate to professors in institutions B, C, and D responsibilities for such activities as planning and sponsoring a seminar, designing an instrument, synthesizing a body of research, etc.

This strategy, as depicted in Figure 3.3, retains the advantages of highly centralized decision-making and coordination, but enables more individuals to exercise leadership, generates more centers of communication, and capitalizes on a larger pool of talent and a broader range of personal contacts. It would probably be more costly than the first strategy, though, and would require greater time commitments for coordinative activities.

Pattern 3. Moderate Decentralization

The distinguishing feature of a moderately decentralized coordination plan is that overall domain-specific planning and control would be the *shared* responsibilities of persons from several different institutions. Within this coordination pattern, each institution would either assume responsibility for particular facets of the program (by mutual consent) or would provide leadership opportunities for persons from other universities as well. Both of these alternatives are represented in Figure 3.4.

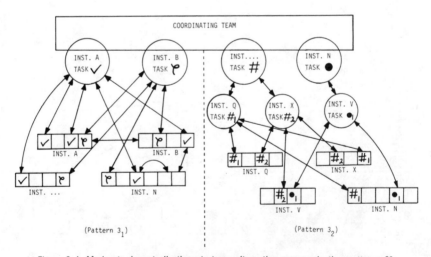

Figure 3.4. Moderate decentralization strategy: alternative communication patterns.[23]

Major advantages of this strategy are that it provides flexibility, diversity, and a broad base of participation while maintaining a degree of centralized planning and coordination. It also entails the added expenses of coordinative activities, however, and requires substantial time commitments of a relatively large number of people.

Pattern 4. High Decentralization

Least coordinated of all the communication and decision-making patterns would be a highly decentralized strategy characterized by independent activity within several different institutions and a loose network of communication among them. For example, professors in one university might decide to sponsor a research development seminar and conduct some research focusing on one domain; professors in another institution might decide to conduct some research on the same domain and engage a group of students in their region in related research; in a third university, professors might decide to sponsor a seminar on the same domain and produce a newsletter on developments in that domain. These activities might be assumed to occur with only informal communication links among all the interested professors and students.

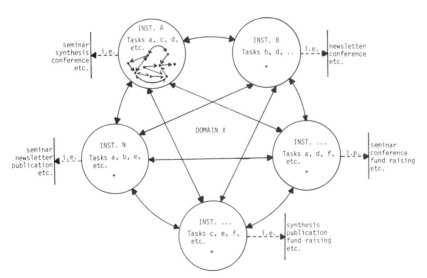

*Within-institution communication as indicated in Institution A

Figure 3.5. High decentralization strategy.

This highly decentralized pattern would capitalize most efficiently on individual needs, interests, and talents of participants but would likely result in many programmatic gaps as well as duplications of effort. As represented in Figure 3.5, this pattern entails a great deal of communication, but of a relatively unstructured nature.

These four "model" strategies for coordinating a research program in a context of inter-institutional cooperation are difficult to assess in the abstract. If the criterion of success is *extensive relevant research productivity*, then clearly the particular circumstances within (and among) participating universities are major factors determining which type of strategy is implemented successfully. Such factors as available institutional resources, individuals' interests and expertise, leadership styles of coordinators, and conceptual styles of coordinators and participants would influence the choice and probably success of a strategy for each domain of research. Nevertheless, a general assessment of the relative probabilities of success among strategies was undertaken.

An Exploratory Study of Strategies

To estimate the relative probable success of the four prototype strategies, an exploratory study was conducted.

Implications of this small study are that the range of support, inquiry, and dissemination activities that would accomplish the goal of extensive relevant research in each domain might be best actualized by a team of coordinators from several different institutions. This team would confer regularly to plan, coordinate, and monitor a number of interrelated activities involving as many participants as possible from its own and other institutions. Key advantages and disadvantages of this strategy are listed in Table 3.1.

Table 3.1. Major Advantages and Disadvantages of the Moderate Decentralization Strategy[1]

Advantages	Disadvantages
1. High degree of participant commitment	1. Diffused accountability
2. Broad range of rewards to participants	2. Little interpersonal communication
3. Close matching of interests to tasks	3. Unclear objectives
4. Varied types of interpersonal communication	
5. Large pool of available expertise	

[1]Items listed are those which were found to carry the greatest weight in a moderate decentralization pattern. They are listed in descending order of importance.

Inter-domain Coordination

As indicated earlier, a second level of coordination is implied by the domain approach to inter-institutional cooperation, that of inter-domain coordination. Here the focus is on procedures and mechanisms for facilitating the entire program, for enabling cross-domain cooperation and analysis, for linking potential participants with leaders in appropriate domains, and for stimulating activity within each domain.

To accomplish these functions a range of supportive and developmental projects could be undertaken by the overall coordinating unit. These might include:

1. Generating external funds to support the research program as a whole.
2. Allocating externally generated funds to domain leaders to support specific research-related activities.
3. Developing lists of potential participants and resource persons and sharing this information with appropriate domain leaders.
4. Referring active participants to appropriate leaders in other domains so that research pertaining to more than one domain of inquiry is "picked up" in the other appropriate domains. (For example, if a researcher working with the "Deans-as-Individuals" domain were conducting a study of the relationship between *deans' conceptual styles* and the *organizational complexity* of their institutions, the ongoing research and findings of the study would be referred to the "Schools of Education as Complex Organizations" domain participants.)
5. Linking researchers (across domains) with like interests so that collaborative research might be encouraged.
6. Stimulating and/or conducting cross-domain analyses and syntheses of findings, an activity that is most directly related to the development of theories of higher education administration.

Quite clearly, the nature and composition of this general coordinating body is of prime importance for the success of the program as a whole. Who participates in this body and how the body functions will greatly influence the eventual contours and directions of the program. Although a detailed analysis of the various mechanisms for

inter-domain coordination was not undertaken, four alternative mechanisms are suggested, as outlined below.

One strategy for overall coordination would be for the UCEA
central staff to assume responsibility for all the types of activity outlined above. The UCEA staff would, in a sense, be a "clearing
house" to and from which all the information would flow. In considering this alternative the heavy burden on the small staff should be
borne in mind, as should the probable efficiency of such a strategy.

Another approach would be the establishment of a steering committee comprised of a UCEA staff member and a leader working
within each of the domains. This strategy has the advantage of enabling the sharing of responsibilities among leading institutions, but it
requires coordination meetings and places an additional burden on
those who might also be deeply involved in domain-specific activities.

A third alternative would be to establish a steering committee
comprised of a UCEA staff member and several higher education
leaders who are not themselves directly involved in domain-specific
activities. This strategy has the advantage of broadening the base of
participants to those who might not have the time for deeper involvement and of engaging the support of additional outstanding higher
education leaders. However, it also necessitates coordination meetings involving people who are not intimately acquainted with the
problems and processes in the various domains.

A fourth strategy would be to have people in one institution assume the overall coordination responsibilities. Whereas this strategy
enables convenient and efficient coordination, it requires a substantial
commitment of time and energy on the part of one institution.

Of the four patterns outlined here, the second and third appear
the most promising in terms of equity and feasibility. Both entail optimal representation of leaders in the field and minimal burden to any
one individual or institution. The ultimate decision regarding a mechanism for overall coordination will be based largely on discussions
here and in the future, as plans for fostering research programs un-
fold.

SUMMARY AND CONCLUSION

The focus of this paper has been on strategies for implementing a
large-scale research program in an environment of constraint. The
question addressed has been: By what patterns of communication and

decision-making can the existing problems best be overcome so as to maximize research productivity in an inter-institutional program?

Two levels of coordination were identified, the within-domain and the inter-domain. Regarding the inter-domain level, four alternative strategies were suggested, of which either steering committee pattern was viewed as preferable to the other two patterns. Regarding the within-domain level of coordination, four models ranging from highly centralized to highly decentralized were outlined. Findings of a small pilot study suggested that a strategy of moderate decentralization might result in the highest probability of successful goal attainment.

Instruments for the pilot study had been based upon consideration of some problems to be confronted or challenges to be met in implementing the research programs. Four interrelated problem areas were reviewed: financial constraints, competition for resources, the perceived theory-practice dichotomy, and interpersonal conflict. Since these problem areas imply the necessity for designing implementation strategies to surmount them, it was suggested that within each domain leaders seek to minimize costs or generate external support funds, promote flexibility and diversity, provide intellectual stimulation and opportunities for publication, and broaden the base of participation as much as possible. The pilot study suggested that a strategy of moderate decentralization—that is, shared responsibility among several institutions—might optimize these recommendations.

In contrast to the problems reviewed earlier, several supportive factors should be noted which portend considerable success in achieving the project's goals. It became clear during this analysis that achievement of the goals of the proposed research program would require not only commitments of many people but ingenuity and creative imagination as well—qualities that have already been demonstrated by numerous participants in the early developmental stages of the project.

UCEA's long history of achievement in cooperative research and development efforts is another favorable factor that should not be overlooked. Both the creative energy of the organization's director and its communication network that spans two nations are key elements in the success of a complex and multi-dimensional program such as projected here.

Finally, the potential of the program for satisfying all types of needs and motivations within the profession should be noted. From the most elemental safety needs of those seeking job retention to the highest order motivations toward self-actualization, to borrow from Maslow's taxonomy,[24] the proposed program potentially offers rewards and satisfactions. From this perspective the proposed project might be viewed not as a challenge in the face of adversity but as an opportunity to meet the needs of a wide spectrum of people achieving a goal of greatest merit, the production of knowledge.

NOTES

1. Paper prepared for the NYU-UCEA co-sponsored Research Development Seminar, "The Deanship in Schools of Education," New York University, January 1976.

2. Appreciation is owed to Jack Culbertson, Nicholas Nash, and Richard Podemski, whose comments and critiques of drafts were most helpful in the development of this paper.

3. Thomas S. Kuhn, *The Structure of Scientific Revolutions*, 2nd ed., enlarged (Chicago: The University of Chicago Press, 1970).

4. Daniel E. Griffiths, in "Some Thoughts About Theory in Educational Administration," *UCEA Review* (Vol. 12, No. 1), p. 13, cautioned "Those who are prone to use theories . . . from other organizations in a thoughtless manner" to apply Katzell's degree-of-isomorphism criteria rigorously. However, since those criteria appear quite subjective, and since the perceived relevance of a theory to a research problem is contingent upon the conceptual style of the researcher, the research program described in this paper should not exclude any theoretical frameworks for which a plausible rationale for inclusion has been offered.

5. The domains of inquiry represent a range of perspectives on the deanship that are differentiated from each other by their degree of globalness. As described by Culbertson in "Conceptual Framework of the Conference" (paper prepared for the NYU-UCEA co-sponsored Research Development Seminar on "The Deanship in Schools of Education," New York University, January 1976), the domains are: (1) Baseline Data About the Deanship, (2) Deans as Individuals, (3) Deans as Individuals-in-Organizations, (4) Schools of Education as Complex Organizations, (5) Schools of Education as Organizations-in-Environments, and (6) Organizational Change in Schools of Education. It is assumed that there is a range of theoretical frameworks rooted in the various behavioral and social science disciplines that are relevant to each domain.

6. Griffiths, *op. cit.*, p. 17, recently used the phrase, "flat descriptions," with reference to atheoretical or non-discipline-based depictions. The term, *baseline data*, refers to atheoretical survey findings. Both of these types of information are useful in identifying population or sample strata, providing implications for theory development, and serving non-research purposes.

7. Jack A. Culbertson, "Efficiency, Large-Scale Research and Innovation Through Inter-institutional Cooperation," *UCEA Annual Report, 1962-1963* (Columbus, Ohio: The University Council for Educational Administration, 1963), pp. 1-10.

8. Emil J. Haller, "Toward a Programmatic Knowledge Production System in Educational Administration." Paper presented at the Annual Meeting of the American Educational Research Association, New Orleans, Louisiana, 1973.

9. Herman Feshbach, for example, in "Graduate Education and Federal Support of Research," in *Daedalus–American Higher Education: Toward an Uncertain Future* (Vol. 2, Winter 1975), p. 248, stated:

   > By and large there is increasingly more interest and more support for programs which have immediate goals of practical importance than for those which can be described as basic and directed toward uncovering new facts and new insights. One can always point to many historical examples demonstrating that such basic studies have been in due course remarkably effective. Characteristically it is usually not possible to demonstrate the direct impact of today's basic research on today's needs.

10. The tradition in UCEA since the founding of the organization has been that member professors contribute their time and expertise to UCEA-sponsored ventures. That is, remuneration is not provided although expenses are generally covered.

11. Culbertson, "Conceptual Framework of the Conference," *op. cit.*

12. Jerome R. Ravetz, "Immature and Ineffective Fields of Inquiry," *Scientific Knowledge and Its Social Problems* (New York: Oxford University Press, 1971), pp. 364-402.

13. Blaine R. Worthen, "Competencies for Educational Research and Evaluation," *Educational Researcher* (Vol. 4, No. 1, January 1975), pp. 13-16.

14. See Ravetz, "Practical Problems," *op. cit.*, pp. 339-363.

15. Peter Seldin and Edward Wakin, "How Deans Evaluate Teachers," *Change* (Vol. 6, No. 9, November 1974), pp. 48-49. Deans in the sample were from accredited liberal arts colleges not affiliated with universities. However, it appears likely that similar or more pronounced trends of this type would obtain in universities and professional schools.

16. *Ibid.*, p. 48.

17. Ravetz, "Immature and Ineffective Fields of Inquiry," *op. cit.*, p. 399.

18. See, for example: Patrick Suppes, "The Place of Theory in Educational Research," *Educational Researcher* (Vol. 3, No. 6, June 1974), p. 3; Feshbach, *op. cit.*; and Ravetz, "Technical Problems," *op. cit.*, pp. 321-338.

19. In his chapter "Quality Control in Science," Ravetz, *op. cit.*, pp. 273-288, discussed many of the reasons for and effects of the "private ownership" of scientific findings.

20. Jack A. Culbertson, in "Facilitation of Research—A Continuing UCEA Mission," *UCEA Annual Report, 1962-1963*, *op. cit.*, pp. 25-29, labeled four patterns of inter-university cooperation in research as: centralized, complementary, segmented, and shared. Each pattern is described briefly on page 25 of the article. These patterns were developed with reference to international research cooperation.

21. Patricia N. Barbaresi described three patterns of inter-institutional research cooperation in "Toward a Programmatic Knowledge Production System in Educational Administration: The Development of Alternative Models." Paper prepared for the Annual Meeting of the American Educational Research Association, New Orleans, Louisiana, 1973. The three models, generated inductively on the basis of a study of research administration in some government agencies and private corporations, were called: Centrally Organized Research Model, Professor Initiated Research Model, and Research Package Model (see pages 26-39). They were designed with reference to dissertation research.

22. The four patterns in Figure 3.2 represent different communication patterns within a highly centralized form of organization. In Pattern 1a, coordinating team members communicate directly with each participant in the other cooperating universities. In

Pattern 1b, a within-institution representative is selected in each cooperating university; coordinators communicate with representatives who, in turn, communicate with participants from their own institutions. Pattern 1c is one in which each coordinating team member assumes a different task responsibility and communicates with those persons in cooperating universities who are participating in the completion of that task. Pattern 1d would be particularly appropriate for a "newsletter" about one domain: in each participating institution, one individual would have responsibility for collecting information and forwarding it to the coordinators; a different person in each institution would be responsible for disseminating information; coordinators would publish the "newsletter."

23. Two patterns in Figure 3.4 represent different communication patterns in a moderately decentralized form of organization. In Pattern 3a, each member of the coordinating team (comprised of representatives from different universities) assumes responsibility for a particular task and communicates with participants in all other cooperating institutions who are helping with that task. Pattern 3b is one in which persons from other institutions (those not represented on the coordinating team) are delegated leadership responsibilities for the completion of particular tasks.

24. Abraham H. Maslow, *Motivation and Personality* (2nd ed.) (New York: Harper & Row, 1970).

Part II

CHAPTER 4

Schools, Colleges, and Departments of Education: Demographic and Contextual Features[1]

by
DAVID L. CLARK
EGON G. GUBA
Indiana University

The purpose of this chapter is twofold: first, to depict the demographic characteristics of the population of schools, colleges, and departments of education (SCDEs) in the United States, and, second, to identify contextual factors within these organizations and their parent institutions of higher education (IHEs) which affect the individual and institutional behavior of SCDEs.

THE DEMOGRAPHY OF SCHOOLS, COLLEGES, AND DEPARTMENTS OF EDUCATION[2]

Twelve institutional categories will be used in this section of the chapter encompassing three major variables associated with SCDEs, that is, degree level offered in education (doctoral, masters, baccalaureate); institutional control (public, private); and involvement of the SCDE in R and D in education within the degree-level classification (likely involvement, less-likely involvement). The categories are exhibited in Table 4.1 where, for example, the 163 doctoral-level institutions are divided into 112 public SCDEs and 51 privates. Within

Table 4.1. Number and Percent of SCDEs by Institutional Category

Category	Number of SCDEs in Each Category	Percent of Total in Each Category
A. Doctoral Research Center		
1. Public	23	1.7
2. Private	11	.8
B. Other Doctoral Programs		
1. Public	89	6.5
2. Private	40	2.9
C. Master-Level Pre/In-service Teacher Education Centers		
1. Public	183	13.4
2. Private	75	5.5
D. Other Master-Level Programs		
1. Public	101	7.4
2. Private	203	14.9
E. Baccalaureate-Level Teacher Education Centers		
1. Public	32	2.3
2. Private	104	7.6
F. Other Baccalaureate-Level Programs		
1. Public	60	4.4
2. Private	446	32.6
Total	1,367	100.0

the 51 privates, 11 are grouped as research center institutions and 40 are not. At the other extreme, the 550 private baccalaureate SCDEs are divided into groups of 104 and 446. All 550 have much more limited involvement in R and D than the 40 private doctoral institutions that were not classified as research centers, but within the degree-level group, the 104 E-Privates are operating programs in teacher education which are more likely to involve their faculty in R and D or field-service activities than the 446 F-Privates.

Number of Institutions

The first observation to be made about SCDEs is their total number. There are 1,367 state-approved programs of teacher education operating in the United States. They are distributed across the 12 institutional categories as noted in Table 4.1. Two comments seem cogent about these data:

1. The sheer number of professional training sites in teacher edu-

cation is far beyond that characteristic of other fields of professional training. In fact, 72 percent of all four-year institutions of higher education maintain state-approved teacher education programs.

2. If one were to rely on the modal institution in teacher education to define the "typical" SCDE, it would not be the doctoral-level, multi-purpose university with which many persons associate teacher training but, rather, the baccalaureate-level private college in which teacher certification programs are offered as a part of undergraduate training (550 of the 1,367 SCDEs or 40.2 percent of the total are of this type).

Institutional Size

As one might have predicted from the number of professional training sites for teacher education, their general demographic characteristics represent the full range of characteristics exhibited by colleges and universities. Table 4.2 indicates that the modal teacher education program (i.e., the program in the private baccalaureate institution) is located in a small college in which the overall student enrollment is usually less than 1,000. Conversely, the most comprehensive and prestigeful of the professional preparation programs (the A-Public and A-Private SCDEs) are located in university settings with enrollments of 15,000 to 30,000 students. Neither of these institutional types, however, prepares the bulk of the nation's educational practitioners. The masters-level public institutions (the C- and D-Publics) are the largest producers of education graduates. If one were to define the typical SCDE as the institution in which most practitioners receive their training, rather than the modal SCDE, the typical school of education would be a public institution in which the highest degree level offered in education is the masters degree.

These simple demographic data on institutional size point to several characteristics of interest about schools of education, to wit:

1. Despite the diversity of institutions of higher education (IHEs) offering teacher education programs, the concentration of students in pre-service preparation programs by institutional type is dramatic. Only one institution outside Type A SCDEs and the B-C-D-Publics had as many as 400 education graduates in 1974-75.

Table 4.2. General Institutional Characteristics of SCDEs by Institutional Type

Type	Control	Median Institutional Enrollment[1]	Median Number of Education Graduates per Institution in Category 1974-75[2]				Median Number of Regular Full-Time Faculty[2]	Total Regular Full-Time Faculty by Institutional Type[2]	Percent Maintaining AACTE Membership[3]	Percent Accredited by NCATE[4]	
			Bacc.	Masters	Doctor	Total				At Some Level	At Highest-Degree Level
A	Public	31,500	963	450	113	1,526	113	2,599	91.3	91.3	91.3
	Private	14,156	150	350	35	535	63	693	81.8	90.9	90.9
B	Public	15,900	550	275	32	857	113	8,781	96.6	87.6	66.3
	Private	8,235	75	100	30	205	27	875	65.0	52.5	35.0
C	Public	6,835	456	173	—	629	47	11,841	98.9	94.0	72.1
	Private	2,354	100	75	—	175	15	1,150	97.3	93.3	52.0
D	Public	4,118	334	150	—	484	30	3,210	54.5	8.9	5.0
	Private	1,530	75	50	—	125	7	1,353	32.0	2.0	1.5
E	Public	2,084	200	—	—	200	13	365	100.0	93.8	93.8
	Private	1,104	78	—	—	78	5	545	100.0	97.1	97.1
F	Public	2,500	100	—	—	100	8	442	51.7	13.3	13.3
	Private	847	68	—	—	68	5	1,987	37.0	1.6	1.6

[1]School year 1974-75 (Education Directory: Higher Education, 1974-75).
[2]Based on sample of 135 SCDEs responding to the study questionnaire.
[3]School year 1974-75 (AACTE Directory, 1975).
[4]School year 1974-75 (NCATE, 21st Annual List, 1974-75).

2. Centers for graduate study and research in education are not isolated from large programs of pre-service teacher preparation. To the contrary, not only do the Type A SCDEs maintain large undergraduate enrollments in comparison with all other institutional types but the research center doctoral SCDEs operate larger pre-service programs than do their doctoral-level counterparts (B-Public and B-Private).

3. The research center institutions also operate extensive masters-level, in-service training programs in education. At all degree levels, the public universities produce the bulk of the masters degrees in the field.

4. The productivity of doctoral students in education is concentrated in the "A-Public" and "B-Public" institutional types. The former produced *circa* 2,600 new doctorates in 1975; the latter *circa* 2,700.

SCDE Faculty

The typical SCDE might also be identified by the concentration of its faculty resources. As noted in Table 4.2, nearly 70 percent of the professors of education are employed in doctoral- and masters-level public institutions. In the former case, it would be reasonable to infer that the concentration of faculty signals their involvement in both R and D functions and training activities, while in the latter institutions the emphasis in faculty activity is probably upon training and service. There are several observations which might be made about the distribution of faculty by institutional type, that is:

1. Less than 10 percent (9.7 percent) of the education faculty are employed in SCDEs which can be typified as research center institutions. Since even in these locations the involvement of faculty in R and D represents a small percentage of their time commitment, the actual full-time equivalent of faculty engaged in R and D in schools of education is very small.[3]

2. A peculiar anomaly exists in the "A-Public" institutions. The size of their faculties in relation to the number of education graduates is smaller than any of the other doctoral-level institutional types. An observer might well have anticipated that both the "A-Public and Private" institutions would have maintained lower ratios of faculty to students than their doctoral

counterparts in the "B" type since research center institutions should find it necessary to allocate faculty time to their more extensive R and D commitments.

3. Future SCDE faculty resources for R and D are concentrated even more heavily than current SCDE faculty. Of the *circa* 7,000 doctoral graduates estimated to have been produced in 1975, 5,280 or 75 percent were produced in the public doctoral categories. Failure to attend to R and D productivity in these sites could have a major long-range effect on the quality of productivity in the field.

Professional Association Membership

SCDE membership in the single, comprehensive organization representing teacher education at the national level, the American Association of Colleges for Teacher Education (AACTE), is a function of the degree level maintained by the institution in teacher education and the type of institutional control, that is, public versus private. This phenomenon is illustrated in Table 4.3.

Table 4.3. Percentage of SCDE Membership in AACTE by Degree Level in Education and Type of Control

Degree Level in Education	Type of Control	
	Public	Private
Doctoral	95.5	68.6
Masters	82.7	49.6
Baccalaureate	68.5	48.5

Almost all public institutions operating programs beyond the baccalaureate level maintain membership in AACTE. Even at the doctoral level, however, only about two-thirds of the privates are AACTE members, almost identical to the percentage of public baccalaureate institutions that maintain membership. Although a very large number of AACTE members are small private baccalaureate-level institutions (since these are the single largest sub-group of SCDEs), the Association represents less than half of the population of these SCDEs. Overall, 62 percent of the SCDEs are AACTE members. Three inferences might be drawn from these data:

1. To the extent that AACTE is influential in representing the

interests of the teacher education community, public institutions and private doctoral-level institutions are overrepresented in AACTE in their influence on the community.

2. To the extent that AACTE can either improve the level of performance in its member institutions or exercise quality control on teacher education, a significant number of institutions is impervious to this influence.

3. To the extent that AACTE is used by policy planners as the sole source for input in assessing the influence of alternative policies on SCDEs, those planners will not account for a significant portion of the affected population.

Quality Control in Teacher Education

At the national level, teacher education institutions are accredited by a voluntary association, the National Council for the Accreditation of Teacher Education (NCATE). Although a considerably smaller percentage of SCDEs are NCATE accredited than are AACTE members, the pattern of accreditation is, similarly, a joint function of degree level and type of institutional control as illustrated in Table 4.4.

Table 4.4. Percent of SCDEs Holding NCATE Accreditation by Degree Level in Education and Type of Control

Degree Level in Education	Percent with NCATE Accreditation at Some Level		Percent with NCATE Accreditation at Highest-Degree Level	
	Public	Private	Public	Private
Doctoral	88.4	60.8	71.4	47.1
Masters	63.7	26.6	48.2	15.1
Baccalaureate	41.3	19.6	41.3	19.6

Voluntary national accreditation in teacher education is a phenomenon of the public institution. Among the doctoral-level institutions, fewer than one-half the privates held accreditation at the doctoral level; fewer than one-fifth of the masters and baccalaureate private institutions were accredited by NCATE at their highest-degree level. To note that 39 percent of all SCDEs are NCATE accredited institutions at some level or that 31 percent are accredited at their highest-degree level is to communicate little or nothing about the actual pattern of national voluntary accreditation in teacher education. These data suggest that:

1. To the extent that a major purpose of national voluntary accreditation is viewed as the enforcement of minimal standards, it would appear not to be working. More than four-fifths of the private baccalaureate SCDEs are not NCATE accredited. These smaller institutions, some of which appear to have little commitment to teacher education other than offering courses needed for certification, are not being rejected by NCATE; they have simply withdrawn from the game by not applying for accreditation. On the other hand, if the assumption is made that larger institutions operating doctoral-level degree programs in education are least likely to be operating minimal programs, these are the institutions being accredited by NCATE. But, of course, all these institutions are operating state-approved programs in teacher education with or without NCATE sanction. When the norm for a group is nonparticipation, as it surely is for the baccalaureate SCDEs, the penalties attached to out-group status can be considered to be inconsequential.

2. Since there is no obvious reason to suspect across-the-board qualitative differences between the public and private SCDEs, the markedly different level of participation by these institutions in a national voluntary accreditation program would seem to indicate that the present system, if it is important to the development of the field, is not working.

3. If accreditation of professional training is important, teacher education as a whole is missing its benefits. Some teachers are still being prepared in institutions which not only are not NCATE accredited but also are not regionally accredited as colleges.

Summary

Teacher education is hardly an ordinary field of professional training. Programs for teacher preparation exist in most four-year colleges in the United States. These training sites, not surprisingly, reflect the diversity of higher education itself. They range from the highly organized professional schools or colleges of education, with large faculties offering a full range of specialized-degree programs through the doctorate, attempting to operate significant R and D and service programs to the smallest baccalaureate-level colleges with, in some instances, only part-time faculty offering certification course requirements to their students who wish to meet state teacher certification requirements. Almost all of the country's 100 most prestigeful colleges and universities offer teacher education programs; and at the other end of the scale approximately 100 of the SCDEs in the country are located in IHEs which are operating without either state or regional accreditation.

The field has two dominant and conflicting characteristics. On the one hand it is so diverse that no generalization fits the population of SCDEs. Policy- and decision-makers stumble and fumble to generate programs or policies that capture the diversity. Conversely, the field is concentrated in institutional types. R and D in education is restricted as an institutional mission almost exclusively to the doctoral-level SCDEs. Faculty and students are heavily clustered in the masters- and doctoral-level public institutions.

In contrast with oft-noted centralization of control over teacher education, the field is loosely organized at the national level. A minority of the SCDEs participate in national voluntary accreditation, and even membership in AACTE falls off to slightly less than 50 percent among two institutional types, that is, masters- and baccalaureate-level SCDEs. Neither quality-control mechanisms nor organized representation of institutional interests in teacher education are well-established at the national level.

THE ORGANIZATIONAL CONTEXT OF SCHOOLS, COLLEGES, AND DEPARTMENTS OF EDUCATION[4]

SCDEs are impacted upon by a variety of external factors which affect the behavior of individuals within these units and the organized response of the units to demands for change or services. Dramatically, within the recent past, major fluctuations in teacher supply and demand has influenced, and in some cases forced, decisions that have altered the normative structure of SCDEs.

But, simultaneously, there are factors internal to the SCDE and its parent IHE which modify the impact of these external pressures. These factors will be labeled individually as contextual factors or conditions and collectively as the organizational context of SCDEs. These contextual factors are more than simply characteristics or features of the SCDE. They have a history within the SCDE and/or the

IHE. They are not transitory; they tend to be, rather, institutional hallmarks. As such, although no organizational condition or factor can be argued to be immutable, they are not easily or casually manipulable.

There are some *caveats* to offer before turning to the discussion of the organizational context of SCDEs. As was noted in the preceding section of this chapter, SCDEs are not a homogeneous community of institutions. The factors and conditions will be of varying significance to SCDEs and IHEs of differing types. The heterogeneity of institutional sub-types has to be taken into account in assessing the validity or impact of any generalization.

Although the authors are willing to argue that no contextual factor or condition which will be discussed was retained except on the grounds of generalizable effect for at least a sub-type of SCDEs, the data presented in this section of the chapter rely heavily on face validity, in contrast with the demographic data presented in the first section.

Finally, the impact of a given factor on individual or institutional behavior obviously varies depending upon the behavior under consideration. What may appear at first glance to be a factor impeding organizational change, for example, emphasis within SCDEs on self-actualization and entrepreneurial behavior of the professor, may, in fact, be a stimulant to change if the direction of desired change is to increase externally supported research activity within an SCDE.

The objective of this section is not to establish a "final set" of factors but to introduce (1) a research tool for inquirers interested in studying SCDEs directly or in more general organizational research using SCDE sites, (2) a discussion tool for SCDE administrators and faculty members interested in understanding and analyzing the present and future of their unit, and (3) a planning tool for decision-makers and change agents concerned with stimulating and institutionalizing change in SCDEs or with using SCDEs as change agents in other educational settings.

Since space does not allow for the enumeration of the full inventory of conditions and factors identified in the study, the section will be organized around a set of seven generalizations which bridge clusters of contextual factors or conditions and which are argued to be (1) critical (of high impact) and (2) valid (of high probability) for a substantial number of SCDEs. Some provocative individual factors and conditions will be included at the end of the section.

The Individual and the Institution

The culture of institutions of higher education (IHEs) is predominantly idiographic (i.e., emphasizing the self-actualization of the professor) rather than nomothetic (i.e., emphasizing the goals of the institution). This general cultural feature is characteristic of most SCDEs and is frequently formalized by legitimating the role of the professor as a private entrepreneur through the release of a portion of time (usually *circa* 20 percent) for individual activity or consulting arrangements. The idiographic culture is strongest in SCDEs emphasizing research missions since national reference groups exist to reward and reinforce professorial productivity independently of the particular SCDE in which the professor is located. Faculty members in such SCDEs frequently view themselves as "cosmopolites" rather than "locals" and derive maximum reinforcement from agents and agencies external to their SCDEs.

IHEs and SCDEs, consequently, have neither the same prudential checks and balances on individual performance nor the ability to deploy or redeploy personnel which is characteristic of many bureaucracies. Administrators and faculty members can and occasionally do enhance their professional status on a national basis while failing to contribute proportionally to the nomothetic goals held by the institution. Administrators are frequently constrained from the pursuit of apparently legitimate institutional goals because they cannot redeploy personnel to staff the programs appropriate to those goals.

> *GENERALIZATION #1:* All organizations operate with the ever-present tension between the attainment of idiographic and nomothetic goals. *SCDEs exist in an organizational culture which is strongly idiographic.*

The Unit and the Institution

SCDEs operate within a broader institution as a competitive sub-system of that institution. Certain structural and organizational features of the IHE affect the SCDE in common with other sub-units; other features affect the SCDE differentially. The competition among the sub-systems of the IHE (departments, schools, colleges) is dulled by what might be termed a condition of *negotiated normalcy*, that is, a form of gentleman's agreement among units concerning what is fair and proper in competing for budget and staff, establishing or deleting programs, or carving out spheres of influence. This condition protects units against massive perturbations in the system but simultaneously limits moves which might lead to significant changes. The state of normalcy is supported by the phenomenon of *loosely coupled units*[5] within the IHE, that is, most departmental, school, college, or center programs within IHEs are minimally interdependent; they are tied together weakly; the success or failure of one does not necessarily determine the success or failure of another. This leads to a live and let live philosophy within the agreed upon normal state at the IHE level and subsequently within school and department levels.

The SCDE is, of course, influenced by these characteristics of the general IHE organization. Since the education unit on almost all campuses has been and is below average in prestige, it is left with a weaker bargaining hand in establishing or modifying the negotiated state of normalcy. This general status position is aggravated by the fact that certain core SCDE activity areas are viewed as of low status in most colleges and universities, that is, undergraduate teaching, development, and service to practitioners.

The placement of the pre-service training program at the baccalaureate level reinforces the low status position of the program at the university (in common with all undergraduate instruction). The fact that the pre-service program is inextricably tied to the arts and science program leads to less autonomy than is characteristic of most of the university's loosely coupled units and especially the autonomy experienced by graduate training programs in other professions. Note, for example, the popularity of the concept of teacher education as an "all-university function."

> *GENERALIZATION #2: The SCDE has been and is typically in a weak bargaining position within the university's system of negotiated normalcy.* This is reflected in the obvious ways, i.e., below average resource allocations, vulnerability in periods of enrollment decline, difficulty in initiating new programs, and difficulty in providing rewards to faculty. *The SCDE experiences less autonomy in operation and decision making than most graduate and professional programs* at the university.[6]

Governance and Decision-Making

Despite the increasing pressures of institutional bureaucratization on the one hand and unionization on the other, the predominant governance pattern within the IHE and, consequently, the SCDE is the collegial mode. This forces, at a minimum, a search for consensus, broad tolerance of disparate views, and, conversely, the use of unilateral decisions by administrators and/or institutional coercion to change only as a last resort. The collegial mode of governance combined with the inexperience and lack of training of many IHE administrators and limited IHE investments in institutional research lead to decision-making processes in IHEs/SCDEs which fit the Cohen, March, Olsen description of decision-making behavior in ". . . Situations which do not meet the conditions for more classical models of decision making in some or all of three important ways: preferences are problematic, technology is unclear, or participation is fluid."[7]

> *GENERALIZATION #3: The decision making system* within most SCDEs, between SCDEs and the university, and between SCDEs and external agencies *is such that few agents can initiate or certify change unilaterally but many groups and individuals can veto change.* A proposal for change within SCDEs can be said to be exposed to double or multiple jeopardy. *The decision making process in SCDEs and IHEs is not accurately reconstructed through the use of rational bureaucratic decision making models.*

The Missions of SCDEs

The only common mission shared by SCDEs is the training of teachers. Despite the widely held assumption that schools of education fulfill multiple missions bridging training, research, development, and service, research is considered a central mission in a small number of SCDEs (25 to 35). No sub-type of SCDE claimed the "D" portion of educational R and D as a significant mission area in the SCDE national survey. Even general service activities (with the exception of *ad hoc* service carried out by individual faculty for a fee) are concentrated almost solely in graduate SCDEs.

This lack of congruence between actual SCDE missions and perceptions held by client groups and, frequently, by superordinate IHE administrators of SCDE missions leads to:

1. *Mission mismatch*—an effort on the part of the SCDE to adopt and fulfill missions which are not synchronized with their faculty strengths, base of fiscal support, or general IHE environment.
2. *Mission overreach*—a condition which builds up over time as

pressures increase on the SCDE to take on all the problems confronted by education in a community, region, or state. The clearest examples of this problem in recent years came from urban-based SCDEs which attempted to solve the urban community's educational problems with a handful of staff employed originally to teach classes for undergraduate and graduate students.

GENERALIZATION #4: To accept and understand the apparent truism that *SCDEs as a whole were conceived and organized and are operated and funded to train educational personnel* is vital to understanding their productivity in R and D, involvement in service and change programs with schools, and responsiveness to the challenge of new missions. *Programs involving the SCDE in such non-teaching areas must be considered complementary, and frequently tangential, rather than integral to the SCDE in all but a few such sites* (perhaps 50-60 of 1,367).

SCDE Budgets and Resources

The regularized operating income of almost all IHEs is derived primarily from student fees and tuition and/or state appropriations and scholarship support tied to student enrollment. Not surprisingly, SCDEs are bound tightly in their fiscal structure to instructional head-count budgeting. The budgets and resources of SCDEs are, moreover, labor intensive, that is, concentrating heavily on professorial personnel costs in contrast to other cost areas.

Investments in R and D and service activities by SCDEs, where they exist at all, show up in the form of reduced teaching loads for faculty. However, such provisions seem to be "bled out" of the budget after the fact rather than being built into the operating budget.

GENERALIZATION #5: Most SCDEs have little in the way of budget and resources to support institutional missions, programs, or activities in research, development, or service to schools. External agencies which frequently assume that SCDEs are staffed and budgeted to undertake significant responsibilities beyond instruction of students are operating on the basis of an illusion.

SCDE Faculty and R and D

Among IHE faculty, SCDE professors can be characterized as involved heavily in instructional assignments, advisement, placement, supervision of student teachers, and service activities with schools. Except in doctoral-degree granting institutions they are infrequently provided with any released time for R and D activity. Many have little or no pre-employment training for or socialization to R and D. Post-employment socialization to research is weak in most SCDEs. It is literally the case that some SCDEs operating doctoral-level programs of preparation in the education professions are staffed by professors who are uninvolved or little involved in research activity.

However, SCDE faculty in all institutional types aspire to, or at least predict, personal involvement in R and D. The contrast between ongoing faculty activities and projected activities by faculty is startling.

> *GENERALIZATION #6: Most professorial personnel in education are weakly socialized to and little involved or uninvolved in R and D activity in education. However, most professorial personnel in education simultaneously predict personal involvement in such activity in the near future. The dissonance between what SCDE faculty do and what they aspire to do or feel they "ought" to do in R and D is so marked as to be almost certain to create personal dissatisfaction and severe role dissonance.*

SCDE Faculty and the Reward System

Reward systems in all IHEs operating doctoral-level programs are attuned to R and D activity on the part of professorial personnel. Without success in R and D, careers atrophy; with success, almost any weakness in performance can be tolerated. Faculty engaged productively in research and scholarly activity are rewarded; faculty engaged productively in less prestigeful function areas (service activities, undergraduate instruction) are commended. Promotion and tenure criteria are applied differentially so that "workmanlike" performance in R and D is sufficient for promotion, but "super" performance is required in emergent (knowledge-utilization) or low status (teaching) areas.

The effect of this emphasis on traditional, high status productivity is felt even in non-doctoral institutions. Although research and scholarly activity is less frequently required for promotion and tenure in such sites, it is almost always recognized and rewarded when it is found. In all institutional types, conventional scholarly productivity is more heavily emphasized in arriving at promotion and tenure decisions than was the case five years ago and is predicted by faculty and administrators to be even more heavily emphasized in the future.

Simultaneously, the demands on SCDEs for field involvements are mounting. Teacher education programs are to be moved into the "real world." On-site, in-service training programs designed to be responsive to the needs of practicing teachers are widely urged. Field service demands continue, and their conventional forms are augmented by emergent change-agent activities—helping schools to identify, adapt, adopt, and institutionalize innovations.

> *GENERALIZATION #7: The clearest route to professorial success in IHEs/SCDEs is through conventional productivity in research and scholarly writing. This situation creates two levels of conflict in SCDEs: (a) the emphasis on non-research activities in such units results in professorial personnel being hard pressed to conform to the conventional reward structure in many institutions; and (b) the external press for SCDEs to respond to school problems moves SCDEs into activity areas that do not fit classical methods of rewarding faculty. Professors caught in this conflict risk their careers; SCDEs caught in this conflict risk their status and power within the institution.*

Some Singular Observations

The following supplementary notations of conditions and factors affecting individual and institutional decision-making in SCDEs were considered by the authors to be either less critical or more conjectural on the basis of the data accumulated over the past three years. They seem, however, to be worth further consideration and investigation:

1. *On SCDE Missions*

   a. The status of an activity within an IHE generally affects the position accorded that activity in the SCDE mission statements, for example, relatively few SCDEs eschew the research mission although the level of research activity in most SCDEs is low. In contrast, the most frequent KPU (knowledge production utilization) activity involving SCDE faculty is field service, especially on an individual consulting basis, but service is seldom mentioned in SCDE mission statements.

   b. SCDEs have what might be considered "mission weights."

There are "mission-heavy" institutions in which almost all faculty understand and are able to verbalize the mission of the institution unambiguously. In some instances, the mission is derived from religious affiliation, geographic location (e.g., urban) or special substantive interests (e.g., art, business, music). Other institutions have traditional mission emphases defined by broad, long-standing reference groups, for example, land grant institutions, national research center SCDEs. The largest group of SCDEs, however, can be considered "mission-light," in the sense that any one of a number of mission orientations would be equally reasonable as an institutional hallmark. Such SCDEs are frequently, if not continuously, searching for or vacillating among mission emphases. A final and large group of SCDEs can be considered "mission-free," that is, they view the activities of the SCDE as a service or support function for the IHE in which they are located and neither maintain nor strive for a set of professional missions that are distinguishable from the overall institutional mission.

2. *On Faculty Deployment*

Beyond the regularized assignment of faculty to class loads, the availability of faculty resources to support new institutional thrusts, especially non-traditional programs involving field-based activity, is often more apparent than real, that is:

a. New faculty are most susceptible to manipulation in assignment but the reward system in IHEs is least responsive to such non-traditional activities. The risk to the career of the new faculty member in using major blocks of his or her time on such activities is very high.

b. Faculty of "star" status represent the skills frequently needed to succeed in new thrusts but they tend to be (1) over-committed, (2) highly idiographic in behavior, (3) oriented to national reference groups, and (4) well-established in conventional productive outlets.

c. The apparently under-employed faculty who have time to devote to the new thrusts are often "drones," that is, they are under-employed because they are unproductive. The

investment of the time and energy required to raise them to
a level of proficiency in a new area is usually dispropor-
tionate to their likely productivity in the area.

   d. The locally-oriented "regulars" while competent to assume
responsibility for the new thrusts, have been called upon
too often in the past and are already over-committed to established line functions. Assigning them to the new thrust
is of limited utility since they must be replaced in the regular function to which they were previously assigned.

   e. Since new thrusts typically involve specialized knowledge
and skills, a significant group of the faculty is technologi-
cally unemployable as a consequence of shifting market
demands and mission emphases.

3. *On New Deans*

   a. All involved parties (faculty, superordinate administrators,
constituents) hold unrealistic expectations for newly appointed deans or chairpersons. With little in the way of
new support, they attribute to the dean the ability to overcome long-standing constraints in the institutional environment. A predicted shortfall in the ability of the new
dean or chairperson to meet these expectations is almost
always correct.

   b. New deans or chairpersons and new missions go together.
The dean or chairperson typically brings a substantive
interest or process specialization to the new role and formally or informally this is translated into a new or reinforced mission.

   c. A change in SCDE administration activates power interests
within the SCDE and sometimes across concerned IHE
departments. At the pre-employment phase, emphasis is
placed on selecting a dean or chairperson compatible to
vested interests. In the immediate post-employment phase,
efforts are made to co-opt the interest and support of the
new administrator. In the final phase, the special interests
are restructured in appropriate offensive and defensive postures.

4. *On Leadership and Change*

   a. The inconstancy of SCDE/IHE administrative leadership

personnel may facilitate the initiation of change in SCDEs (i.e., new deans and new missions) but may undercut the institutionalization of change. Professorial personnel are sometimes hesitant to respond to nomothetic demands which may turn out to be transitory aberrations in the institution's development.

b. During periods of marked change within SCDEs, the dean or chairperson is often viewed by faculty as the singular change agent upon whom the success of the innovation depends. This is an especially powerful factor in instances where the new thrust is not endemic to the mission of the SCDE. In R and D, for example, less prestigeful institutions seem to have fits and starts of R and D involvement and productivity, a reasonably heavy emphasis during a period of time when the SCDE administrator emphasizes the area, and a diminishing period of activity if the successor is less interested in R and D.

c. Some IHE/SCDE administrators are planning for the future in a time frame that corresponds with the tenure they anticipate in their current assignment. The time frame of many administrators is insufficient to deal with the core problems confronted by the SCDE.

5. *On Images of SCDEs*

a. R and D production units and individual departments that are high R and D producers project strong external national images for the SCDE. They may, over time, become the dominant image.

b. Undergraduate, pre-service education reflects dimly to external audiences. In the case of national reference groups and R and D influentials it could be said not to reflect at all, for example, qualitative rankings of SCDEs nationally are based typically on such activities as R and D, scholarly productivity, and advanced graduate-study programs.

c. The image held by outsiders of the SCDE is influenced unduly by their perception of the dean or chairperson. Again, this is more likely to confuse national reference groups than local practitioners. The incumbent SCDE administrator is frequently symbolic of the primary mission image which the SCDE wishes to convey.

    d. During periods of mission and activity transition, SCDEs suffer from an image "time-lag." In some instances, this may mean that the institution is living on its reputation; in others, opportunities may be thwarted because the potential of the SCDE is underestimated.

6. *On Mythologies in SCDEs*

SCDEs maintain and nurture local myths about the institution which seem demonstrably false to the external observer. Some are debilitating: they eliminate the consideration of alternatives and serve as *ex post facto* explanations of failure, for example, cultural or geographical isolation, teaching overload, budgetary inflexibility. Others are supportive: they serve to raise the *esprit de corps* of the institution, for example, perception of the SCDE as an elite R and D oriented unit, or the best regional liberal arts college, or the producer of sought-after teachers. One of the most remarkable current myths involves teacher placement. Despite national figures to the contrary, SCDE personnel in all types of institutions insist that their record of teacher placement has been, is, and will continue to be excellent.

7. *On Personnel Development*

    a. Beginning professors are not subject to the patterns of supervision or personnel development characteristic of most bureaucracies.

    b. SCDEs/IHEs have minimal in-service or retraining opportunities for faculty members during their careers. The consequence of this personnel development deficiency is apparent with the recent emergence of surplus professorial staff in SCDEs in one specialization while shortages exist in another within the same SCDE. The less dramatic, but more general, consequence is that professorial personnel tend to retain pre-service training deficiencies throughout their careers.

8. *On the Changing Reward System*

    a. In the immediate past (three to five years) and for the foreseeable future, IHEs/SCDEs have placed and will continue to place a heavier emphasis on research and scholarly productivity in assessing faculty for promotion and tenure than has been the case previously. Substitute criteria for R and D productivity are being allowed less frequently.

b. Despite protestations to the contrary by most administrators, IHEs/SCDEs are screening younger faculty for reappointment, promotion, and tenure more closely than they screened the senior faculty colleagues. Budgetary limitations and the availability of large numbers of new doctorates are affecting decisions about selective retention of faculty. Superordinate review of SCDE level personnel decisions is more thorough. The criteria are not being modified but the application of the criteria has changed.

c. The tightening of promotion and tenure standards is felt more sharply in SCDEs (and a number of other professional school settings) than in some of the predominantly graduate arts and science departments since a university-level emphasis on R and D productivity tends to disadvantage the professional school by definition. The SCDE, for example, is obliged to fulfill a series of missions beyond teaching and research that involve faculty in-service, development, field-based activities, etc., which constrain R and D activity options.

9. *On Problem Avoidance Responses*

Some SCDEs are responding to needed changes in what appear to be necessary and sufficient ways. However, current circumstances are complicating the ability of SCDEs to respond. Conventional tools of change (higher budget, more faculty) are missing. Some of the problems confronted by SCDE administrators and faculty have reached a level of severity where their satisfactory solution would place what is perceived as an impossible drain on limited financial resources, challenge long-held value systems or traditions of the institution, and remove the job security of the faculty. Faced with these situations many SCDEs have:

a. Asserted a degree of change (accomplished or contemplated) which outstrips the evidence the external observer can assemble that change has taken place. In some instances, the word replaces the action so completely that the institution creates a new "local mythology."

   b. Turned to ritual non-solutions to buy time or avoid con-
      fronting the problem altogether. Popular non-solution tac-
      tics (which may, of course, in some instances be serious
      planning efforts) include committees, commissions, task
      forces, etc.
   c. Initiated dysfunctional responses which give the appear-
      ance of targeted actions. The most popular of these is a
      low-cost move in a problem area in which the institution
      cannot afford to face up to the central problem, for exam-
      ple, the appointment of a part-time administrator to coordi-
      nate or stimulate activity in an area where released time for
      broad faculty involvement would be required to solve the
      problem.
   d. Formally denied that a problem exists, typically by assert-
      ing that "natural" processes will take care of the problem
      over time.

Summary

   Schools of education are complex organizational sub-units within
a complex superordinate structure. The contextual features of these
organizational units are not easily classifiable in gross terms, for
example, they are neither bureaucracies (although they exhibit many
bureaucratic characteristics) nor collegial organizations (although collegiality is a goal stated and pursued by institutional members). They
do, however, exhibit their own set of organizational features which
make rational what may at first appear to be irrational or random
individual behaviors and institutional decisions.

   The preceding discussion of contextual factors and conditions in
SCDEs was designed not only to open up the systematic study of
these organizational features in SCDEs but also in IHEs, in general,
and in their multiple sub-units.

NOTES

1. The data reported in this chapter are based upon a project performed pursuant to a
   grant from The National Institute of Education, Department of Health, Education,
   and Welfare. The opinions expressed herein do not necessarily reflect the position
   of The National Institute of Education.
2. This section of the chapter summarizes responses to an institutional questionnaire
   completed by 135 SCDEs from a national sample of 176 schools of education. A
   detailed treatment of the procedures and data is available in David L. Clark and

Egon G. Guba, *A Study of Teacher Education Institutions as Innovators, Knowledge Producers, and Change Agencies* (Washington, D.C.: National Institute of Education, April 30, 1977), pp. III-1 through III-80.

3. Subsequent studies of SCDE productivity confirmed the assumptions about individual and institutional involvement in R and D reflected in the category system, for example, 49 percent of the publications in research journals by SCDE faculty were produced by the 34 Type A institutions. Further details on R and D productivity in SCDEs is available in Clark and Guba, *op. cit.*, pp. V-1 through V-60.

4. This section of the chapter relies heavily on site visits to 20 SCDEs which were completed as a part of the national study of schools of education conducted by the authors from 1974-77. A more detailed treatment of these contextual factors is available in Clark and Guba, *op. cit.*, pp. VII-1 through VII-33.

5. This term was borrowed from Karl E. Weick, "Educational Organizations as Loosely Coupled Systems," *Administrative Science Quarterly* (Vol. 21, March 1976), pp. 1-19.

6. SCDE influence, prestige, and autonomy are enhanced in situations where (a) SCDE enrollment is a significant percentage of the total institutional enrollment, (b) the SCDE has acquired substantial external financial support for its programs and activities, and/or (c) SCDE faculty have actively pursued and attained membership on influential university committees.

7. Michael D. Cohen, James G. March, and Johan P. Olsen, "A Garbage Can Model of Organizational Choice," *Administrative Science Quarterly* (Vol. 17, March 1972), p. 16.

CHAPTER 5

The Education Deanship: Who Is the Dean?

by
FREDERICK R. CYPHERT
NANCY LUSK ZIMPHER
The Ohio State University

It is apparent that various groups within the education profession have increasingly elevated the question of leadership training for deans in schools, colleges, and departments of education to a high-level priority. Organizations such as the University Council for Educational Administration, Harvard University, the American Council on Education, the American Association of Colleges for Teacher Education, and the Association of Colleges and Schools of Education in state universities and land-grant colleges have all been engaged at one time or another in this kind of activity.

Educators have long recognized the need for the specific training of personnel within the profession. Historically this training has been organized around programs for the certification of teachers, principals, superintendents, and other school personnel. Ironically, those individuals who have been chosen for leadership positions in schools, colleges, and departments of education which offer these certification programs have not had the benefit of prior job-specific training. Instead, we have assumed that past experience, chiefly as a professor in higher education, could provide sufficient orientation for becoming a dean of a school of education. Concurrently, the responsibilities of these leaders have increased, and the pressing problems of higher education have demanded an even higher level of expertise in virtually all facets of this leadership role, for example, budgeting, collective bargaining, program improvement, and the "management of decline." It seems unreasonable to continue to assume that persons who come to these leadership positions will be able to respond to the demands of the role without the opportunity for job-specific training.

The end result of this and related studies, we hope, will be the creation of programs designed to enhance the effectiveness of deans. Theoretically, any training program for education deans must be based on a body of knowledge about the role responsibilities of deans as well as an understanding of the persons who execute these role responsibilities. In effect, a training program for deans involves the successful interrelating of these two sets of prerequisite data. This study was aimed at the second of these two factors, namely, an answer to the question of who is the dean. For instance, we know virtually nothing about the goals of incumbents in these leadership positions: where they come from, what their backgrounds are, what their personal characteristics are. Neither do we know who might be potential candidates for these administrative positions. We know more about the processes by which these individuals are selected than we do about the survivors of this screening process. We are not knowledgeable about the career aspirations of incumbents in leadership positions. In addition, we know very little about why recent deans have left their positions. Likewise, we have no knowledge about the characteristics of future deans. Is the commitment of incumbents to the job significant enough to warrant their training and further development or should our attention be focused primarily on prospective candidates? And finally, although we are currently giving some consideration to institutional differences, we do not know what effect these differences have on the leaders in these institutions.

Without knowledge of the above illustrative concerns, we are attempting to organize training programs with a shortage of knowledge. At the very least, we must depend on the participants in these programs to provide us with a set of concerns for which they need solutions. Yet we have no evidence to suggest that these concerns are the ones that will effect improved performance in the administrative roles involved.

In summary, both the university presidency and the university professoriate have been the object of numerous studies. However, university "middle management," the deanship, represents a void in our data base, even though its importance is increasingly recognized.

THE STUDY

The purpose of the study was to identify personal, professional, and job-related characteristics of deans of schools, colleges, and departments of education. These characteristics provide a basis for making inferences about the preparation for and the responsibilities of the education deanship.

More specifically, the study was organized around the following 9 objectives (with illustrative sub-questions):

I. Phase One (as reported in this paper):
   A. Identify and describe personal characteristics of current deans.
      1. What is the personal profile of deans (age, race, sex, health, geographic background, etc.)?
      2. What is the family background of deans (parental education, occupation, etc)?
      3. What value structure guides a dean's personal behavior (politics, religion, etc.)?
   B. Identify and describe professional background characteristics of current deans.
      1. What are the career patterns of deans?
      2. In which institutions do deans study?
      3. What factors influenced incumbents to become deans?
   C. Identify and describe current professional activity data regarding practicing deans.
      1. What are the role expectations of deans?
      2. What do deans perceive as their successes and failures, needs and expertise?
      3. What are the future plans and desires of deans?
   D. Identify, describe, and compare the perceptions and role expectations which superordinates have of current deans with the incumbents' self-perceptions.
      1. Is the dean perceived as satisfied with the position?
      2. What are the personal attributes or competencies needed for somebody to be successful in the position vacated?
II. Phase Two (to be reported at a later date):
   A. Describe the characteristics of persons who recently left a deanship for any reason other than death. Responses to appropriate questions from the survey of current deans will be

solicited from past deans. In addition, the following unique questions will be addressed:

    1. What were the reasons for leaving a deanship?

    2. What are the personal attributes or competencies needed for somebody to be successful in the position vacated?

B. Describe the characteristics of prospective school, college, and department of education leaders. Responses to appropriate questions from the survey of current deans will be solicited from future deans.

    1. What are the personal/academic characteristics of this pool?

    2. Would those identified in this pool consider taking such a position?

C. Probe more extensively into some questions treated only superficially in the present inquiry.

    1. What are the causes of varying leader behavior?

D. Identify and describe characteristics of deans in fields other than education.

    1. How do the characteristics of non-education deans compare with those of education deans?

    2. What are the generic and unique profiles of deans?

E. Interrelate the findings of this research with those of Clark and Guba regarding universities as complex organizations.

    1. How do leadership persons affect organizations?

    2. How do organizations affect the behavior of deans?

Methodology

The population of this study[1] included deans of schools, colleges, and departments of education from all institutions which have a teacher training program. Further, the total population of schools was divided according to a taxonomic category system shown in the Appendix to Chapter 5. A 20 percent sample was drawn from each of the eight categories. In addition, prior to this drawing, the institutions within each category were ranked from low to high according to their total enrollment to assure that the sample was representative of size as well as of the other factors mentioned previously. With the use of a table of random numbers, a stratified random sample of institutions was drawn. At the time of the drawing (October, 1975), discounting institutions for which data were not yet available, the population of schools, colleges, and departments of education totalled 1,360 institutions. The 20 percent sample and the population to which questionnaires were sent totalled 271.

The original organization of the questionnaire was intended to capture a sense of the deans' past and present characteristics and future aspirations. Rather than organize the questionnaire into these three parts, however, an instrument was designed to include questions about past, present, and future characteristics from a different three-part division. This new organization was as follows: (1) personal data, (2) professional background data, and (3) job-related data. The process of developing questions was one of beginning with a general area considered to be important, such as career path, and then developing specific key questions which would enable us to generalize regarding the original area. After arriving at an initial list of questions, other relevant studies were surveyed. As a result, the instrument was modified to generate data comparable to the information in the Stanford project on academic governance,[2] the Cohen/March study[3] of the university presidency, the Bagley study[4] on education professors, and the Campbell/Newell study[5] of professors of educational administration.

The first draft of the questionnaire was quite lengthy, so every attempt was made to structure the questions into a multiple-choice or short-answer mode, and the number of open-ended questions was reduced. Locally, the questionnaire was field-tested in September 1975, with deans of the state-assisted institutions in Ohio and heads of five private institutions in Ohio. Nationally, it was tested by seven deans, associate deans, and former deans. Of the total population, 89 percent responded to the field test. As a result of the suggestions received, the instrument was again shortened, and several ambiguous questions were deleted. The final questionnaire which went to the population of this study had an eight-page printed format and was divided into three parts as follows: personal data (with 22 questions), professional background data (with 14 questions), and current professional data (with 40 questions).

After the 20 percent stratified random sample of institutions was drawn, it became necessary to identify the name and title of the head of teacher education in each school, college, and department of education. The primary source of these addresses was the information on file at the Center for Research on Institutions of Teacher Education. This information was supplemented by the directories of the American Association of Colleges for Teacher Education and the American Council on Education. For the new remaining respondents, calls were made to the institutions to identify the correct individual. To assure the appropriateness of the respondent, an information sheet was attached to each questionnaire asking that the individual identified please forward the questionnaire, if it was incorrectly addressed, to the head of teacher education. The cover letter explained the purpose of the study and also advised respondents that completion of the questionnaire could be facilitated by enclosing a current résumé with the return. About 30 percent of the respondents took advantage of this opportunity.

The questionnaire, complete with cover letter and return envelope, was mailed to the entire sample on November 3, 1975. Approximately three weeks later, 32 percent, or 89 responses, had been returned. Follow-up letters were mailed to the remainder of the population between November 21 and 26. Again, within three weeks an additional 51 responses were in, making the total responses 51 percent. Follow-up calls were made to the respondents. By the cutoff date necessary for mailing a preliminary report of this study, 181 respondents had returned usable questionnaires for a total response of 68 percent. Three respondents indicated that they were unwilling to complete the questionnaire. The stated reasons were that the information requested was too personal and that the questions appeared to be irrelevant to the specified purpose of the study.

The profile of the non-respondent population by sex, title, and terminal degree was comparable to the respondent population. In some instances, institutions identified in the original sample were no longer preparing teachers, and in those instances, a second institution was drawn to complete the sample.

Of the 76 questions in the instrument, approximately one-third of them allowed for open-ended responses. The initial task in the analysis of the data required the derivation of several systems to classify responses. For the first 40 questionnaires which were returned, responses to the open-ended questions were compiled. A broad and complex classification system with repeated applicability was derived to permit direct comparisons of open-ended responses regarding respondent feelings and functions in role. What follows is a brief explanation of the elements of this major classification system:

1. Leadership—used only when the respondent used the word, almost always unspecified.

2. Planning—used for goal setting, fact-finding, seeking more or better knowledge of the field, knowledge of the law in higher education.
3. Organizing—executing, facilitating, climate-building, decision-making, administrivia.
4. Student development—anything related to students: recruitment, advising, etc.
5. Evaluation—related to accreditation activities, self-study.
6. Program development—related to program stimulation, course organization.
7. Staff development—in-service training of faculty, recruitment, tenure, promotion.
8. Budgeting—resource allocation/acquisition, financing.
9. External relations—public relations, liaison for educational unit to those outside unit (central administration, community, legislature); building a politically viable constituent base.
10. Professional duties—teaching, research, reading (activities commonly associated with the professorial role).
11. Power—personal influence, autonomy, authority, personal pay-off.
12. Unclassifiable—other.

Each open-ended question was coded into one of the above classifications, and information from the submitted résumés was transferred onto the instrument. Instruments were key punched and verified, and a computer program was selected. The number of variables totalled 180. Variables appear to cluster and can be viewed in some combination. Variables can also be cross-tabulated. Means and frequencies were tabulated for responses in each of the eight categories, both separately and categorically combined. Because the rate of response was unequal among categories, it was necessary to weight each category to find a mean response for the total population.

In addition to being able to view the eight categories separately or totally, it was possible to divide them into several meaningful clusters for analysis. One approach was to combine the private institutions and to contrast them with the public institutions. Another sort combined the doctoral-granting institutions and compared them separately with both the master-level institutions and the bachelor-level colleges. A third way of analyzing the data compared chief administrators who are entitled "dean" with those who are called "chairpersons." Other efforts compared females with males and whites with racial minorities. And finally, the data compiled from new deans were contrasted with those from deans with longer tenure. Means and frequencies were computed for each of the clusters. In addition, a chi square was computed to test the degree of significance for frequency responses, and an analysis of variance was employed to measure the significance of mean response. (Due to the quantity of data retrieved in this study, tables are not incorporated in this discourse.)

Analysis of the Data (Findings)

I. First, the data revealed the following profiles of the *personal characteristics* of deans:

    A. The mean age at which respondents assumed their current deanship is 43 years, with the category means ranging from the age of 37 to 48. Because only 3 percent of the respondents have had more than one deanship this is also the mean age for assuming an initial deanship. In looking at the mean age within individual categories, the only significant relationship (at the .05 level) occurs by type of degree offered at the respondent's institution. The deans of doctoral- and bachelor-degree-granting institutions assume the deanship at an older age (Ph.D.—45; B.A.—44), than do the leaders of master-degree-granting institutions (age 41).

    B. A physical picture of deans reveals that the current mean age for all deans is 48, with the age of deans at doctoral and bachelor institutions being slightly above the mean and that of the deans at master institutions slightly below this average. Some perspective on these data can be gained from the Campbell and Newell study (p. 17) which shows that the mean age of practicing professors of educational administration is 48 and from the Cohen and March research (p. 8) which lists the mean age of presidents in office as 53.
Women deans average 5 foot 2 inches in height and 138 pounds in weight. The men included in this study average 5 foot 10 inches in height and 178 pounds in weight.

    C. Eighty-four percent of our respondents are male, and 16 percent are female, with no women heads of teacher education appearing in public or private doctoral-level institutions, and with the highest percentage (25 percent) of women heads of teacher education employed in private bachelor-degree institutions. Women are more likely to carry the title "chairperson" in contrast to men, who are more often called "dean."

Ferrari reported in Cohen and March (p. 12) his findings that 11 percent of college and university presidents are female, while only 2 percent of the educational administration professoriate are women (Campbell and Newell, p.18). However, 20 percent of the doctorates in the broad field of education are awarded to women (Bagley, p. 87). As with women presidents, women deans appear to be chiefly in the smaller institutions and in the Catholic-affiliated institutions.

D. Of the respondents to this study, 93 percent are white, 6 percent are black, and 1 percent are Oriental. There are no blacks in the population of private doctoral, private master, or public regional institutions, but rather they are most heavily represented in what formerly may have been all black institutions in the public bachelor-institution category. Parenthetically, 97 percent of educational administration professors are white, and precise data regarding presidents are not available.

E. Of the entire population of respondents, 73 percent describe themselves as being in excellent health. Only 2 percent of the population identify themselves as being in less than good health. When asked if they saw themselves as hyperenergetic—having more energy than most people, or having average or less than average energy—71 percent felt they had more energy than most, and 7 percent felt they were hyperenergetic.

F. Of the respondents, 86 percent are married, 4 percent are widowed or divorced, and 10 percent never married. Among categories, 100 percent of the deans of doctoral institutions are married in contrast to 78 percent of the deans of private bachelor institutions who are married. There is a highly significant relationship between one's sex and marital status. Ninety-three percent of all male respondents are married as contrasted with only 44 percent of women heads of teacher education who are married. Moreover, 44 percent of women deans have never been married.

Other studies show that approximately 74 percent of *all* professors of education are married (Bagley, p. 92), that 94 percent of the educational administration professoriate are married (Campbell and Newell, p. 19), and that virtually all unmarried presidents are members of celibate orders (Cohen and March, p. 12).

The mean number of children for the total population sampled in this study is 2.1. In drawing any conclusions about data on children, marital status must obviously be considered. There is a high proportion of unmarried females entitled "chairperson" in the private institutions. This causes a significant relationship between one's sex and the number of children and one's title and the type of institution where one is employed.

G. Fifty-nine percent of the spouses of those respondents who are married are currently employed. Ninety-four percent of the spouses of non-white respondents are employed, in contrast to 54 percent of the spouses of whites who are employed. The spouses of deans in private doctoral institutions are those that are most likely to be employed, that is, 80 percent of these persons are currently working. Of those spouses who are employed, 61 percent are educators (elementary/secondary school teachers, instructors in higher education), and 16 percent are practicing a profession other than in education (e.g., law, nursing, accounting), although these spouses in non-educational professions do not seem to marry deans in doctoral institutions. In each category, more than half of the working spouses are in education, with the sole differentiation being that 33 percent of the female deans are married to small businessmen while 65 percent of the male deans are married to educators. Of the spouses who were previously employed, as this differs from being currently employed, 73 percent were educators.

H. In regard to family background and youth, 96 percent of the respondents were reared at home by their parents, and 56 percent of the population are either middle- or last-born children. All totalled, 93 percent of the respondents come from multi-child families. These data are quite comparable to those for educational administration professors which show 55 percent as being middle- or last-born children and 90 percent as coming from multi-child families.

I.   Although 92 percent of the respondents have doctorates, 54 percent of their mothers and 58 percent of their fathers received no education beyond high school. Twenty-six percent of both parental groups attended college with 14 percent of both parents receiving degrees. There seems to be no major difference between the level of education of the mothers and the fathers, with the unique exception that the mothers of female deans have a higher educational level than the mothers of male deans.

The 41 percent of university presidents' fathers who attended college and the 27 percent who completed college are both substantially above the general United States figures for the appropriate age group. Even more distinctive was the proportion of presidents' mothers who attended college (34 percent) and those who completed college (16 percent) (Cohen and March, p.17).

J.   Forty-eight percent of the fathers of deans were employed as owner/managers of small businesses or as skilled laborers or artisans. Only 4 percent of the fathers were employed in an education-related occupation, in contrast to 21 percent of the mothers who were working. However, 55 percent of the mothers of male deans were not employed outside the home, in contrast to the 47 percent of the mothers of female deans who were employed, primarily as educators.

For purposes of comparison, 14 percent of education professors in general had fathers with professional employment. Fifty-four percent of the fathers of professors were white-collar workers, and 33 percent were semiskilled or unskilled laborers (Bagley, p.92). While presidents appear to come from all occupational groups, working-class and farmer fathers tend to be under-represented relative to their proportion of the nation's population, and professional, executive, manager, and proprietor fathers tend to be over-represented. Fathers who were secondary school teachers appear to be particularly over-represented (Cohen and March, p.16).

K.   Seventy-five percent of the respondents in the sample were reared or spent the majority of their youth in rural areas, small towns, or small cities (rather than in large cities and their suburbs). In addition, 98 percent of the deans spent their youth in the United States. Of those few who did spend a large percentage of their youth outside the United States, they are now almost exclusively found in doctoral-level institutions. Of the states identified by the respondents as the state in which they were born, the largest dean-producing states are Pennsylvania, New York, and Wisconsin. Fifty-eight percent of today's deans practice in a state other than the one in which they were reared. However, most movement is confined to adjoining states, and the few who move out of their native region follow the trend of the general population westward and southward. Like presidents (Cohen and March, p.18), most deans are employed within 500 miles of their birthplace. Larger schools are more likely to draw leadership from a great distance than are smaller schools.

L. In an effort to measure the perceived change in social class of deans, we asked the respondents to identify their class standing at three periods in their life: youth, age 30, and currently. The stratification used was upper, upper-middle, middle, lower-middle, and lower class. In youth, 55 percent of the respondents viewed themselves as lower or lower-middle class, and 40 percent viewed themselves as middle class. At age 30, 70 percent identified themselves as middle class, and the upper-middle class category showed an increase of from 11 to 16 percent. Thirty-five percent of the deans identify their current class standing as middle class, and 59 percent identify their current class standing as upper-middle class. Clearly, the results indicate upward social mobility. In youth, only 12 percent of the respondents perceived themselves as above middle class. Consistently, the women studied view themselves as occupying higher socio-economic status than do men respondents. The continuum of perceived current social status declines from deans in public doctoral institutions at the upper level to chairpersons in private bachelor institutions at the lower level.

M. Two other demographic indicators of political preference and religious identity reveal that 52 percent of the deans who responded are Democrats, 24 percent are Independents, and 22 percent are Republicans. The mean range is from 80 percent Democrat in the doctoral institutions to 42 percent Democrat in the bachelor-level institutions. Therefore, it follows that there are fewer Democrats and Independents and more Republicans proportionately in private institutions than in public colleges. Political preference appears to shift by degree orientation but appears to be unaffected by central or regional status. In this value preference, deans appear to be closer to professors of administration (where the choices are 46 percent Democrat, 26 percent Republican, and 26 percent Independent [Campbell and Newell, p.22] than to presidents who register as 41 percent Democrat, 37 percent Republican, and 22 percent Independent [Cohen and March, p.13]).

In religious preference, 61 percent of the respondents are Protestant, 21 percent are Catholic, 4 percent are Jewish, 6 percent have some other religious preference, and 8 percent have no affiliation. Unlike the political pattern across categories, there appears to be no real pattern in religious identity other than that in most cases, the religious affiliation of the dean is the same as that of the institution, and a higher percentage of non-affiliation is reported by doctoral respondents. The data show that the deans of education in non-church-related schools in the United States are overwhelmingly Protestant. In this respect, deans resemble presidents. Similarly, 71 percent of the professors of administration are more likely to be Protestant than Catholic (Campbell and Newell, p.22).

II. Next we come to a profile of the *professional background* of the dean.

A. Of the respondents who received doctorates (again, 92 percent), the mean age for completion of the degree was 37, with the category means ranging between the ages of 31 and 40. This figure is similar to the mean of 38 which is the age at which the average professor of educational administration receives a terminal degree (Campbell and Newell, p. 26). In general, female respondents, those who are employed in private institutions, those who carry titles other than "dean," and those who work in bachelor-level institutions obtain doctorates at a later age than do their public, male counterparts.

B. In a population of 178 deans, there were doctorates from 79 different institutions. No single institution prepared more than seven deans, although there were several institutions clustered in the six- to seven-graduate range. These institutions, as identified in our study, are Harvard University, Indiana University, The University of Wisconsin, and The University of Iowa. Three of these four institutions are identified in the Blau[6] study as within the top 12 prominent institutions.

C. For purposes of classifying areas in which respondents have engaged in study, instruction, and research, we devised a system of subject areas as follows: (1) education, unspecified; (2) social and historical foundations of education; (3) teacher education (elementary/secondary, teaching of specific subject areas, general instruction); (4) guidance, counseling, and student personnel services; (5) educational administration and supervision; (6) psychology; (7) research, measurement, and evaluation; (8) higher education; and (9) others. The highest percentage (34 percent) of the deans took their doctorate in teacher education, with 28 percent majoring in educational administration. It is interesting to note that no surveyed dean of a private doctoral institution received the doctorate in administration, which contrasts with public doctoral institutions which have the highest percentage of respondents who did. We asked as well how many respondents had been involved in some prior training in administration. The affirmative response was 67 percent. Even though category two respondents had not pursued a doctoral major in educational administration, 60 percent of them had had prior administrative training.

D. We also asked the respondents to identify activities in which they had participated during the last year for the specific purpose of improving their competence as a higher education administrator. The responses were categorized as yes (unspecified); yes, through relatively insignificant activities (meaning attendance at annual conferences, etc.); yes, through more significant activities (training institutes, leaves of absence for further study in an area related to role, etc.); and no. Sixty-eight percent of the respondents recorded that they had not engaged in such activities in the last year. Twenty-seven percent revealed they had engaged in self-improvement activities of minor significance. Only five percent of all respondents, largely from private institutions, indicated that they had participated in programs with a clear and specific professional growth dimension.

E. The respondents were also asked to identify those areas in which it would have been most helpful to have had prior or additional training, and their responses were categorized according to the system described earlier (ranging from "leadership" to "power"). Twenty-seven percent of those responding wanted more help in "organizing" (executing, facilitating, making decisions), and 20 percent wanted prior or additional help in budgeting. In terms of leadership and program development, females reported a need for additional training which exceeded that reported by males. In addition, respondents in doctoral-level institutions indicated a need for prior training in coping with power relationships in complex organizations. Although clearly current deans want additional training, only one-third of them appear to have sought or found any of it available last year.

F. The survey instrument included a cluster of questions related to the career paths of deans. It may be best to begin the explanation by citing the breakdown of our respondent population by title. Thirty-seven percent are deans or acting deans; 40 percent are chairpersons or acting chairpersons; and the remaining 23 percent are heads, directors, or professors or have other titles. The title "dean" is used for 80 percent of the leadership persons in doctoral institutions. In the remaining public-institution categories, 50 to 60 percent are deans. In the private institutions below the doctorate, fewer than 25 percent are titled "dean." In general, this means that a higher proportion of men are likely to carry the title "dean" than are their female counterparts. (Even though this breakdown exists, we will continue to refer to the entire population as "deans," and will refer to "chairpersons," etc., only to indicate significant relationships according to title.)

G. Eighty-nine percent of the respondents took their current deanship from another position in higher education, and 57 percent of the population took their position from within the same institution in which they were already employed. A dean is more likely to have come from another institution in categories one, two, and three than in the remaining categories.

H. We also reviewed information on previous employment to find that only 27 percent of the respondents had held prior administrative positions in higher education. Twelve percent had been chairpersons, 12 percent had been associate or assistant deans, and 3 percent had been both. Less than 1 percent of the population had held another deanship prior to the current one. Seventy-two percent of the respondents have had prior experience in elementary/secondary schools. Of those who have had experience, 40 percent had been classroom teachers, 22 percent had been administrators, and an additional 38 percent had been both teachers and administrators. Respondents were also asked when (i.e., in what year) it first occurred to them that they were interested in becoming a dean. In general, those who acquire a deanship do so about two years after first giving it serious consideration. One's sex is a significant factor in relation to career planning since males take slightly more than this amount of time (2.2 years), while females take considerably less time between consideration and acquisition (0.65 years). It is interesting to note that 91 percent of the current deans feel that their behavior has been influenced by an administrative-role model. Far and away the biggest percentage (36 percent) of these role models are other deans.

I. Another cluster of questions within professional background deals with scholarly productivity. Fifty percent of the respondents report that they had published books and/or monographs, although this percentage is above 80 percent in the doctoral-level institutions. Deans of doctoral-level institutions, particularly those in public colleges, report that they published from two to three books/monographs each, prior to entering the deanship. This rate of productivity decreases to less than one such publication for all other categories. For all categories, the rate of book publication decreases after the respondent enters the deanship.

Seventy-three percent of the respondents report that they have written articles. The mean number of articles written prior to entering the deanship is 4.3, and during the deanship, 2.0. If the number of books and articles reported during the deanship is combined and divided into the mean number of years current deans have served, the rate of productivity for deans is one publication every year. In general, males write more than females. However, this discrepancy in productivity appears to be more an institutional pressure to publish than it is a function of one's sex.

J. The total respondents report authorship of a mean of 2.2 research and development proposals, and 2.0 training proposals during their careers. The major producers of training proposals are public doctoral-level deans. Forty-six percent of the respondents are currently engaged in research (only 3 percent related to their job and 10 percent related to their educational specialty). "Deans" appear to engage in more research than do persons carrying other administrative titles.

On the average, deans engage in paid consulting about six days per year. With consulting and other outside activities, 82 percent of the deans, individually, generate less than $2,000 income per year in excess of their regular salaries. In general, the higher the degree level of the institution, the higher the "other" income level of the dean.

Respondents were asked to rank the amount of time spent on research and development, training projects, and consulting prior to the deanship as more, less, or the same as the amount of time spent during the deanship. Forty-nine percent of the respondents report that they spend less time now on research and development, 40 percent report more time spent on training projects, and 51 percent report less time spent in consulting. The greatest reduction in the amount of time spent on developing training projects and consulting occurs in public doctoral-level institutions.

K. At this point we should note that it becomes increasingly arbitrary to separate professional background data from current professional data. A case in point is the question asked concerning membership in professional organizations. We asked first how many memberships and offices were held other than because the respondent was dean. Eighty-nine percent of the respondents belong to three or fewer national organizations, with the largest percentage of membership occurring in doctoral institutions; 2 percent of these same persons hold top offices in these organizations (president, vice-president); and 5 percent of the population hold middle-range offices (committee chairperson, etc.), in national professional groups. Ninety-six percent of deans, chiefly in public institutions, belong to three or fewer non-national (state, regional, or local) organizations; 5 percent hold top offices; and 10 percent hold middle-range offices in these organizations. Similarly, when asked about memberships and offices held because they are deans, 95 percent responded that they belong to two or fewer national and two or fewer non-national organizations. The most predominant joiners tend to be "deans" in public doctoral institutions. One percent hold top national offices in dean-related associations, 3 percent hold top offices in non-national groups, 9 percent hold middle-range national offices, and 8 percent hold middle-range non-national offices. All persons who hold top offices for either professional or dean-related reasons fall within categories one, two, and three. The respondent population spends 11 days at conferences yearly, with the highest attendance occurring among deans in the doctoral category.

L. We also asked questions about time away from the job other than for professional reasons. Of those responding, 35 percent take all of the vacation to which they are entitled. Sixty-one percent of those who do not take all of their vacation do so because of the press of work demands. Fewer than 10 percent of the respondents at doctoral institutions take all of their vacation. "Chairpersons" from private institutions are most likely to utilize all of their vacation.

M. Respondents were also asked how they spend their recreational time. The mean number of hours per week spent in recreational activities is 24. That figure includes a mean of four hours for physical recreation, five hours for recreational reading, nine hours for professional reading, and five hours for other types of recreation. Women are more likely to engage in professional and recreational reading, in contrast to men who spend more of their recreation time in physical activities. Non-white respondents spend more time on professional reading than do white respondents. In addition, 83 percent of the respondent population feel that the deanship restricts them from pursuing personal and professional activities.

N. When asked what professional activities deans would pursue if they had eight working hours a week free, 64 percent said they would pursue activities related to their professorial interests (reading, writing, conducting research, etc.). For other, less important desires, indications were that 8 percent would engage in program development, and 8 percent would engage in liaison or public relations work. There is a significant relationship between length of tenure in the deanship and increasing interest in spending more time on activities related to staff development. Female respondents report interest in spending more time in activities related to the power dimension of administration. Deans in private institutions would pursue program development activities if they had more time. Non-whites report an interest in spending free hours on professional activities.

Somewhat ironically, the ways in which deans would spend this additional time if they had it are unrelated to the kinds of help they state they need. Whereas deans report needed assistance in organizational matters and budget, fewer than 2 percent would spend newly acquired time on either organizational or budgetary problems.

III. Data which resulted from the third part of the questionnaire present a *current professional profile* of deans.

   A. Today's typical dean has held this position for 70 months (nearly six years). His or her predecessor served a mean of eight years in the deanship. There is a significant relationship between one's title and how long one anticipates remaining in the deanship. The mean expectancy for "deans" is four to six years of additional service, while "chairpersons" anticipate remaining in that role for only one to three years. Non-whites expect to remain in office for a longer period of time (seven years or more), than do their white counterparts. In general, the same tenure expectation discrepancy exists between deans in doctoral institutions and those in bachelor-level units. When comparing the data from respondents with less than one year of service as deans with those from respondents having more than two years in the role, one finds that there are few significant differences between the characteristics: perceptions of role and responsibilities, productivity, and personal and professional characteristics. This indicates that length of tenure is unrelated to the factors measured by our study.

   B. An analysis of the employment condition suggests that 97 percent of the respondents hold academic rank, 64 percent are professors, and 23 percent are associate professors. In general, the higher percentage of full professors occurs among males, who carry the title "dean" in public doctoral institutions. Of those who have academic rank, 74 percent also have tenure as a faculty member. One hundred percent of the respondents in the doctoral institutions have faculty tenure. In contrast, 92 percent of the total array of respondents do *not* have tenure as deans. Sixty percent of the respondents have 11/12 month contracts, and 40 percent have 9/12 month contracts. There is a direct relationship between 11/12 month contracts and male respondents who carry the title "dean" and are employed in public doctoral institutions.

C. Thirty-four percent of the deans reported that they are currently earning a salary of between $15,000 and $19,000, 17 percent are earning less than $15,000, and 16 percent are earning between $20,000 and $24,999. Only 3 percent of the respondents earn $40,000 or above. The highest mean salary is reported for doctoral institutions, with the lowest salaries occurring in bachelor institutions, while salaries in private institutions fall below those in public institutions. To illustrate, 40 percent of the private doctoral-level respondents make above $40,000. In contrast, 58 percent of the respondents from private bachelor institutions make $20,000 or less.

D. Another cluster of questions in the current professional background arena describes the dean's span of control. Forty-eight percent of the respondents report that they have professional assistance on their immediate staff. An analysis of individual category response reveals that the majority of the subordinates exist in the doctoral institutions and in public master-degree institutions. Respondents reported the responsibilities of their immediate staff members. Of these staff members, 13 percent work in the area of teacher education, 12 percent work in student services, 10 percent work in laboratory experiences, and 43 percent are classified as other, including administrative assistants. Only 6 percent of those respondents who have assistants assign them to fiscal affairs, and another 6 percent have assistants for graduate programs.

E. An additional cluster of questions focused on the professional dimensions of a dean's job. Eighty-six percent of the respondents report that they teach classes. The lowest mean number of courses taught annually by those deans who teach is 1.2 in doctoral-level institutions as contrasted with 4.2 in private bachelor-level institutions. The mean number of courses taught last year by all respondents was reported as 3.2 courses. White respondents teach more courses than do non-white respondents. The data show that 50 percent of the instruction which deans execute is offered in "the teaching of" a particular subject field and in general methods of instruction courses. In several cases it includes the supervision of student teachers. The next area most frequently taught by deans is educational foundations (15 percent).

F. The bulk of the student advisement carried out by deans occurs in public and private bachelor-level institutions. The mean number of undergraduates being regularly assigned to a dean is reported at 19. Deans at doctoral-level institutions, when they advise at all, do so at the graduate level.

G. A significant portion of the questionnaire and, consequently, of the data, relate to what we have previously called respondent perceptions of feelings and functions in role. It seems appropriate to describe initially the responses recorded in relation to the question: "What do you consider to be the major functions and responsibilities of the deanship?" Using the system developed to classify the responses to open-ended, role-related questions, 17 percent of the respondents recorded organizing responsibilities as a major function of the deanship. Significant percentages were recorded for other functions, as follows: 16 percent for staff development, 14 percent for liaison and public relations functions, 13 percent for program development, and 9 percent for budget-related activities.

Statistically significant differences in functions reported were:

1. More females than males report that student development is an important function of the deanship.
2. Respondents from doctoral-level institutions assign a higher priority to planning than do their colleagues in other types of institutions.
3. Deans in public doctoral-level institutions consider budget with greater concern than do deans in private doctoral-level institutions.
4. Deans, more than respondents with other titles, view staff development as an important function.
5. Non-white respondents report evaluation as an important function more often than do their white counterparts.

H. With the same classification system used above, an analysis of other questions related to the functions which the respondents identified as appropriate to the deanship follows. Deans were asked to identify one of their most successful and one of their least successful activities during the past year of their deanship. A mean of 42 percent of the respondents experienced success in the area of program development. Eighteen percent recorded success in evaluation-related activities (such as reaccreditation), and 14 percent identified success in staff-development activities. In contrast, the highest percentage of failures (25 percent), paradoxically, was recorded for activities related to staff development. Twenty-one percent of the respondents experienced failure in program-development activities, and 15 percent experienced failure in budgetary activities. In both success and failure, program and staff development appear to be important considerations. Not surprisingly, only 3 percent of the respondents felt successful with regard to financial matters. There were no significant differences in the successes and failures reported by respondents among categories.

I. Another sequence of related questions asked deans to list three each of their most significant satisfactions and frustrations. Eighteen percent of the respondents indicated that deans receive the most satisfaction from activities associated with that portion of their role which is professorial (e.g., research, instruction, and writing). "Chairpersons" spend more time in this activity and appear to get more satisfaction from it than do "deans." Before reporting other satisfactions, we will insert further explanation of perceptions related to the professorial role. It is interesting to note that 60 percent of the respondent population, if given a sabbatical leave, would prefer to engage in activities related to the professoriate (further study, research, writing, or a visiting professorship), rather than more administratively allied activities. While 55 percent of the respondents feel that their administrative position is one of the most important aspects of their life, this feeling is primarily exhibited by deans at public graduate-level institutions. Another 40 percent feel that their administrative position is only one of several important career activities, with other activities, such as teaching, research, and service, being of similar importance. Also, 59 percent of the deans feel that they are *likely* to become a professor after leaving the deanship. When asked what position they would prefer to assume, 55 percent again specified the professorship. Ascension to the presidency and academic vice-presidency is more desired than expected—very few want to become dean at another institution—but nothing competes with the professorship.

Other satisfactions noted are as follows: 16 percent in the area of program development, 14 percent in activities related to student development, 13 percent in staff development (especially by respondents in public institutions), and 11 percent in activities related to organizational responsibilities (particularly by doctoral-level respondents). Additionally, a significant number of women report satisfactions from activities related to the liaison function of the deanship.

These results can be contrasted with items reported as frustrations. Twenty-four percent of the respondents report that they have experienced frustration in activities related to organization (i.e., execution, facilitation, climate-building, etc.). Eighteen percent of the respondents report frustration in the area of fiscal affairs, 16 percent in liaison/public relations, and 15 percent in staff development. There is a significant relationship between certain of these frustrations and respondent groups as follows:

1. Women respondents are more frustrated by activities related to student development and power relationships.
2. Respondents at master-level institutions report more frustrations with matters related to organization.

J. Closely allied to the above responses, deans say that they might be most expert in helping deans in organizational activities (25 percent response) and in program-development activities (also 25 percent response). The next most frequently recorded area of expertise (11 percent) is in staff-development activities. A more detailed analysis of these data reveal the following respondent patterns:

1. Doctoral-level respondents report expertise in evaluation and in fiscal affairs. Bachelor-level respondents appear least secure in these same areas.
2. Female respondents report that they could be helpful in functions related to leadership and staff development more than do their male counterparts.
3. Private deans describe themselves as having student-development skills in contrast to public deans who report expertise in staff development.
4. "Deans" appear to feel more secure with program-building activities than do non-deans.

As reported previously, deans collectively say that it would have been most helpful to have had prior or additional training in the areas of organization, program development, and fiscal affairs. Surprisingly, needs and expertise appear to fall in the same groupings.

K. Questions related to mode of operation of deans reveal further information about role perception. We asked deans to describe faculty/administration roles in the decision-making process in their administrative unit. The format for this question was multiple choice, and, as such, 46 percent of the respondents felt that their unit was characterized by strong leadership from officials but much influenced by a broad spectrum of faculty through committees, faculty senate, etc. An additional 40 percent felt that their unit differed by being more or less democratically run by faculty and administrators working together instead of being dominated by faculty, college or central administration, or other external forces. It is significant that domination of the teacher-education unit by the central administration increases as the degree-granting level of the unit decreases.

L. Deans were also asked on what basis they made their decisions on a continuum from almost exclusively politically to almost exclusively substantively. Fifty-four percent of the respondents reported that they made their decisions on a primarily substantive, but somewhat political, basis, and 23 percent felt that their decisions were almost exclusively substantively based.

M. Also related to the decision-making process, deans report that they typically seek advice on matters of serious professional concern primarily from their administrative superior. Sixty-eight percent responded affirmatively to this choice, which was the highest positive percentage received for any of the possible choices. Other choices which received a high percentage of "yes" answers were: (1) the faculty (collectively), (2) a professor in the same college, and (3) a member of the immediate administrative staff. Clearly rejected were such choices as professional association or agency persons or an elementary/secondary school colleague. There seem to be no differences among the responses of varying types of deans on this question.

N. Another general question about decision-making asked deans to estimate approximately how much influence they have over institution-wide policies that affect their administrative unit, compared to their perception of the average dean. Forty-nine percent of the respondents feel that they have more than average influence. An additional 38 percent of the respondents report that they have about the same influence as other deans.

O. All of the above questions which relate to respondent feelings and functions should be juxtaposed to the responses which follow. To the question, "If you had it to do all over again, would you still become a dean?," the response was an impressive 83 percent "Yes." To the question, "Which statement describes your feeling toward your current deanship?," 24 percent find the role highly satisfying to them personally, 50 percent enjoy it most of the time, and 20 percent find it equally satisfying and frustrating, for a 94 percent total response indicating moderate to high satisfaction.

IV. Data solicited from *deans' superordinates*.

One of the goals of this study included the examination of the perceptions of current deans' superordinates (i.e., provosts or vice-presidents) on their role expectations for current deans and their perceptions of their current dean's job satisfaction, frustrations, successes, and failures.

In the first step of this phase of the study, a letter was sent to the 181 deans who responded to the original questionnaire, requesting permission to contact their immediate superordinates (provosts or vice-presidents) for their perceptions of the dean's role expectations. Affirmative responses were received from 125 deans, and letters were sent to the provosts of these deans, requesting that they respond to certain questions on the original questionnaire. Provosts were asked to respond in regard to the dean rather than to themselves. The 93 provosts who responded were evenly divided among institutional types. Means, frequencies, and standard deviations were calculated between responses of provosts and current deans.

What follows is an initial reporting of the data reported in the survey of the provosts:

A. Sixty-five percent of the responding provosts view their dean of education as possessing more energy than most persons, with an additional 5 percent of the provosts viewing their dean as hyper-energetic.

B. Provosts were asked to identify those persons whom their education dean consulted for administrative advice. The highest percentage of responses (73 percent indicated that the dean sought advice from an administrator in the university outside the dean's administrative unit. Of all the other possible sources of advice, none received more than a 34 percent positive response.

C. Provosts were asked to identify one of their dean's most successful activities during the last year. Thirty-five percent of the respondents identified successful activity in program development, with an additional 24 percent of the responses indicating success in evaluation activities.

D. When asked about the least successful activities of their dean, 21 percent of the provosts noted lack of success in their dean's staff-development activities, with an additional 20 percent of the provosts noting lack of success in the deanship with program-development activities (the same area in which 35 percent of the provosts said their dean had experienced some success).

E. Provosts were asked to identify areas of expertise in which their dean could assist other deans. The areas of expertise which received the highest ratings were: (1) program development, (2) external relations, (3) organizational activities, and (4) activities related to the dean's professorial role.

F. Provosts were asked to identify what they perceived to be the major functions of the deanship. Three activities received the highest responses as follows: (1) program development, (2) staff development, and (3) organizational activities.

G. Provosts were also asked to respond to several questions related to institutional climate and the dean's role in the institution. Fifty percent of the provosts characterized the unit their education dean administers as being guided by strong leadership from officials, but with much influence being exercised by a broad spectrum of faculty through committees, faculty senate, etc. Provosts characterized their dean's institutional involvement (according to 61 percent of the respondents) as being one of the most important aspects of the dean's life. Accordingly, provosts believe that for their dean, the deanship is that person's prime job and consumes most of the dean's non-family time. Fifty-eight percent of the provosts responded that their dean has about the same influence over institutional policies as the average dean has. Fifty-nine percent of the provosts believe that their dean makes decisions on a primarily substantive, but somewhat political, basis. And finally, 40 percent of the provosts believe that their education dean is equally satisfied and frustrated in the deanship, with an additional 39 percent of the provosts noting that their dean enjoys the deanship most of the time.

In essence, there appear to be no major differences between deans' self-perceptions and their superordinates' perceptions of education deans.

Inferences, Interpretations, and Projections

The purpose of this study was to collect descriptive baseline data in an area of significant interest, where heretofore there has existed only a data void. As such, this is a low inference, descriptive study. The data which have evolved will be added to and tested repeatedly, both by us and by other interested researchers.

We have drawn from these data some correlations and levels of significance among and between types of respondents. To this end we offer substantive generalizations regarding the personal and professional background and role perceptions of today's deans of education.

I. Substantive generalizations:
   A. *Personally,* American deans of education today are most commonly healthy and energetic, middle-aged, married, male, white, Protestant, Democrat, and from a relatively non-college educated, lower-middle class, nonprofessional-managerial, native-born, small-town, multi-child family background.

For those who are only moderately familiar with the deanship today, there were only a few major surprises to be found in the data. Not only are heads of teacher education as a group what might have been expected, but also most of the differences between "deans" and "chairpersons" could have been predicted.

While using the deanship as a means of upward social mobility was expected, the relatively low level of education in the homes from which deans come was unanticipated. Similarly, the high level of spouse employment and the professional nature of that employment were surprising.

B. *Professionally*, American deans of education today normally hold the doctorate degree, have had some training in educational administration, entered the profession through public school experiences, advanced from there to the university faculty, and took the deanship directly from a position in higher education. Despite their administration duties, they manage to engage in as much research and writing as do their professorial colleagues. They find that the deanship does constrain both their personal and professional activities, however, they do belong to several national and regional professional associations, and acknowledge the need for professional self-improvement, even though they engage in relatively little of it.

Although a common perception may have been that deans, as chief administrators of colleges of education, have therefore primarily been graduates of administration doctoral programs, they are instead predominately graduates of programs in the teaching of specific subject areas and in general instruction.

Also surprising is the apparent lack of a clear career path to the deanship. The myth of academe suggests a move from professor, to department chairperson, to assistant or associate dean, to dean, with the terminal move to the deanship generally not occurring within the same institution. Our data show that a high percentage of deans come directly from the professoriate and are as likely to be promoted from within as to change institutions to acquire a deanship.

C. The profile of the American college education dean's *current status* is far less clear than are the personal and professional background profiles. First, and foremost, deans obviously are happy, satisfied, and secure and perceive themselves as relatively influential.

Today's dean reports that the faculty is involved democratically; reaches decisions primarily on their substantive, as opposed to their political, merits; and consults regularly with administrative superiors on professional problems. In addition to administrative responsibilities, the dean does a modicum of teaching, advising, and consulting. The dean is normally a tenured full professor on an extended administrative contract who is paid a salary slightly in excess of regular faculty.

Deans are capable of identifying their feelings and functions associated with role (i.e., the satisfactions and frustrations and the successes and failures inherent in the deanship), and they recognize a need to improve upon skills related to the deanship.

The preceding profiles are descriptive of the total population studied in this research. Other combinations of the respondents suggest two emerging profiles which do not deny the validity of those presented earlier, but which constitute contrasting and perhaps more meaningful ways of viewing the administrative heads of teacher-education programs.

D. It is reasonably clear that there is one head of teacher education (type A) characterized by persons who are male, who are called "dean," and who are employed in relatively large doctoral-awarding universities. These persons are productive scholars, are active in national associations, and take an administrative, as opposed to a professorial, perspective of their role. They appear to be relatively autonomous in their decision-making capacity, work year around, hold full professor rank, earn a reasonably high salary, have relatively little direct student contact, and consult moderately. They tend to take little vacation and have the job security of long-expected tenure in the deanship.

E. It is equally clear that a type B head of teacher education is confirmed by our data. This classification consists of males and females in equal number who are called "chairperson" and who are employed in relatively small bachelor-degree-granting colleges. They spend little time writing and researching but have considerable student contact through teaching and advising. These persons are active in state and regional professional associations. Professorial functions and duties are as important to them as are administrative responsibilities. The central administration impinges significantly on the decisions they make. They are employed on an academic-year contract, are likely to hold a rank below full professor, earn low to moderate salaries, consult irregularly, and take all of the vacation they earn. They tend to see their administrative role as temporary.

F. There is a third and far less distinct profile which we shall label transitory. Persons in this category exhibit some characteristics of both types A and B but have relatively few unique attributes. They do appear to have more problems with organizational questions than do their colleagues. They are employed chiefly in master-degree-granting institutions. By inference, and without statistical verification, it appears that the role and function (and hence the setting and responsibilities) of both bachelor- and doctoral-level respondents are relatively stable and well defined. Master-granting institutions, on the other hand, appear to be neither "fish nor fowl" and consequently reflect this inconsistency in their leader characteristics and role demands.

II. Implications for Training

One of the major objectives of this study was to derive some understandings which would be helpful in organizing programs for improving the performance of deans. What follows are some generalizations, derived from our findings and impregnated with inferences, concerning the substance, process, and desirability of such programs for deans.

A. Deans express a clear desire for further training. It is equally apparent that practicing deans are not receiving such instruction. It is probable that this dilemma exists because the training which deans desire is simply not available.

B. Deans are able to identify their own problems and needs. Deans are also able to identify their own areas of administrative expertise. There is a high degree of similarity between the needs of some deans and the expertise of others. Consequently, deans appear to be invaluable to the education of other deans.

C. Deans as a group need assistance with the management of their time. Not only should such assistance be part of the substance of training programs for deans but also it should become one of the factors to be considered in program design.

D. Deans appear to have generic needs or problems (e.g., staff-development activities). However, it appears that variability in the settings of deanships produces differences in the expectations and applications of the incumbents involved. For instance, the issue of fiscal affairs may be a common problem for many deans, but the solution for a dean in one institution may be quite different from the solution for a dean in another.

E. The needs and competencies of deans appear, in the main, to be unrelated to the length of time that an individual has occupied the deanship. Consequently, one need not be concerned with grouping deans of similar length of experience when organizing training programs. Clearly this means that dean-training programs need not be national in order to achieve the critical mass necessary for success.

F. There is only a brief span of time between when one first considers assuming a deanship and when one is successful in acquiring such a position. Therefore, the time when one is receptive to pre-service training for the deanship is severely limited. In effect, it appears that in-service education for deans may be the most feasible approach.

G. We close on what we believe to be an extremely encouraging note. The fact that we received a 68 percent response to a complex questionnaire leads us to be confident that not only are deans as a group interested in improving their effectiveness, but also they are highly receptive to inquiries and findings of researchers and to their efforts to devise training programs for them.

APPENDIX TO CHAPTER 5

Institutional Categories

I. Public Doctoral-Level Institutions
   22 institutions sampled
   17 responses received

II. Private Doctoral-Level Institutions
   10 institutions sampled
   5 responses received

III. Public Master-Level Institutions
   49 institutions sampled
   38 responses received

IV. Public Master-Level Institutions, Regional Campuses
   8 institutions sampled
   7 responses received

V. Private Master-Level Institutions
   55 institutions sampled
   30 responses received

VI.   Public Bachelor-Level Institutions
      13 institutions sampled
      10 responses received

VII. Public Bachelor-Level Institutions, Regional Campuses
      5 institutions sampled
      3 responses received

VIII. Private Bachelor-Level Institutions
      109 institutions sampled
      68 responses received

      271 Total Institutions Sampled
      178 Total Usable Responses Received

NOTES

1. Although data from the survey of deans' superordinates will be reported later in this paper, the major portion of this report is devoted to the subject of current deans.

2. J. V. Baldridge, D. V. Curtis, G. Ecker, and G. L. Riley, *Diversity in American Higher Education: A National Study of Academic Governance, Faculty Activities and Professional Climates* (San Francisco: Jossey Bass, Autumn 1977).

3. Michael D. Cohen and James G. March, *Leadership and Ambiguity: The American College President* (New York: McGraw-Hill, 1974).

4. Ayers Bagley, *The Professor of Education: An Assessment of Conditions* (Minneapolis: Society of Professors of Education, 1975).

5. Roald F. Campbell and L. Jackson Newell, *A Study of Professors of Educational Administration* (Columbus, Ohio: University Council for Educational Administration, 1973).

6. Peter M. Blau and Rebecca Z. Margulies, "The Reputations of American Professional Schools," *Change* (December 1974).

Part III

CHAPTER 6

Some Notes on Deans as Individuals and the Role of the Dean[1]

by
ARTHUR COLADARCI
Stanford University

I was appointed to the decanal chair after two decades of service in the American professoriate—a carefree period during which I carefully learned little and cared even less about institutional administration, other than ready participation in the academic tribal rituals of expressing paranoia and vouchsafing disinterest. Accordingly, in the guilty realization that I was assuming a role for which I was most unprepared, I set about to locate and study the accumulated knowledge and wisdom bearing on employment as dean of a school of education. I found, with Adamic surprise, that the literature addressing this honorable estate could be read comfortably between a late breakfast and an early lunch—and that the dearth in volume was not compensated for by substance. It appears that educational researchers, even those given to extended fits of intemperate empiricism, essentially have been disinterested in examining a role that, in their own profession, is rumored to be consequential but is charged frequently to be ineffective.

The roles and performances of public school administrators have been studied, modeled, "criterionized," criticized, and evaluated with high frequency for several decades. The role and behavior of the persons under whose presumed aegis people are prepared for those positions are generally accorded benign neglect, except for an occasional *cri de coeur*—a passionate protest against the sorry state of professional preparation. If the observation is generally correct, it is surprising that (1) the studies of public school administration largely are initiated and encouraged by members of education faculties and (2) education deans (in my admittedly unsystematic recollection) frequently come from and continue reference to the corps of school administration specialists.

Nor, in my impression, are the competent studies of public school administrators easily generalizable to collegiate administration generally or to decanal performance more specifically. The two institutional contexts differ substantially in purposes and dynamics. Furthermore, if James March (1976) is correct, the administration of higher education functions in ambiguity of purposes. I believe there is more explicit purpose definition and constraint in public school administration—for weal or woe. Governance and administration in American higher education, furthermore, is characterized by definable heterogeneity across institutions. These institutional differences may be sufficiently great as to puzzle rather than encourage the study of the decanal (or any other administrative) role in post-secondary education.

My own instinct is that the facts of institutional diversity should compel us, in studying administrative roles, to utilize paradigms and methodologies different from those modally used heretofore—rather than to give up the chase as too risky or undefinable. Therefore, without gainsaying the importance of other sub-sets of the domain, "The role of the dean of education," I restrict my attention here to only a small portion of the possible domain.

At an earlier time, I would have suggested that this question be engaged with a bias for nomothetically oriented inquiry. However, my recent experiences in the role, my conversations and observations, and my perusing of some literature persuade me that the search for long-lived usable applications, universal explanations or high derivative-yielding theoretical formulations have been and will continue to be premature, at best.

This is not to reject the possible and even probable existence of nomothetic lawfulness across persons, situations, and time—neither is it an assumption of inherent idiosyncrasy of events. Indeed, I suspect that, when the last datum is in, we will read more sense than humor in a great line from T. S. Elliot's, *The Cocktail Party*:"'All cases,' observes Sir Henry to his patient, "'are unique—and very similar to others.'" Rather, I argue (and not alone) for a temporary but healthy intellectual agnosticism about a *science* of administrative behavior— i.e., about the near-term productivity of nomothetically oriented designs and inquiries.

Where behavior research and analyses have yielded descriptions, generalizations, explanations, and theories that purport to have or to approach universal application, they have done so at levels of abstraction far removed from the referential events to be accounted for. The search and analyses will go on, of course, and may drive the power of prediction and explanation further down the ladder of abstraction.

We probably are in some agreement on why social and psychological research has been less productive of universals than research in the physical domains. The former, we often point out, must engage more variables and, more importantly, the behavior events, their correlates, and their contexts are demonstrably more *interactive* and in more complex ways.

I submit that we should believe what we say—that, in inviting research on the dean and his role, we should urge and persuade that such inquiry be rationalized and designed with explicit engagement of three realities: (1) heterogeneity of schools of education and their host institutions, (2) multiplicity of variables in decanal roles and performance, and (3) the near-certainty that the performance of a dean (or anyone else) is explainable most usefully in terms of interactions among personal and situational characteristics.

(1) *HETEROGENEITY:* I dare say that we easily can agree that schools of education scarcely comprise "birds-of-a-feather." The differences across these institutions and their hosts are patent and, surely, must be consequential in the topic we pursue here. Indeed, some observers (e.g., Baldridge, *et al.*, 1975) feel that this diversity has increased with time. Others argue that the movement may be in the direction of more homogeneity because of "prestige imitation" (as in Jencks and Riesman, 1968, and Newman, *et al.*, 1971, 1973), or program "mainstreaming" (Pace, 1974), or a movement from private to public institutions. Although I find the predictions of increased diversity more persuasive, the fact of great diversity is real and it will continue to be our natural habitat for a long period, even if the trend is contrary.

The existence of marked differences among the institutional contexts in which administrative roles are defined and performed should not be ignored in mounting inquiry into these definitions and performances.

(2) *MULTI-VARIATION*: The *number* of variables that presumably and possibly may bear on an understanding of the decanal role is exceedingly large, even if one restricts attention to only a single institution in a particular time period. My impression, however, is that the multi-variate reality of administrative roles, generally, is underestimated and oversimplified among those who propose and conduct analyses—and even more so, perhaps, among those who perform those roles. If we at this moment undertook to list the variables we think have identifiable or probable relevance in the study of decanal roles, our catalogue quickly would exhaust the patience of a *rapporteur*. If we should add to our midst some specializations not now represented, the list of variables would increase rapidly and probably exponentially. We cannot (or, better, should not) ignore the variables relating to person, interperson, or institutional process, among others. To be sure, we have seen studies that acknowledge and delineate some of the diversity. They are informative and suggestive, but their grasp is far short of the reach we need. One recent investigation, confining itself to organizational characteristics only, identified five dozen variables for which there were available data across a sample of higher-education institutions and produced an impressive matrix of zero-order coefficients of correlation among all variables—from which we learn that, with few exceptions, the correlations are low or modest. The result should not be surprising, as I will suggest below. There *were* some very high correlations, incidentally; you may find it reassuring, for example, to know that the correlation between "institution size" and "number of faculty" is greater than .90.

(3) *INTERACTION:* I have suggested that heterogeneity and multi-variation are inescapable conditions of the dean's role (or *any* administrative role). These conditions, alone, should provide justification of the role and its performance as "complex." The inherent complexity, I submit, is probably greater than past inquiry suggests, and—to touch upon the gravamen of my current concern—probably lies more in presumed *interactions* among variables and characteristics.

I here use the term *interaction* in the special sense in which it has been applied by recent scholars (e.g., and notably, Cronbach and Snow). For example, consider the case in which a given situation has one effect on one kind of person and a different effect on another. Or, for another example, where the relationship between an independent variable and criterion performance differs at different points of the independent variable and the criterion.

This is to say that the ways in which institutional and personal characteristics bear upon the role and performance of a dean probably vary with the differing contexts for the role and performance. Hence, as I have noted, it is neither surprising nor confusing to find that the correlations among putatively "important" variables across institutions are modest.

Should we not also design our studies of the decanal role on the assumption that such interactions may be present in a single institution? We do not know about the ways in which any institution demonstrably changes in purposes, structure, agenda, and relationship over time; therefore, it is difficult to answer the question negatively. These ways and rates have, indeed, increased markedly in the last decade—a period that has witnessed marked changes in schools of education and their parent universities—changes in clientele, agenda, governance, resources, etc.

If the foregoing general limning is sensible, or even partially sensible, what does it suggest by way of profitable approaches to knowledge-building?

1. At the most general level, I submit, we should encourage and support more (and more competent) inquiry that is flavored by what I earlier termed *agnosticism* about nomothetic explanations. I would go further and encourage temporary, explicit, calculated, secular atheism on this matter. The assumption that there can be "an administrator for all seasons," I submit, should not control all or even most of the search. We may find more heurism in particularistic inquiries and analyses. This is much easier said than done, of course. The recent and continuing culture of educational research distributes its rewards and prestige symbols among those who profess allegiance to model-building, theory-generation, and hypothetico-deductive intellectual strategy. We need to encourage the brave soul (at least the tenured soul) to indulge his or her more inductive instincts.

   Context-constrained research does not mean the inevitability of context-limited generalizations and explanations. Rather, it places most of the logical burden on inductive processes and techniques. One of my distinguished colleagues, who scarcely can be called "soft-headed" about science-building, recently has argued on this general direction for the discipline of psychology (Cronbach, 1977). His position is equally relevant and perhaps more urgent for the phenomena we are discussing here.

2. More specifically, we need, and the foregoing posture requires, studies of the administrator *in situ*—"case studies." "Case studies," as you know, abound in melancholy number. What we *do not* need is more of the same. Rather, I suggest, we encourage studies of deans-and-deanships-in-context that are maximally inclusive of the known and hypothetically relevant parameters of person, interperson, institutional processes, and agenda, to name only a conventional few. Such comprehensive case analyses should provide better illumination for the particular dean and institution. This is more than a call for the use of ethnography and ethnographic techniques in studies of administrative role and performance. And it is more than a call merely for the utilization of the most powerful techniques for quantitative analysis. Both of these are indeed applicable and under-utilized in such inquiries. What additionally is called for, in my own view, at least, is the willingness (and competence) to introduce less palpable and more interpretive parameters of role-context. One of my colleagues, Elliot Eisner (1977), is making a persuasive case for fuller contextual analyses and evaluation. He and his students seem to have articulated a different conception of evaluation—to which I only direct your attention lest I garble a highly complex approach in brief description.

The overriding objective is to generate something we now seriously lack if an inductive strategy is to be nourished—a competent and growing basis for fruitful, inductive quests for commonalities and for working inductive hypotheses about relationships between and interactions among given role definitions, performances, personal attributes, institutional characteristics, etc. Over time, such studies, if they adequately inform each other, also will permit the development of a more useful taxonomy of variables, which can serve the dual purpose of advising new studies and inviting more similarity of attack among them.

The case studies called for here clearly cannot be single-person enterprises. Each, by definition, should be planned and conducted by a collectivity that matches the range of substance and methodology inherent in this kind of "case": for example, political, economic, sociological, psychological, anthropological, normative. That is, such research should be genuinely interdisciplinary in nature if it is to be more productive of role knowledge than earlier efforts have been.

NOTE

1. This paper is a *précis* of the full presentation made by Dean Coladarci at the Seminar.

REFERENCES

Baldridge, J. Victor, David V. Curtis, George P. Ecker, and Gary L. Riley. "Diversity in Academic Governance Patterns," *Research Memorandum, No. 130*. Stanford Center for Research and Development in Teaching, School of Education, Stanford University, Stanford, Calif., January 1975.

Cronbach, Lee J. "Beyond the Two Disciplines of Scientific Psychology," *The American Psychologist*, Vol. 30, No. 2, February 1975.

Cronbach, Lee J., and Richard E. Snow. *Aptitudes and Instructional Interactions*. New York: Irvington, 1977.

Eisner, Elliot W. "On the Uses of Educational Connoisseurship and Criticism for the Study of Classroom Life," *Teachers College Record*, February 1977.

Jencks, Christopher, and David Riesman. *The Academic Revolution*. New York: Doubleday, 1968.

March, James G., and Johan P. Olsen. *Ambiguity and Choice in Organizations*. Bergen, Norway: Universitetsforlaget, 1976.

Newman, Frank, *et al*. *Report on Higher Education*. Washington, D.C.: Department of Health, Education, and Welfare, 1971.

Pace, Robert C. *The Demise of the University: A Comparative Profile of Eight Types of Institutions*. New York: Carnegie Foundation for the Advancement of Teaching, 1974.

CHAPTER 7

Deans as Individuals-in-Organizations

by

DORIS W. RYAN
The Ontario Institute for Studies in Education

THE PROBLEM

The North American university began in the 1960's to experience an enormous increase in the complexity of its role and function in society. Political and social concerns were lumped with the more traditional academic and vocational functions to create a "volatile new mix" that defied stable organization (Mollenberg, 1976). During the same period, the academic profession was changing. As the emphasis on research increased, the profession became an amalgamation of segments, specialties, and sub-specialties, and these interest clusters were reflected in the university organization (Ryan, 1974). Decision-making and governing processes became more and more complex and were fraught with potential conflicts (Riesman, 1956; Kerr, 1963; Walton and Dutton, 1969).

By the mid-1970s, the North American university was confronted with new problems. Declining student enrollments, shrinking funds for research, reduced operating budgets, and increasing cynicism with regard to its products provided the ingredients for what March (1974) has called a "period of neglect" or decline. University organization has just begun to reflect the impact of these trends. Little is known about the impact on governance and decision-making as yet.

Even less is known about the role of academic administrators and about the effects of current issues and strains on that role. Discussing the hazards of academic administration, Mollenberg (1976) argued that the extreme complexity of the role that a modern university administrator must play and the rampant mistrust of authority have placed the incumbent in a "no-win" situation. The impossibility of the institutional role, he reasoned, often invades private life. The kinds of role conflicts and role ambiguities described by Mollenberg and reinforced by Cohen and March's (1974) analysis of leadership in an organized anarchy are logical and provocative. Educational researchers, however, have rarely attempted to document and analyze these dynamics.

Reviewing over 500 reports on higher education completed within the past decade, Peterson (1974) concluded that the role activities, attitudes, and values of crucial officers in universities and colleges have not been well researched. Studies of leadership, decision-making, functional impact on the organization, and other aspects of administrative behavior seldom have been undertaken. Very few studies have examined the causes and consequences of congruent and/or conflicting role expectations, and complex models of role behavior which utilize empirical data and multivariate analysis techniques have not been attempted. Studies of academic administrators, according to Peterson, have made little use of conceptual variables or theoretical models. In short, the dean's role has been described primarily through survey methods, and little is known about the dynamics of that role or about interrelationships among societal, institutional, and personal variables and their effects on role behavior and attitudes.

Administrative roles have been studied more comprehensively in other institutional settings, but typical studies of role conflict have focused on the role expectations of individual organizational members as direct predictors of conflict and stress in an administrative position. Other contributing factors, such as group and organizational characteristics, have been treated at best as exogenous variables, differentiating the contexts within which role conflicts may occur. Few attempts have been made to examine rigorously the organizational sources of role tensions that might explain the meaning of relationships among variables in typical survey studies.

It is the author's thesis that organizational factors and accompanying social processes have potent explanatory potential in studies of the deanship. In the first place, both university organization and the internal organization of academic sub-units reflect sociocultural factors in the institution's environment. That is, changes within the society and culture produce changes within the academic profession (one sub-system), which together provide the impetus for modifications within university organization. The author has argued elsewhere (Ryan, 1974) that the concept of normative diversity (or heterogeneity) provides a means for theoretically linking organizational factors to their societal and cultural sources.

This conceptualization is consistent with Blau's (1970, 1973) theory of differentiation in organizations, in which inter-unit heterogeneity was presented as an inferred (not operationalized) concept to explain some of the hypothesized relationships in the model. It is also consistent with Parsons' (1951) general theory of social action and with his recent (1973) focus on the institutionalization of cultural patterns in the social system of the university. Smelser (1973) further illustrated this theoretical chain of impact when he noted that the external provisions (or sanctions) for specialized research in the 1950s and 1960s in the United States created an impetus for professional differentiation (academic research specializations) and, therefore, fostered tensions within the university organization. One might expect other tensions in the 1970s and 1980s as societal norms and sanctions change and as resources for continued expansion of specializations decrease. Whether normative diversity among and within academic sub-units will subsequently decrease is an empirical question. The impact on university organization and the organization of sub-units, whatever its form, nevertheless will affect the dean's role and the stress experienced in that role.

One might use the concept of normative diversity to explain variation among the role pressures sent by individual organizational members to the dean. It will become clear in this paper, however, that the author believes that, for large institutions at least, the dean's potential role stress arises primarily from tensions emanating *among* sub-units under his administration.

Thus, in the second place, studies that treat organizational factors as endogenous variables would allow researchers to identify factors among member groups *qua* groups that impinge on the dean's role. Normative diversity would be one such factor, and relative sub-unit autonomy would be another (see Ryan, 1974). The author, in an earlier study of academic sub-units within The Ohio State University, was able to differentiate among departments in terms of internal organization and of research-teaching emphasis (a normative variable) and was able to relate values of individual faculty members, group emphasis on research, and professional differentiation to departmental organizational structures and processes (see Ryan, 1969, 1970, 1972). Furthermore, tests of structural effects revealed that, regardless of an individual faculty member's orientation to the profession or to the institution, his length of service, his rank, and his possession or non-possession of a research grant, he tends not to deviate from the norms and attitudes of his departmental colleagues (Ryan, 1969). Departments tended to differ in terms of their relationships with their deans and in the salience which they placed upon inter-departmental or college-level governing bodies. Thus organizational variables are important keys to interpreting role conflict, ambiguity, and stress and to predicting effective administrative coping strategies.

OVERVIEW OF THE CHAPTER

The author's basic assumption in this paper is that the behavior of deans as individuals-in-organizations cannot be understood without some prior understanding of the nature of the organizations they inhabit. In another place, the author has argued that theory developed for organizations in general must be refined in the academic setting by knowledge of the day-to-day dynamics and processes peculiar to that institution (Ryan, 1974).

The academic context is examined in the first section below. In particular, the discussion illustrates how higher educational organizations differ structurally and functionally from other organizations. Three dimensions along which differences can be viewed are introduced—namely, control mechanisms in a dual structure, normative diversity or heterogeneity among and within sub-units, and differential sub-unit autonomy.

From the descriptive and analytical material in the initial section, the author then develops hypotheses relating structural and normative characteristics among groups in the college or school to variation in the dean's coping strategies. A third section continues the development of hypotheses, including ones related to sub-unit actions designed to offset the influence of changes in the profession (through inbreeding, for example) or to offset the influence of the dean and/or academic governing bodies on sub-unit resources and autonomy.

In the fourth section of the chapter, a theoretical model developed by Kahn and his associates (1964) will be described as a viable starting point for approaching multivariate studies of deans as individuals-in-organizations. Kahn's model is essentially psychological in focus, and it conceives of role expectations and sent pressures as the direct links to administrative role conflict and behavior. While a causal chain is conceived to include personal, group, and organizational variables, the core factors are role pressures sent by individual members of the role set.

The author presents a modification of the Kahn model based on the discussions in this paper. The alternative causal chain conceives of organizational variables (both structural and procedural) as directly impacting on the dean's role stress and behavior. This modification highlights the importance of characteristics of academic groups *qua* groups in predicting administrative role conflict. As well, the author's modifications allow researchers to treat the relationship between administrative behavior and organizational variables as reciprocal rather than uni-directional as Kahn does.

The final section of the chapter speaks to implications for research. Sets of research questions with suggested methodologies for answering them are based both upon Kahn's model and upon the author's modified one. If role studies provide data for testing both conceptualizations, it will be possible to assess whether individual role expectations (easily operationalized via survey methods) can serve as "proxies" for the underlying social processes within universities or whether field studies focused on examining organizational dynamics are needed to explain the links between cultural, social, institutional, and personality variables.

THE ACADEMIC CONTEXT

While institutions of higher education are commonly referred to as professional organizations, it has been observed that, as universities grow larger, their organizations become more bureaucratic in form (Dykes, 1968). In the discussion that follows, it will be argued that academic institutions are neither purely bureaucratic nor purely professional in their organization structures and procedures. Rather, they are characterized by a dual-organization structure, the administrative and the academic. While the dual structure is a fairly stable organizational factor, the blurring of responsibilities, procedures for decision-making, and informal influence processes may vary among institutions and within institutions (for example, among constituent colleges, schools, etc.). Two variables that affect the dynamics are inter-unit and intra-unit heterogeneity (or normative diversity) and relative sub-unit autonomy.

Institutional Blend of Professional and Bureaucratic Attributes

Weber (1947) theorized that responsibilities in a bureaucracy are distributed in a fixed way as official duties, creating a division of labor and a high degree of specialization and requiring that positions be filled by professionally or technically qualified specialists. As positions become differentiated, a formal status hierarchy develops. The principles of professionalism have much in common with Weber's description of bureaucratic principles, but there is one major difference. Control in the bureaucracy resides in the hierarchy, while professional control stems from a body of expert knowledge and an internalized code of ethics and from the support of self-control by the external surveillance of peers (Blau and Scott, 1962). Professionalism is thus conceptualized as an alternative to bureaucracy (cf. Etzioni, 1964; Vollmer and Mills, 1966).

Dykes (1968) has argued that, as universities grow larger, structural superordination and subordination is accentuated, rules and regulations become more important, hierarchical authority increases, and the institution moves away from the characteristics of collegiality toward those of bureaucracy. Weber (1947) wrote that bureaucratic authority in large-scale organizations always weakened collegiality as an effective control.

Nevertheless, institutions of higher education do not meet the distinguishing criteria for bureaucratic organizations. Responsibilities of academic sub-units, for example, are not reduced in scope by administrative assignment of official duties. While the work of sub-units may be specialized (and, therefore, illustrate structural differentiation), all perform relatively similar functions (for example, instruction and research). The choice of priorities among functions depends more upon individual values (emanating, to some extent, from norms within the academic profession) than upon direct administrative assignment. Administrative control in the bureaucratic sense is manifest at best in the provision of opportunities and in administrative encouragement. The division of responsibilities in the university creates roughly parallel sub-units devoted to specialized subject matter and specialized inquiry. The need for administrative (or hierarchical) coordination and control is less than that in organizations in which division of labor produces interdependent sub-units performing parts, but not all, of a common task (Blau and Scott, 1962).

Further, the development of a formal status hierarchy with concomitant emergence of distinct official positions occurs only among the administrative group, and the "control" exercised by this structural arrangement may be quite limited. Within the academic community, there is no parallel expansion of "distinct official statuses"; that is, the status of "faculty member" is not differentiated typically in terms of functional specialty in the hierarchical sense. Just as in any other social grouping, academic groups develop status-ordered positions over time. The major difference between this development and the hierarchical positions of bureaucracies is that, within the academic community, these positions are not conceived as part of the formal organizational blueprint, and they do not fall into strata of superordinate and subordinate positions. Rather, they tend to develop into positions of influence among the collegium or faculty "group of equals" (Ryan, 1969).

The academic institution, then, does not reflect many of the basic premises of bureaucratization. Rather, there are two organizational structures, the administrative and the academic. Parsons and Platt (1973) posited that bureaucracy is concentrated in the university administration and deals largely with non-academic functions while the core social structure (for example, academic faculties and sub-units) is notably non-bureaucratic and constitutes a stratified collegial association.

The author would argue that, while the administrative organization resembles a bureaucracy in structure, its functions and procedures reflect many aspects of professionalism. The discussion above provides the rationale for the thesis. Further, the author contends that the co-existent academic organization itself is not totally free of bureaucratic attributes. For example, even though faculty members participate in administrative functions and in decision-making, their organizational structures begin to resemble hierarchies. Clark (1961) reasoned that the institution of a counter-system of faculty committees and representative bodies worked to reduce the conflict between administrators and faculty members, but these organizational mechanisms were evidence of the bureaucratization of the faculty itself, as a hierarchy of committees emerged with "proper channels" for influence. Note that even Parsons and Platt (1973) recognized that the core social structure constituted a *stratified* collegial association.

As noted, the position of a faculty member is not further differentiated in the university's formal organization. (Indeed, the position of department chairperson may not even be included in organizational charts.) Nevertheless, a division of labor and the institution of distinct official statuses may occur *below* the position of faculty member. Since these developments occur *within* academic sub-units, they are not recognized in the university's formal organization. As faculty members become increasingly involved in activities outside of the institution (e.g., research, consultation, attendance at disciplinary meetings, public service), Smelser (1973) noted that a number of new positions ancillary to faculty activities begins to increase—teaching and research assistants, research administrators, administrative assistants, and clerical personnel. Indeed, this internal bureaucratization may be a variable upon which to compare sub-units within universities and their differential relationships with their deans.

Where such ancillary positions are present, the supervising professor functionally acts as an administrator in his own right, although the "position" does not appear in the university's administrative hierarchy. The dean's relationship with sub-units in his college or school must be studied with this variable in mind.

> The researcher must appreciate the difference between the professor in the humanities who shares an office with one or more colleagues and argues with his dean for more budgetary allocation for books, and the professor in the natural sciences whose personal "empire" may include a laboratory manned with research and technical assistants. (Ryan, 1974, p. 62)

The Dual Organization

From the discussion above, the author would argue that the conceptualization of neither the bureaucratic nor the professional organization is useful, in and of itself, in generating variables by which to differentiate among the organizations that deans inhabit. It is much more fruitful to conceive of the higher-education institution as an organization with a dual structure and to examine the distinguishing properties and processes that are associated with that unique organizational type.

Figure 7.1 depicts the dual structure within a typical large university. The college (or school) exists as one level within both "hierarchies." Within the administrative organization, the deanship exists as a position with some "line" responsibilities, but the counterpart in

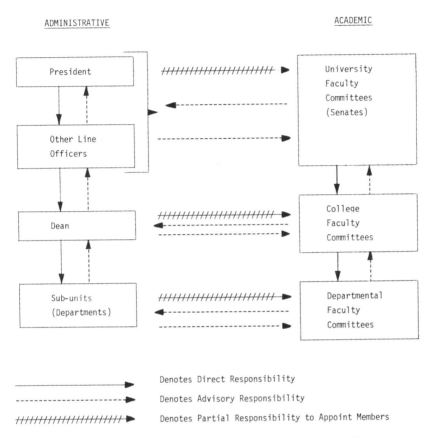

Figure 7.1. Administrative and academic organizations in the university.

the academic organization may be a college-level faculty committee. The formal division of responsibilities between the administrative and academic organizations may be modified by advisory relationships.

Typically, college-level (or school level) authority is differentiated into administrative responsibilities of the dean and into prescribed powers of the college faculty. The dean of a college within a large university generally has two major responsibilities: (1) recommending the annual college budget to the president and allocating the received budget and (2) recommending the appointments to, and all promotions within, the staff and membership of the college faculty (cf. Corson, 1960:77, Dibden, 1968). The by-laws of the university may or may not define an explicit procedure for faculty involvement

prior to the dean's personal recommendations. The fiscal responsibilities of the dean may extend to a right to review departmental[1]
program priorities, where program budgeting is used. Other duties
might include appointing college committees, presiding at meetings of
the college faculty, approving student courses of study, and recommending student disciplinary action.

The responsibilities assigned to the college faculty, on the other
hand, typically revolve around the instructional program. Most institutions grant the college faculty the right of adopting, altering, or
abolishing courses and curricula subject to approval at the university
level, that is, typically through a university-wide faculty committee,
then to the president and the board of trustees (Corson, 1960:102-
106). Other typical responsibilities include the adoption of admission
requirements; the creation or abolition of schools, bureaus, and departments within the college; the adoption or abolition of academic
degrees administered to them; and the recommendation of candidates
for degrees. These responsibilities are subject to approval by some
university-wide faculty committee and/or by the president and the
board of trustees.

The formal division of responsibility between the administrative
and academic organizations is modified by advisory relationships.
While the dean makes the final personnel and budget requests to the
university level, the recommendations may be made after consultation
with department chairpersons and/or college faculty. In turn, the dean
may advise college faculty committees before their curricular recommendations are sent to the university level. The dean may establish
additional committees consisting of both administrators and faculty
(e.g., executive committees), and the individual may delegate a portion of his authority to these groups. In Ohio State (Ryan, 1969), for
example, some of the deans appointed faculty committees to allocate
college monies for individual research projects.

The dean's role, therefore, must be studied as it relates to both
organizational structures within the university setting. Organizational
members may hold one set of expectations for the dean's role in the
administrative organization and another set for his role in the
academic organization. While the two structures appear to serve different institutional functions and thus to be conceptually independent,
in practice there may be a blurring of responsibilities. The dean may
have more control over this "blurring" in some situations than in
others. Where the dean's influence is greater, or where sub-unit autonomy is less, the dean indeed may be able to help shape expecta-

tions for his own role. The particular characteristics of the dean's so-called subordinates (e.g., sub-units), on the other hand, may constrain the incumbent's decisions with regard to organizational and functional responsibilities.

Sub-unit Heterogeneity and Autonomy

Two major attributes that impinge on both role expectations and role behaviors of the dean are the relative heterogeneity and relative autonomy of the sub-units within the dean's administrative unit (e.g., college or school). The two variables are interrelated, as we shall see.

Heterogeneity is both a structural and a normative concept. Structurally, heterogeneity is illustrated in the differentiation within the university organization by academic specialty—for example, the establishment of colleges and departments. The prototype for the differentiation by specialty, in North America at least, is the academic department. Ben-David (1971) documented the emergence of academic departments as a key American innovation that fostered specialization. Blau (1973) recognized that structural differentiation in universities, rather than making the work of academics more routinized, has provided opportunities for the work to become more specialized. As North American society sanctioned the academic commitment to create knowledge, the ascendence of research and scholarship encouraged structural differentiation, and the academic profession became more and more heterogeneous (cf. Clark, 1963; Parsons and Platt, 1973; Veysey, 1965; Bucher and Strauss, 1961.)

Thus the academic department has become the structural counterpart of faculty members' preoccupation with their specialties (cf. Demerath, Stephens, and Taylor, 1967). The organizational differentiation reflects not only heterogeneity among academic specialties but also normative diversity within the academic profession. To understand those aspects of heterogeneity or normative diversity that could create conflicts in academic decision-making, the work of Thompson and his associates (1969) is useful. Thompson reasoned that cultural differences among academic specialties or departments are revealed in sets of rules to guide searches for knowledge, for example, truth strategies. The particular truth strategy employed, he argued, affected a department's standards and demands for curricula, space, pay, promotion, recruitment of personnel, esteem, academic excellence, and the quality of inter-departmental relations. These relationships have obvious implications for the dean's role and for the potential conflict felt. Thompson posited that governance was troublesome, for example, where departments with diverse truth strategies (i.e., demands and standards) were grouped together organizationally. Thus the concept is useful in studies of deans among colleges within single universities.

As noted, North American society in the past sanctioned the rise of the commitment to create knowledge, and the academic profession responded by emphasizing specialized knowledge. The emergent clusters of experts were institutionalized as separate departments, within the larger universities at least. The type of heterogeneity being discussed here may or may not be present in particular institutions of higher education. This variable will affect the dean's role. As Clark (1961) argued, institutions of higher education vary in the extent to which their work requires coordination. Less administrative coordination is required in universities heavily committed to research, since the specialist's work is more nearly an entity in itself. More coordination is needed in institutions committed almost exclusively to teaching (or, perhaps, to inter-disciplinary research and development). The concept thus may be useful in cross-institutional research—comparing deans of education, for example, in various institutional settings.

Heterogeneity, both structural and normative, may emerge not only among the sub-units under the dean's administration but also *within* particular sub-units. The author (Ryan, 1969) was able, for example, to differentiate among academic departments in terms of their internal formal designation of areas (sub-specialties within the academic specialty). Where formalized areas were present, the department's faculty committees tended to be structured on the basis of area representatives. The normative nature of this development can be inferred from the finding that departments stressing research tended to be internally differentiated, while those departments emphasizing teaching were not. Thus one could profitably study the dean's role within a single college and his relationships with sub-units within the college that may vary on the basis of internal heterogeneity.

The more specialized the work of academics becomes, the more autonomous they become. Thus the two concepts are related, both for individual faculty members and for entire academic sub-units under the dean's jurisdiction. Academic autonomy has its roots primarily in normative sources, although it may subsequently affect both structure and procedures for decision-making within higher-education institutions.

The individual faculty member may stress research or teaching on the basis of personal values and orientations, and individuals enjoy relative autonomy in dealing with their own subject matter on the basis of expertise. Academic tenure is the institutionalized form of professional autonomy. As Parsons and Platt (1973) argued cogently, autonomy here does not mean freedom from responsibility and from evaluation. It implies that much of the control, coordination, and evaluation of academic work comes from outside the institution itself through universalistic standards applied by disciplinary associations. Increasing structural differentiation (i.e., heterogeneity) not only encourages disciplinary specialization, then, but also implies the commitment of individuals to specialized modes of inquiry which are subject to external evaluation.

This ideal form of academic autonomy has been modified, to some extent, by the presence of external groups with resources to offer research grants. The devotion to universalistic disciplinary standards among granting agencies may be questioned, but the impact they have had on the work of academics and on their relative autonomy vis-à-vis institutional administrators is difficult to dispute. Logically, those academic sub-units attracting external research monies may enjoy relative independence from the dean's potential financial "control."

One would expect institutional differences in sub-unit autonomy as well as within-institutional differences among sub-units. In effect, then, autonomy is differentially distributed, both between and within universities. Sub-unit autonomy may vary directly with commitment to research and with cultural sanctions from outside the institution, for example, in the form of research grants. One would expect the high-prestige institutions to be more differentiated structurally at the departmental level than would lower-prestige universities or single-purpose institutions, because they would tend to have the necessary faculty resources and facilities for formally differentiated research specializations. Similarly, one would expect their sub-units to be relatively independent of one another and to enjoy more autonomy than in an institution lacking both structural differentiation and resources for research specialization. The dean's role would vary accordingly. Nevertheless, even within the high-prestige university, particular sub-units under a dean's jurisdiction might also differ in both respects.

The variable of sub-unit autonomy, like that of heterogeneity, affects structures and processes for decision-making and governance within the institution. Autonomy in this sense is different conceptually from that of decentralization. The latter concept is used typically to describe organizational patterns in which members are provided opportunities to share decision-making responsibilities. The presence of an academic organization with elaborate committee structures might then be described as indicative of a decentralized organizational structure. Yet faculty members in relatively autonomous sub-units may not choose to participate in this structure. Autonomy, then, implies relative independence from the organization itself, whether or not that organization is decentralized.

The concept of academic autonomy, as it pertains both to individual academics and to sub-units, has not received adequate attention in research designs or in models of administration and organization. The author here simply can urge that researchers recognize this as an important variable in the academic setting. The salience of this variable can be inferred from the author's finding (1969) that both colleges and departments in The Ohio State University differed in terms of numbers of faculty committees and in proportions of faculty participating in committee work. These differences could not be related solely to size but rather appeared to be related to normative differences and to relative independence among groups. For example, the large arts and sciences college had only four college-level faculty committees (with 5 percent of the college faculty participating) while the relatively small agriculture college had 21 college-level faculty committees (with about 50 percent of the total faculty participating). The former college appeared to have much broader goals than did the latter, which seemed to stress instructional functions. Similarly, departmental emphasis on research seemed related to faculty time devoted to committee service at that level (with 50 percent of the faculty in research-oriented departments serving on department-level committees compared to 85 percent participation in departments emphasizing instruction).

In summary, this section has argued that institutions of higher education are characterized by a dual organization structure, both arms of which have some bureaucratic and some professional attributes. Institutions may vary in the formal distribution of responsibilities between their administrative and academic organizations, but, more importantly, they may vary in the blurring of responsibilities and in the dynamic processes that emerge. While the dual structure itself may be a fairly stable organization characteristic, other factors are more subject to changes in the sociocultural environment.

Two variables of major importance, relative sub-unit heterogeneity and autonomy, were discussed as viable bases for differentiating among institutions and among the jurisdictions of deans.

As we shall see, the dean has some influence on the degree of impact of such socioculturally based variables on his organization and administration. How does the dean respond to normative diversity among college sub-units? How does the dean deal with sub-unit autonomy? What strategies may the dean employ to manipulate influence patterns among the sub-units in the academic organization? The next section addresses these issues.

COPING IN ACADEMIA: THE DEAN'S USE
OF FORMAL RESPONSIBILITIES

The dean of a college or school is given formal responsibilities that could affect the constituent departments in significant ways. The actual use of formal "authority" may vary and the extent of professional decision-making may vary accordingly. Several alternatives to centralized administrative decision-making are discussed here, and the limitations of each on professional judgment are linked to differential sub-unit autonomy and heterogeneity. The major thesis is that the dean's use of the responsibilities vested in his office (his coping strategy) reflects the degree to which these two variables are present among member sub-units. Indeed, his role behaviors may well influence the opportunities of member departments to respond to changes in the external sociocultural environments that sanction heterogeneity and autonomy.

The dean's use of budgetary responsibilities, for example, can affect the attractiveness of college sub-units or members to external funding as well as their ability to recruit quality graduate students and faculty (cf. Page, 1968; Freeman, 1965; Meltzer, 1956; Orlans, 1963). Since sub-unit budgets are typically "tagged" by the dean for instructional salaries, wages, supplies and equipment, and travel, there is little room for "juggling" by the department chairperson (cf. Williams, 1965, Chapter 9). Finally, the dean can affect a department significantly through the review and approval of faculty appointments, promotions, tenure decisions, and salaries. Thus the dean's administrative role behavior may have enormous impact on organizational members, despite the presence of the academic structure.

The dean's use of responsibility to appoint faculty committees (or to allow for elected committees) may affect the potential interaction among member departments or other sub-units. In other words, the dean's behavior may directly affect both the formal organization and the interpersonal relations among his constituents. In Ohio State, for example, one dean confided that he deliberately established several faculty committees in an effort to encourage some communication between departments (Ryan, 1969). Obviously, a dean could elect to avoid appointing faculty committees if the interaction is perceived to be detrimental.

Since the dean has formal responsibility to review departmental decisions or recommendations, and since his recommendations, as well as those that have passed through the series of faculty committees, are subject to review by university-level hierarchical offices, the ideal form of professionalism could not exist in the large university. Within these constraints, however, the test of professionalism is still met when one can assume that the dean, the president, and all other officers with review powers possess the "expert knowledge." The fact that most administrative officers in the university are themselves academics has been used to support the notion that professionalism survives and controls the university (cf. Parsons, 1966; Etzioni, 1964). However, this argument is based on the implicit assumption that professionals share a common value system and a perspective of the world. Differentiation within the profession occurs because that assumption is no longer valid.

Structural differentiation is more than a reflection of institutional size; it is an outgrowth of the complexity within the academic profession as well. The proliferation of specialties as separate departments in the university makes it difficult for the dean to possess the basis for professional judgment (cf. Clark, 1963; Kaplan, 1959; Joughlin, 1963). A concrete example will illustrate this dilemma. A department chairman at Ohio State asked the rhetorical question in interview, "How is the dean to establish a priority between the psychology department's request for more rats and the art school's request for a piece of sculpture?" The dean of one college studied at Ohio State reversed the program priorities of one of his larger departments, but explicitly stated in his report to the university officer that he had no real basis for reviewing departmental priorities (Ryan, 1969).

Another alternative for allowing professional control within the bureaucratic administrative organization is the delegation of the dean's responsibilities to college-level faculty committees. Here, too, structural and normative differentiation shape the outcome. Lacking a common knowledge base, the departmental representatives may engage in "vote-swapping" as was the case in some units in Ohio State (Ryan, 1969). Riesman (1956) has likened departments to political and social blocks in society, each preventing the other from growing too large, each acting to prevent new potential disciplines from becoming established as competitors for funds and students.

Long ago, Weber (1947) observed that where there is a conflict of interest of socially established groups, it may work out to the advantage of a "chief" through a process of negotiation and struggle with the various groups. Weber argued that, especially where conflicts of interest emerge in representative bodies, the outcome cannot be the result of a vote; the outcome must be either a negotiated compromise or a decision of the "chief" after each side has spoken. In more modern though congruent terms, Kerr (1963) has suggested that in academia, administrative coordination has increasingly taken on the attributes of mediation, and Clark has written of the university's need for faculty politicians and mediators, "Men who serve on central committees, men with cast iron stomachs for lunch-table discussions and cocktail parties, men who know how to get things done that must be done for the faculty as a whole or for part of the faculty" (1963:50).

Obviously, where professional responsibility is delegated to representatives, individuals do not participate as equals. One of the most telling pieces of data from Dykes' (1968) study of the participation in decision-making by a liberal arts faculty in a large university was the finding that 47 percent of the faculty members interviewed did not *know* whether the faculty was, in fact, excluded from decisions in which it should be involved. The most logical explanations, according to Dykes and to many of his interviewees, were the shift in the locus of decision-making from lower to higher levels of the organizational hierarchy and the shift in the pattern of decision-making from town hall to representative government. Both shifts were related to the size and complexity of the university. The basic dilemma posed by normative and structural differentiation in the universities is that as the identity of faculty members increasingly focuses upon the department, the decision-making arena is shifting upward to the college level and beyond. This phenomenon affects both the administrative and the academic organization.

Even where decision-making is delegated to total faculties, there is no basis for judgment in a "common body of expert knowledge." The total faculty council at the college level may be an arena for compromise, however. Weber (1947) wrote that collegiality might serve as the mechanism to reconcile the points of view of different technical specialists and divergent interests by discussion, but collegiality unavoidably obstructs the promptness of decision, the consistency of policy, and the clear responsibility of the individual. For these reasons, Weber argued that large-scale tasks which require quick and consistent solutions fall into the hands of administrators, and where collegial bodies have executive responsibilities, the trend is for the leading member to become pre-eminent. The total size of the group would obviously affect the potential contribution to be made by individual faculty members.

While there are no data available on actual decision-making processes among college faculty councils, interviewees in four colleges at Ohio State rather consistently stated that meetings of total college faculties, even though infrequently held, were attended only by roughly 10 to 20 percent of the faculty, except in very rare situations. For example, a discussion of reorganization of the arts and sciences into six colleges at Ohio State drew roughly 40 to 50 percent of the faculty, a very unusual turnout in the opinion of the interviewees (Ryan, 1969).

A final alternative for allowing professional control within the restraints of hierarchical authority emerges through the dean's flexibility in granting autonomy to the major faculty grouping of equals, that is, those of the departments. Operationally, the dean could "rubber-stamp" the requests and recommendations of the department chairpersons. Degree of professional control is then dependent upon the autonomy granted the faculty by the department chairperson, since this alternative assumes the chairperson to be spokesman for his group of equals who have considered issues at the department level.

Blau (1970), however, has noted that normative and structural differentiation in an institution is paralleled within sub-units. Applied to the university, this means that departments also grow larger and more internally differentiated. Decisions delegated to the large department must, therefore, be the outcomes of compromise or mediation. Clark (1963:48) wrote, "The intense specialization alone makes many a man into king of a sector in which few others are able to exercise much judgment. Thus, *within* a department, men increasingly feel unable to judge the merits of men in specialties they know nothing about." Whether a department chairperson makes unilateral decisions which are communicated to the dean, or whether he allows the faculty to attempt a compromise of interests is problematic. The choice is at least partially dependent upon size of department, which, in turn, is correlated with presence of formalized areas of subdivisions and with emphasis on research. (See Ryan, 1969, Chapters 5 and 6, or Ryan, 1972, for a discussion of organizational types, administrative style, and use of faculty committees among departments in The Ohio State University.)

There are obviously institutional differences in the autonomy granted faculties at the departmental or college levels in decision-making. Clark (1961) reports data from another study as evidence of a positive correlation between the academic quality of universities and faculty authority, and other evidence suggests that strong faculty authority aids in attracting and retaining competent professors (cf. Barton, 1961; Lazarsfeld and Thielens, 1958; Wilson, 1955). These studies do not report the particular organization of departments into colleges within the institutions studied, however. If Blau's (1970) theory of structural differentiation is relevant to the academic organization, the high degree of faculty authority could be explained in two ways. First, one might infer that the organizational pattern of departments into colleges is based on relative homogeneity of departments, and that administrative supervision and coordination is unnecessary. Alternatively, one could infer that, while supervision and coordination are needed, the college faculty committee or council accepts these responsibilities. More data are needed about control mechanisms of both the administrative and the academic organizations.

The dean of a college, as we have seen, has a choice of behavior in using the formal powers of the office. First, the individual could make unilateral, arbitrary decisions (or, more accurately, recommendations). Indeed, there is nothing in the organizational rules to restrain a dean from initiating, rather than reviewing, the choice of new faculty for member departments. While the dean must consult department chairpersons in budgetary and personnel matters, he is not forced by the formal rules to accept their requests or priorities. As a second alternative, the dean could "rubber-stamp" the recommendations of department chairpersons. Finally, the incumbent could establish college-wide faculty committees and accept their recommendations. Where faculty committees are established, however, the dean or assistant dean typically has *ex officio* membership and often serves as chairperson of the council. Thus, the dean could still influence faculty decisions or could serve as mediator.

While it might be argued that the personality of the dean shapes the administrative style, it is posited here that the characteristics of the particular group of departments (i.e., normative diversity and degree of autonomy, both within and among departments) will constrain the choice of behavior in significant ways. From his observations of the governing process in a number of institutions, Corson (1960) reported that the role of the dean varies depending upon appointment as dean of a professional school or of an arts and sciences college. A careful reading of Corson's observations reveals that the diversity of groups (i.e., departments) under the dean's administration is a key variable in affecting the role definition.

Specifically, where the departments in a college represent a wide diversity of specializations, it is posited here that the dean will not delegate responsibilities to the college faculty because of the potential for inter-departmental conflict. Corson (1960) differentiated the dean's role by size of institution as well, with the dean in large institutions having more power. This is congruent with the hypothesis that the greater the departmental differentiation, the less likely is the dean to allow faculty collegial decision-making and the greater is the need for administration centralization, that is, non-delegation of the final decision (cf. Abrahamson, 1967; Hagstrom, 1967).

Financial resources, for example, are always less than optimal, requiring that priorities be established. It is difficult to conceive of a situation in which chemists could sit down with philosophers and agree to priorities in terms of budget. Further, salary schedules are dependent somewhat upon "market demand," leading to discrepancies among academic specialties on issues which may cause much inter-departmental conflict if committees are given decisional information. Finally, inter-departmental differences would make it difficult for faculty committees to make choices about new personnel. In all these examples, the issue revolves around the basis of professional control—a *common* body of expert knowledge. This foundation for faculty self-governance might be present in a college composed of homogeneous departments, a situation Corson (1960) observed in many professional schools. On the other hand, departments in a large arts and sciences college might be closer to a collection of academic guilds than to a collegium.

When a college is composed of departments with very diverse orientations, it is possible that neither the dean nor a faculty committee would have a viable basis (i.e., professional expertise) for reviewing departmental requests and recommendations. The alternatives, if the dean wishes to avoid inter-departmental confrontations of differences, are arbitrary decisions or general acceptance of the priorities outlined by individual department chairpersons. (If the dean allows direct confrontation of department chairpersons as a group or as an executive committee, he again must expect inter-departmental conflicts.) Where the dean elects to make unilateral decisions, department chairpersons may appeal to the central university administrator for funds (cf. Scott, 1966). This violation of the formal structure is more likely in the case of department chairpersons representing politically powerful or high-status departments (cf. Ryan, 1969). Indeed, Corson (1960) posited that the dean's power is inversely related to the influence of department chairpersons.

On the other hand, where the dean's practice is to accept the recommendation of department chairpersons within budgetary constraints, he is subject to the informal pressure, or bargaining power, of the various chairpersons. In short, the dean's retention of formal responsibility in his office serves to avoid open interaction and confrontation among his departments. It does not, however, eliminate the emergence of informal modifications. The informal pressures may be exerted by each department separately, not directly through the college group *qua* group, and they may be responded to by the dean in terms of departmental differences in professional or institutional status.

It is still possible for the dean to follow faculty committees to share financial and personnel responsibilities but to reserve the right to make final recommendations. Indeed, this could be a strategy based upon the intended resolution or compromise of inter-departmental differences through interaction and open confrontation. Where this strategy is adopted, the dean may need to use other integrative devices as well. Walton and Dutton (1969) have presented a coherent analysis of inter-departmental conflict and its management, a discussion that is relevant to deans of heterogeneous colleges. For example, they note that where a lateral relationship involves joint decision-making, each unit can bias the decisions in its own favor by controlling (and distorting) information relevant to these decisions.

One conclusion of Walton and Dutton's review of studies is that where patterns of conflict appear between departments, the administrator may intervene by manipulating the extent of direct interaction and by setting up rules and specific limits to guide the joint or group decision-making process. This inference is similar to Baum's (1961) conclusion that decentralization of authority, to be effective and proper, depends upon a clear concept of the limits of that delegation and upon a system of review of the exercise of responsibility. It has been argued by other students of organizations that the larger the group and the greater the functional differential within the group, the more elaborate is the internal structure of the organization in order to maintain coordination and control (cf. Hagstrom, 1967; Haas and Collin, 1963). Walton and Dutton, however, concluded that regardless of administrative interventions and attempts at coordination (including reorganization of the units), the effort will be effective only if the units "find a new culture in which to view and understand each other" (1969:83).

The dean has a vehicle for studying the exercise of authority and the possible emergence of a "new culture" in college-level faculty committees, since the faculty has responsibility for curricular decisions. Here, too, the placement of responsibility in the formal structure may be modified by the informal organizations that arise within the group. It is posited that the more diverse the departments concerned, the greater is the possibility for faculty politics to enter the picture, since there is no rational basis for reviewing departmental recommendations. Where informal social relations have been established between two or more departments within the college, "vote-swapping" may appear. Further, the committee becomes an arena for informal status differentiations among departments to influence decisions (cf. Cleveland, 1960; Dibden, 1968).

Like the dean with regard to financial or personnel decisions, the college faculty committee could use its authority in various ways. The continuum of practices could range from the automatic "rubber-stamping" of departmental recommendations to the group's initiation of curricular recommendations that affect member departments. More abstractly, the faculty committee could elect to perform routine tasks, or it could choose to become a policy-making body. The pressures that arise from informal organizations will take various forms, according to the committee's choice of behavior. The choice, in turn, may depend upon the group's normative diversity and potential for interdepartmental conflict. Further, if Walton and Dutton's (1969) interpretations are valid, the shifting of responsibility from the dean's office to the college faculty committees will be an effective vehicle for promoting homogeneity only if the units "find a new culture"—that is, if the college becomes a group, in the sense of establishing social bonds that make possible the enforcement of common norms (cf. Blau and Scott, 1962).

ROLE STRESSES AND STRAINS:
THE SUB-UNITS FIGHT BACK

The author has argued that organizational factors, including the presence of two distinct structures with blurred functional responsibilities, may affect potential role conflict and ambiguity for the dean and may constrain the choice of coping strategies or actual role behavior. Among the important organizational factors in the university setting are the relative autonomy and normative diversity among and within sub-units under the dean's "control." The dean's use of formal responsibilities, it has been argued, will vary depending upon factors such as these. It may now be inferred that the greater the heterogeneity (or normative diversity) of member departments or sub-units, the more likely are informal pressures to emerge in order to reduce the impact of the dean's authority on departmental practices, that is, to ensure that college-level decisions are congruent with departmental needs. The source of responsibility for decisions will determine the mode of applying informal pressure.

The author has already noted that where responsibility remains centralized in the dean's office, informal pressures may be directed by each department separately, and success may vary according to the department's status and influence. Assuming resources are not unlimited, departmental autonomy (in the sense of directing one's own destiny) will vary; the "have's" may continue to obtain requested resources, and the "have not's" may continue to fall behind.

Where responsibility is decentralized, however, and faculty committees promote inter-departmental interaction, departments must direct informal pressures on the group. Informal norms may arise as group phenomena, and these informal standards may tend to make the group more homogeneous. The strategy here is for individual departments to use their status and influence in taking a strong role in shaping group norms. Alternatively, political alliances may emerge. In either case, unless priorities are agreed upon by individual departments in the group, "autonomy" may again vary. In short, decentralization of decision-making may create informal control mechanisms, and the impact on individual departments will depend upon the initial heterogeneity of interests and standards. Over time, heterogeneity will be reduced, or some of the departments will ignore the group and seek resources elsewhere.

In an earlier section, the concept of heterogeneity (or normative diversity) was discussed, and the work of Thompson and his associates (1969) was mentioned. Thompson developed a typology of truth strategies, defined as sets of rules to guide searches for knowledge. Examination of sub-unit truth strategies, Thompson argued, would operationalize cultural differences among academic specialties. Since the particular truth strategy employed by an academic sub-unit affected the group's demands and standards, governance was hypothesized to be difficult where sub-units with heterogeneous truth strategies were grouped together. (Recall the contrast between the professors in the humanities and in the natural sciences and their very different demands.)

Thompson (1969) further theorized that departmental truth strategies were amenable to change, as departments adapt to informal norms of particular colleges in the university. Where such changes occur, the departments concerned would tend to become more homogeneous over time in research strategies and, consequently, in terms of standards and demands. For example, where a sociology department is located in a college dominated by professional groups such as business administration or social work, the direct truth strategy is usually adopted; where sociology is located in a college dominated by the behavioral sciences, the scientific truth strategy seems to predominate. Thompson pointed out that some disciplines appear to exert considerable influence on others. Spatial and administrative location may not be sufficient to guarantee that such influences will operate, but he argued that the opportunity to interact appears to be at least a necessary condition.

Departmental truth strategies, however, may change over time in yet another way—through developments in the discipline as a whole. One thinks at once of the growing emphasis on quantitative or scientific methodologies in disciplines such as political science or geography. Even for the "certain" disciplines, moreover, the rise of interdisciplinary specialties such as biochemistry and biophysics may affect organizational homogeneity.

Intra- and inter-disciplinary changes may or may not affect departments in a particular university, however, and it is posited that the existing institutional organization influences the continuing congruence or incongruence between departmental "cultures" and those of the more universal disciplines. For example, a political science department could scarcely adapt itself to new behavioral methodologies without appropriate staff and facilities, resources which are dependent at least in part upon the dean's authority. Thompson (1969) posited that the dean evaluates budget proposals or requests for space and staff in the light of the truth strategy in which he was trained and which he practiced as a faculty member.

Further, in line with the framework in this chapter, a major shift in resource allocation may leave the dean vulnerable to pressure from other departments in the group. Depending upon the "market demand" for newer men in certain fields, the department in question may need to offer unusual salary, time, and travel incentives. The dean might have difficulty in justifying wide differences between departments in financial matters (linked, as we have seen, to truth strategies). Thus, the more heterogeneous the departments, the more apt is the dean posited to make unilateral decisions and to keep member departments relatively isolated from one another.

Departments, on the other hand, may not want to adapt themselves to new developments in their disciplines. In a study of a single northeastern state university, Lewis (1966) found that an informal process of co-optation may be used by the oligarchy of a university to minimize threats to its position by retaining the faculty persons who should be less likely to question the distribution of power within the institution—for example, inbred professors, trained in the truth strategy prevailing in their departments at the time.

McKelvey (1969) studied expectational non-complementarity and style of interaction between professionals and organization in a federal research agency, and he concluded that where the organization is not fulfilling professional research and career expectations (non-complementarity), cynicism and activity (i.e., attempts to change organizational expectations) occurred. Cynical active professionals (called insurgents), however, received the lowest promotion eligibility rankings from their supervisors. In contrast, idealistic passive professionals (called ritualists) tended to receive the highest promotion eligibility rankings. McKelvey inferred that reducing non-complementarity expectations would tend to promote organizational stability. Applied to the framework in this paper, where departmental members of a college are heterogeneous, the informal reward structure may punish insurgents and reinforce conformists. As a result, a more homogeneous orientation may arise among the group's units, contributing to organizational stability and to a reduction in role stress for the dean.

Thompson (1969) also argued that departments consisting of a homogeneous faculty may be reluctant to bring in "new blood," especially if the status and reward structures could be expected to change. He noted that the introduction of faculty with different orientations could create "Old Guard-Young Turk" schisms. Similarly, where college faculties have responsibility to approve departmental personnel appointments, the existing group norms might operate to keep the homogeneity intact. Etzioni (1965) has argued that the degree to which an organization selects its members affects the amount of resources and effort that must be invested to maintain the level of control considered adequate. In other words, the more effective the selection process, the less need for socialization.

The college dean could intervene to encourage departments to recruit new faculty trained in newer truth strategies, but in reality, this leadership role may be rare. Even where new persons are hired, their power to reshape departmental or college norms is lessened by the control of the more conservative faculty over organizational structures and decisions. As Clark (1961) has noted, it is the "Old Guard" rather than the "Young Turks" who are recruited into faculty oligarchies. A summary report on a follow-up study of doctorate cohorts from 1935 to 1960 (NAS Profiles, 1965) revealed that 25 years after the doctorate, administration occupied the greatest single sector of time of the doctorate-holders, and this growth of administrative responsibility occurred chiefly at the expense of research time. For persons receiving their doctorate in 1955 and in 1960, on the other hand, the tendency was to spend 48.5 percent of their time in research during the first post-doctoral year, with only around 9 percent of their time devoted to administrative activities.

There is no reason to expect faculty governance at the college level to reside in the hands of persons oriented to the discipline rather than in those oriented to the institution. Inbreeding, then, could be another key variable in shaping the informal norms that emerge in the college as a group, and in the tendency for truth strategies of heterogeneous departments to become more homogeneous over time.

In applying Thompson's concept of truth strategies to the framework in this chapter, the focus necessarily has been upon knowledge production and its concomitant effect upon departmental resource needs. The formal and informal organizations of the college, however, may shape the other major activities of departments—knowledge utilization and application. A department may find itself, because of its location in the institution, offering many undergraduate service courses and few graduate seminars. (This possibility occurred for social science departments located in the commerce college in Ohio State, e.g.) Similarly, a department's basic truth strategy may be largely unaffected by its location, but it may be influenced to limit its inquiry largely to areas having direct application to certain groups in the community, for example, natural science departments located in colleges of agriculture. Informal organizations may establish a reward structure based upon instructional or service activities. Certainly the dean's budgetary responsibilities can affect the use of faculty resources in research rather than in instruction and the availability of space and facilities for particular research activities.

Clearly, departments exist in unusual organizational locations without apparent effects as hypothesized here. Whether the formal and informal organizations actually change the direction of particular departments from those of their disciplines may well depend upon the department's abilities to ignore the institution and to seek resources from external agencies (cf. Blau and Scott, 1962; Clark, 1963). In thus adapting itself to the organization, the department adopts entrepreneurial strategies. Vollmer (1966) studied entrepreneurship in different organizational contexts and concluded that scientists are not necessarily at the mercy of the organization. Vollmer hypothesized that entrepreneurial activity can be expected to be associated with markedly increased professional productivity among scientists only in those organizational contexts that are less bureaucratized. Indeed, entrepreneurship was viewed by Weber (1947) as a viable alternative to bureaucratization.

However, the ability to attract external funds is at least a partial function of the institution's support and provision of necessary staff, facilities, and equipment. Although a department chairperson can release individual faculty members from some instructional duties, he must be able to replace them in the classroom, create larger and larger staffs of teaching assistants, and/or enlarge the size of undergraduate courses (cf. Williams, 1965). In all these respects, negotiation with the dean is probably necessary.

One can conclude, moreover, that the emergence of differential entreprenurial strategies is congruent with the hypothesis that the greater the heterogeneity of departments, the more likely are informal pressures to emerge in an effort to reduce the impact of the dean's authority on departmental practices. Finally, the more successful the entrepreneurial activities of member departments, the greater is the potential for informal status differentiations in the group, and the greater may be the successful department's influence on the norms of other member departments. Role stress in the deanship, then, must be studied in relationship to these organizational dynamics.

The empirical observations made in the last two sections of this chapter are derived primarily from studies conducted during the period of expansion in institutions of higher education. Patterns of coping strategies and of departmental attempts to offset the influence of deans and college-level faculty committees may be expected to change during the next decade. For example, there may be fewer "Young Turks" around to challenge prevailing norms and standards for inquiry. Departments may be hard-pressed to adopt entrepreneurial strategies as external funds for research dwindle.

Nevertheless, it is important for research in the deanship to be based upon an approach that recognizes the interrelationships between developments in the cultural system and the social system. Since the concepts of heterogeneity and autonomy provide such linkages, and because they have affected university organization and the dynamics of organizational and administrative processes, it will be fruitful to examine these variables in the current context.

KAHN'S THEORETICAL MODEL OF ROLE DYNAMICS

The theoretical model developed by Kahn and his associates (1964) had as its goal the provision of a means to understand the effects of the contemporary environment on the individual. The environment is conceived as consisting largely of formal organizations and groups, the characteristics of which are assumed to be major determinants of the individual's behavior. The model seems very appropriate to studies of deans as individuals-in-organizations. Nevertheless, the model requires modification for use in the higher-education setting. In this section, Kahn's model is presented, and a modification is suggested to reflect the arguments presented in this chapter.

The organization in which a person holds a job is defined as an open, dynamic system, dependent upon its environment for the absorption of its products and services and for providing the necessary input which reactivates a process of transformation (Katz and Kahn, 1966). According to Kahn et al.,[2] the organization holds together and functions only so long as people can be motivated to perform needed behaviors. The major determinants of the behavior of each person, moreover, are to be found in the behavior of other members.

The key concept for linking individual and organization is office, a unique point in organizational space which defines one's position in terms of its relationship to others and to the system as a whole. Associated with each office is a set of activities or potential behaviors which basically constitutes the role to be performed by the incumbent. The occupants of those offices which exist in a functional relationship constitute a role set. Typically, a role set consists of those offices adjacent to the one of interest (the focal role) in the work-flow structure or in the hierarchy of authority.

Because the members of a person's role set depend upon his performance in some degree or fashion, they develop beliefs about what the incumbent should or should not do as part of the role. These prescriptions and proscriptions held by members of a role set are designated as role expectations and, when communicated to the focal person, are conceived as defining that role. Members of the role set, therefore, are seen as role senders, and their communicated expectations are called the sent role.

In the process of role sending, information is communicated and attempts are made to influence the focal person to conform with certain expectations. Such influence attempts are viewed as role pressures, which may vary according to a number of dimensions such as sign, magnitude, specificity, intensity, and range of conditions under which compliance is intended (see Gross *et al.*, 1958). Consequences for compliance and non-compliance typically take the form of sanctions. The availability and visibility of such sanctions are important in determining the strength of role pressures.

The members of the role set and the pressures which they direct are part of the objective environment of a person occupying a particular office. The individual, however, also responds to that representation of the organization which is his psychological environment. The congruency between psychological and objective environments depends upon the individual's ability and opportunity to perceive organizational reality. Thus for any individual in an organization there is a sent role and a received role, the latter consisting of the person's perceptions and cognitions of what was sent and having the most direct influence on behavior.

Every individual is subject to a variety of internal role forces in addition to those stimulated by role pressures from the role set. One of these forces stems from the intrinsic satisfaction derived from the content of the role. In addition, each person is a role-sender to himself in that the person, too, has a conception of the office and a set of attitudes and beliefs about activities and behaviors relevant to that position. Indeed, the individual concerned may have been instrumental in developing the formal responsibilities of the office. Thus the individual has an occupational self-identity, shaped through a long

process of socialization and formal training, and is motivated to behave in ways that enhance that identity (Miller, 1962; Dai, 1955).

Role behavior in Kahn's model is limited to system-relevant behavior, whether or not it is congruent with the expectations of others.
Forces or pressures originating outside the organization may influence
role behavior, but the major focus in the model is upon the study of
causes from among those forces generated in the work situation itself.

Role conflict is viewed as a fact in both the objective and
psychological environments of the individual. The former is called
sent-role conflict, defined as the simultaneous occurrence of two or
more sets of pressures such that compliance with one would make
more difficult compliance with the other(s). Four kinds of role conflict
are conceived—intra-sender, inter-sender, inter-role, and person-role
conflict.[3] Role overload is a concept used to describe the existence of
more pressures than can be met. In this type of conflict, all the expectations are legitimate, but their cumulative total simply exceeds the
capabilities of the role incumbent. The conflict lies in the demand for
establishing performance priorities.

Whereas role conflict is defined as the product of incompatible or
excessive-role pressures, role ambiguity reflects inadequacy of role-
related information and is defined as the degree to which information
is available to a given position. Information may be nonexistent or
inadequately communicated, both of which are objective conditions.
Psychologically, individuals differ in their response to ambiguity (see
Frenkel-Brunswick, 1949; Cohen, Stotland, and Wolfe, 1955).

Building upon the concepts discussed above, Kahn and his colleagues developed a theoretical model for exploring the effects on the
individual of role conflict and ambiguity. The core of the model consists of a role episode, a complete cycle of role sending, response by
the focal person, and the effects of that response on the role senders.
The complete model includes both antecedent and intervening factors.
(See Figure 7.2.)

Boxes I through IV contain the factors in the core-role episode,
and they represent events at a given moment in time. The directed
lines represent a causal sequence such that sent pressures (II) lead to
experienced conflict (III), which leads to coping responses (IV),
which are perceived and evaluated in relation to expectations (I),
causing the cycle to resume. The circles A through C, in contrast,
represent enduring states of the organization, the person, and the interpersonal relations between role senders and the focal person.
These factors contribute to the sequence of events in a role episode

and represent, in combination, the context within which the episode occurs.

To determine the likelihood and nature of sent-role pressures, the expectations of each role sender in an identified role set are investigated. Similarly, role ambiguity is assessed by investigating the availability of relevant information within the role set. In general, Kahn expects that a focal person's experience of a situation will be a function of the objective demands and pressures to which he is subjected at the moment.

The person who is confronted with role conflict or ambiguity must respond to it in some way. Possible coping responses include utilizing direct attempts to solve the problem by complying or by persuading role senders to modify their incompatible demands, employing attempts to avoid the sources of stress, using defense mechanisms which distort the reality of a conflictual or ambiguous situation, or forming affective or physiological symptoms. Regardless of the nature of the coping response, the individual's behavior can be assessed in relation to the expectations and role pressures of the role senders. These factors, making up the core-role episode, can be studied as an integral whole.

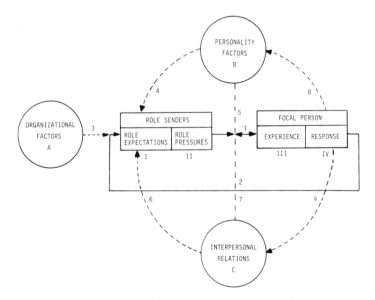

Figure 7.2. A theoretical model of factors involved in adjustment to role conflict and ambiguity. (From Kahn *et al.*, 1964, p. 30)

Role expectations, however, emerge in an organizational context, and fuller understanding of the dynamics of role conflict requires attention to this set of factors. Arrow 3 in the model represents a causal relationship between various organizational and ecological variables and the role expectations and pressures relevant to a particular position. Similarly, role responses are related not only to experienced conflict but also to personality traits (arrow 5). As well, some personal characteristics of the individual may tend to evoke certain responses (pressures) from the role senders (arrow 4). Finally, the more or less stable patterns of interaction between a person and the role senders may affect both differential role-pressure elicitations (arrow 6) and differential responses (arrow 7).

A complete study of role dynamics involving the dean as an individual in an organization would include investigations of each of the major factors in the model and the relationships among them. In the author's view, Kahn's theoretical model could provide a fruitful basis for such inquiry. Nevertheless, the particular context of concern (institutions of higher education) demands additional clarification of factors and causal sequences. Further, the lack of a direct impact of organizational factors on role behavior and the lack of a feedback loop from role behavior to organizational factors require some conceptual modification. The model fails to recognize role pressures and strains emanating from groups *qua* groups. Finally, the absence from the model of the external environment (culture) as a factor in role dynamics is conceptually inadequate. These refinements are included in the revised model in Figure 7.3.

The revision depicts the external environment of the higher-education institution, that is, society and culture and the academic profession sub-system, as impinging on institutional goals, size, and structural differentiation. The revision also includes the institution's response to societal demands and to developments within the academic profession (professional differentiation) that promote the establishment of specialized sub-units and the emergence of specialized areas within academic sub-units. Institutional goals, as pictured, not only affect the degree to which the external culture becomes institutionalized (e.g., the number of separate departments) but also may determine the organizational grouping of departments into administrative units (colleges). (See Ryan, 1974, for a fuller discussion.)

The influence of external professional differentiation, with its concomitant emergence of heterogeneity (or normative diversity) and demands for autonomy among specialized groups of academics, is felt

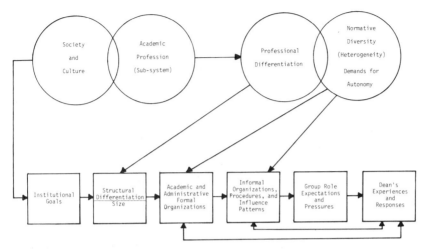

Figure 7.3. Modification of Kahn's theoretical factors in role conflict for studies of deans as individuals-in-organizations.

in the dual academic and administrative formal organizations. Institutional decision-makers are assumed to affect the broadly defined goals of the university, its structural differentiation into colleges and departments, and the dual formal organizations. At any of these junctures, one might expect conflicting views between institutional decision-makers and organizational members (who bring the influence of professional sub-systems of society with them). The formal organizational variables would include the formal division of responsibilities between the two structures, the nature of the actual decision-making structures, rules and regulations that guide decision-making, and the like.

Heterogeneity and differential demands for autonomy among academic departments affect the informal structures and processes that emerge to supplement or modify formal organizations. For studies of the deanship, the departments of concern would be those within the college jurisdiction. Variables here would include provisions for determining membership on decisional committees, procedures used in making decisions, influence structures and patterns, political cliques, and the like. (See Ryan, 1971, for a discussion of the operationalization of both formal and informal organizational variables in studies of academic governance.)

Notice that formal structures and the informal procedures that emerge within that context not only influence group (departmental) role expectations and role pressures communicated to the dean directly but also directly influence the dean's experiences and responses, in and of themselves. Since the organizational structures (both formal and informal) reflect the heterogeneity and autonomy demands that arise through professional differentiation, the dean's experiences and behaviors are hypothesized to reflect , indirectly, the impact of these variables to some extent, regardless of communications that may be sent directly by organizational members or groups. Note, too, that the dean has a hypothesized direct effect on both organizational structures. That is, there is a reciprocal relationship. As we have seen, the dean may establish various decision-making structures and may constrain the membership, procedures, and influence structures that emerge subsequently.

The modifications in this model are heavily biased toward a sociological, rather than psychological, approach to research into the deanship. The author must stress, nevertheless, that changes in society and the professional sub-system have impact on institutions of higher education not only at the institutional level, but also at the individual level. That is, the values and orientations of individual professors recruited to the institution provide avenues through which socio-cultural developments are or are not transmitted in the day-to-day operation of the university. It is assumed that, where institutional goals stress specialized inquiry, like-minded academics will be recruited. The reality of decisional processes within large universities at least demands a model that would recognize academic groups, rather than individuals, as the key sources of role stress in the deanship.

IMPLICATIONS FOR RESEARCH

Research in higher education has included some investigations of deans as individuals and of academic institutions as organizations. Rarely, however, have studies systematically been directed to the role of deans as individuals-in-organizations. There appears to be general agreement among students of higher education that the functions and roles of deans vary with such factors as the nature and size of the institution or academic sub-unit, the dean's own qualities, local custom, written regulations, presidential assignment, the influence of other deans, and the group impact of faculty members (e.g., Dibden, 1968). Researchers must approach a study of the dean as an individual in an organization with a conceptual framework that encompasses these and other variations and that provides a means of identifying and explaining generalizable patterns.

The author has presented a summary of Kahn's (1964) model of role behavior as a viable starting point for multivariate research. The author has also argued that, to understand the dean as an individual in an organization, one must first understand the organization itself. Kahn's model should be modified to reflect our existing knowledge about the academic organization and its underlying dynamics. While typical role studies ask respondents to describe to what extent a particular content area is or should be the administrator's role, they do not typically study to what extent responsibility is blurred or to what extent the content areas or functions are shared responsibilities. The latter concerns are especially important in an academic context because of the potential for professional heterogeneity, autonomy, and decentralization of decision-making.

Bridges (1975) has suggested that the leader of an educational organization is likely to overestimate his potential for influence. Arguing that leaders are not masters of their own fate, Bridges cites some recent studies that raise doubt about the treatment of leadership factors (e.g., managerial styles) as independent variables rather than as dependent variables (cf. Lowin and Craig, 1968; Crow *et al.*, 1972) in organizational studies. Administrators whose "occupational self-identity" is based upon an unrealistic view of influence potential, according to Bridges, may suffer agonizing stress in the everyday role. In a higher education institution, this stress is likely to be even more pronounced because the optimal manager-subordinate distance does not exist (cf. Jaques, 1970), and the dean's actions and decisions may well be subject to the questioning of "subordinates" who know more about their own work than he does.

In this chapter, the author has noted that all academic sub-units (departments) are subject to some influence because of the dean's authority to make budgetary and personnel recommendations and to allocate resources. However, the dean's use of formal authority was hypothesized to be a partial function of the heterogeneity (or normative diversity) of departments in the college. Several associated hypotheses were presented to describe the conditions under which the dean would tend to adopt certain coping behaviors. The decision to delegate responsibility, for example, was posited to depend upon the existence of a common body of expert knowledge among member departments or upon a desire to induce compromise or homogeneity of departmental norms and standards through interaction. Where homogeneity does not exist and where interaction is likely to lead to confrontation, the dean might use delegation in order to increase the likelihood of the group turning to him to arbitrate differences. The dean might also attempt to offset or foster heterogeneity by playing an influential role in personnel decisions.

It was also argued that the greater the heterogeneity of departments in a college, the greater the hypothesized emergence of informal pressures seeking (1) to reduce the impact of college authority (the dean's or a faculty committee's) on departmental practices or (2) to create an informal structure of norms, rewards, and sanctions that would promote homogeneity and organizational stability.

Heterogeneity (or normative diversity) was conceived in terms of truth strategies characteristic of various disciplines or academic fields, linking the concept to differentiation within the academic profession. The existing institutional organization of departments into colleges, moreover, was posited as influencing the congruence or incongruence between departmental truth strategies and those of their disciplines. Faculty inbreeding was conceptualized as a key variable in promoting organizational homogeneity (and, perhaps rigidity) through the perpetuation of existing truth strategies in line with the group's informal norms and reward structures.

As part of the informal attempt to distort the power of the dean (or the college faculty committee) over individual departments, it was posited that departments might attempt to ignore the institution and seek resources from external groups. The more successful the entrepreneurship of individual departments, the greater is their hypothesized status in the group and the greater is their influence in shaping group norms. As the corresponding power of sub-unit or department chairpersons increases, that of the dean is expected to decrease.

While Kahn's (1964) model of role conflict depicts administrative role behavior as a dependent variable, it gives directional influence to sent-role pressures and conceives of organization, personality, and interpersonal relations as factors representing the *context* of a role episode. The author has argued that the organizational factors (both formal and informal) may have more direct effect upon the dean's behavior and upon the role conflict, ambiguity, and stress that he experiences. In particular, the normative diversity and relative autonomy among the dean's sub-units are reflected in many organizational patterns and structures in the academic setting.

Research questions flowing from Kahn's (1964) model might include the following:

1. What is the role of the academic dean, as perceived by members of the role set?
   a. Does the role vary with variations in certain situational or personal variables such as:
      (1) Size of organization?
      (2) Type of administrative structure?
      (3) Existence or non-existence of a clear statement of duties or responsibilities?
      (4) Hierarchical level at which respondent functions (inter-role perceptions)?
      (5) Extent or nature of a respondent's formal training or experience?
   b. Is conflict in the role made evident in different perceptions of the respondents?
   c. Does ambiguity characterize the role?
   d. Does role overload characterize the role?
2. Does the dean perceive these role expectations accurately? (What is the perceived role?)
3. What role pressure and sanctions does the dean perceive?
4. What role forces exist within the dean as an individual (satisfaction from job content, occupational self-identity)?
5. How does the dean respond to role conflict, role ambiguity, and/or overload? What are the dean's coping responses?

Methodologically, such questions could be answered through the administration of survey-type instruments, with respondents representing various members of the dean's role set, whose responses could be compared with those of the dean. Many types of comparisons would be needed to address various questions, but the basic data could be collected easily through surveys.

In this chapter, the author has criticized briefly some typical operational definitions of organizational concepts as applied to the university setting. (A fuller discussion is found in Ryan, 1974). Further, only part "a" of question "1" above addresses itself to relationships between role expectations or behavior and the organizational settings in which deans work. Since the concepts of sub-unit heterogeneity and differential autonomy are viewed as critical for understanding the findings of academic role studies, research designs must go beyond simplistic surveys.

Other methodologies must be employed to describe the differences among colleges and the sub-units or groups within them in terms of both administrative and academic organizations, processes by which authority is shared or delegated, processes of interaction that modify the dean's use of formal authority, and the like. In short, research questions must go well beyond the search for easily quantifiable differences among members of the role set (e.g., extent of respondent's early training) or formal organizational differences (e.g., number of committees) to examine the characteristics of the role set as a group or as groups competing for influence and to examine the actual processes of governance and the dean's role vis-à-vis that of the faculty in such processes. A methodological starting point has been provided by Ryan (1971).

The research questions flowing from this discussion would be broad in scope and would require qualitative analysis based upon field data. Typical questions might include:

1. What structures represent the administrative and academic organizations relevant to the dean's role?
   a. What role does the dean play in determining the makeup of such structures, and why?
2. What is the functional division of responsibilities for decision-making between the two organizations? What rationale explains this?
   a. How is formal responsibility modified by advisory relationships?
   b. How are decisions actually taken? What procedures are followed?
   c. To what extent do faculty members share in administrative responsibilities?
   d. What decisions are made solely by the dean? Who influences these decisions? How and why?
3. Do the structures and processes related to the two organizations reflect sub-unit heterogeneity and differential autonomy? (Comparisons among colleges).
   a. How homogeneous are sub-units in truth strategies, emphasis on research, etc.?
   b. Who determines personnel decisions? What effect does this have on inbreeding or on recruitment of "Young Turks"?

    c. What division of labor is present within sub-units under the dean?

    d. Do sub-units seek resources elsewhere? Does their entrepreneurship create tensions in the organization?

    e. Does the dean identify such factors as important in establishing mechanisms for sub-unit interaction and for decision-making?

    f. Is there evidence to suggest that more heterogeneous departments attempt to reduce the dean's authority?

4. How do organizational patterns affect the dean's role in the sense of promoting role stress and in influencing coping strategies?

5. Have changes in resources affected these patterns?

    a. How has the dean responded to tensions for change?

    b. Has the dean made organizational changes?

    c. How does the dean cope with changes in personnel needs?

    d. How do issues get resolved when resource changes occur?

    e. Do sub-unit heterogeneity and differential autonomy reflect these changes?

These questions are merely suggestive of the types that could be asked in a field study of the day-to-day functioning of a university sub-unit and an examination of the rationale behind the identified processes. While the questions are posed broadly, the discussion in this chapter has provided both theoretical and empirical direction to field efforts. Essentially, the researcher would be guided by an attempt to operationalize the concepts of normative diversity and differential autonomy through his examination of organizational processes, and he would attempt to test the potency of such factors in shaping the dean's role. Direction for studying organizational processes is provided in Ryan (1971).

Since field studies are both time-consuming and expensive in terms of labor, one compromise might be to conduct survey studies of the dean's role first. Based upon the findings of questions such as those flowing from Kahn's model, one might then select a smaller sample of institutions (or colleges within a single institution) which appear to vary in terms of potential role conflict and ambiguity for the dean, and in which gross organizational factors appear to be related to role stress. Through interviewing and observation, the settings might then be examined more fully. In this effort, attention could be paid to the effect of group characteristics (heterogeneity and autonomy) on role stress and on coping strategies. As well, the dean's leadership in addressing group factors could be examined, and his relative influence vis-à-vis group coping strategies could be traced.

Studies in other domains are addressed more directly to the organization *per se* and to the dean as boundary administrator (organizations-in-environments). Yet the need for cross-domain analysis cannot be met unless studies in each domain are informed by knowledge of the important variables linking cultural (or normative) and structural factors to organizational behavior. As changes occur in the larger society, changes will also occur in the academic profession itself and in the institution in which academics work. The dean's role must be studied in the light of these dynamics. Role behavior must be related to both organizational patterns and to the cultural and normative underpinnings they reflect. In the author's view, sub-unit heterogeneity and autonomy are concepts that reflect those cultural ties and that largely determine organizational structures, role behaviors, and role stress for the dean. Research must examine not only conflict inherent in varying expectations for a focal role but also the underlying causes that *explain* those findings.

One further comment seems appropriate. Concepts like role conflict, stress, and ambiguity seem to have negative connotations, at least in the sense of the incumbent's mental health. We have spoken of governance as being troublesome where heterogeneity exists among the dean's sub-units. While research into the deanship might provide bases for developing coping strategies to reduce sub-unit heterogeneity and autonomy, the author would hope that developmental models would be informed by research so that coping strategies recognize the positive outcomes of these culturally linked variables. Heterogeneity and demands for autonomy arise within the context of commonly held commitments of academics to liberal education and inquiry (cf. Parsons and Platt, 1973).

Numerous examples come to mind of deans and department chairpersons selected in the past for the purpose of upsetting established norms in a college or a department. The attempt has been made to recruit new persons, to break up faculty inbreeding and oligarchic influence patterns, and the like. In other words, academic administrators have been challenged to increase heterogeneity among members. Where this has occurred, the motivation typically has been to encourage research and newer modes of inquiry in keeping with institutional goals and professional developments. The challenge to leaders in the forthcoming decade will be even greater, as recruitment may dwindle and as organizational stability could come to mean organizational stagnation.

NOTES

1. The intention in this chapter is to discuss research appropriate to the dean's role in various institutional settings. Where "departments" are mentioned, therefore, the word "sub-units" could be substituted. Colleges of education in particular may not be subdivided formally into departments, but rather into special fields or areas. The College of Education in The Ohio State University, for example, in 1969 included a single school of education, which consisted of four divisions and 24 areas, each having a coordinator or head. (Ryan, 1969).
2. The discussion that follows in this section is summarized from Kahn *et al.*, 1964, pp. 11-35.
3. See Kahn, 1964, for conceptual definitions. Also see Sheehan, 1972, for an example of operationalization of these concepts.

REFERENCES

Abrahamson, M. "Informal Groups in the Research Laboratory," in M. Abrahamson (ed.), *The Professional in the Organization*. Chicago: Rand McNally, 1967. pp. 63-70.

Barton, A. H. *Organizational Measurement and Its Bearing on the Study of College Environments*. New York: College Entrance Examination Board, 1961.

Baum, B. H. *Decentralization of Authority in a Bureaucracy*. Englewood Cliffs, N.J.: Prentice-Hall, 1961.

Ben-David, J. *The Scientist's Role in Society*. Englewood Cliffs, N.J.: Prentice-Hall, 1971.

Blau, P. M. "A Formal Theory of Differentiation in Organizations," *American Sociological Review*, Vol. 35, April 1970, pp. 201-218.

Blau, P. M. *The Organization of Academic Work*. New York: John Wiley, 1973.

Blau, P. M., and W. R. Scott. *Formal Organizations*. San Francisco: Chandler, 1962.

Bridges, E. "The Nature of Leadership." Paper delivered at the conference "Educational Administration Twenty Years Later 1965-74," The Ohio State University, Columbus, April 1975.

Bucher, R., and A. Strauss. "Professions in Process," *The American Journal of Sociology*, Vol. 66, January 1961, pp. 325-334.

Clark, B. "Faculty Authority," *American Association of University Professors Bulletin*, Winter 1961, pp. 293-302.

Clark, B. "Faculty Organization and Authority," in T. F. Lunsford (ed.), *The Study of Academic Administration*. Boulder, Colo.: Western Interstate Commission for Higher Education, 1963. pp. 37-51.

Cleveland, H. "The Dean's Dilemma: Leadership of Equals," *Public Administration Review*, Vol. 20, Winter 1960. pp. 22-27.

Cohen, A. R., E. Stotland, and D. M. Wolfe. "An Experimental Investigation of Need for Cognition," *Journal of Abnormal and Social Psychology*, Vol. 51, 1955, pp. 291-294.

Cohen, M., and J. March. *Leadership and Ambiguity: The American College President*. New York: McGraw-Hill, 1974.

Corson, J. J. *Governance of Colleges and Universities*. New York: McGraw-Hill, 1960.

Crowe, B. J., *et al*. "The Effects of Subordinates' Behavior on Managerial Style," *Human Relations*, Vol. 23, 1972, pp. 215-237.

Dai, B. "A Socio-Psychiatric Approach to Personality Organization," in A. Rose (ed.), *Mental Health and Mental Disorder*. New York: Norton, 1955.

Demerath, N. J., R. W. Stephens, and R. R. Taylor. *Power, Presidents, and Professors*. New York: Basic Books, 1967.

Dibden, A. J. (ed.). *The Academic Deanship in American Colleges and Universities*. Carbondale: Southern Illinois University Press, 1968.

Dykes, A. R. *Faculty Participation in Academic Decision Making: Report of a Study*. Washington, D.C.: American Council on Education, 1968.

Etzioni, A. *Modern Organizations*. Englewood Cliffs, N.J.: Prentice-Hall, 1964.

Etzioni, A. "Organizational Control Structure," in J. G. March (ed.), *Handbook of Organizations*. Chicago: Rand McNally, 1965. pp. 650-677.

Freeman, R. A. *Crisis in College Finance?* Washington, D.C.: The Institute for Social Science Research, 1965.

Frenkel-Brunswick, E. "Intolerance of Ambiguity as an Emotional and Perceptual Personality Variable, *Journal of Personality*, Vol. 18, 1949, pp. 108-143.

Gross, N., *et al*. *Explorations in Role Analysis*. New York: John Wiley, 1958.

Haas, E., and L. Collin. "Administrative Practices in University Departments." *Administrative Science Quarterly*, Vol. 8, June 1963, pp. 44-60.

Hagstrom, W. O. "The Scientific Community," in M. Abrahamson (ed.), *The Professional in the Organization*. Chicago: Rand McNally, 1967. pp. 75-84.

Jaques, E. *Work, Creativity, and Social Justice*. New York: International Universities Press, 1970.

Joughlin, L. "The Faculty and the Dean," *Liberal Education*, Vol. 49, December 1963, pp. 502-512.

Kahn, R., *et al*. *Organizational Stress*. New York: John Wiley, 1964.

Kaplan, N. "The Role of the Research Administrator," *Administrative Science Quarterly*, Vol. 4, June 1959, pp. 20-42.

Katz, David, and R. Kahn. *The Social Psychology of Organizations*. New York: John Wiley, 1966.

Kerr, C. *The Uses of the University*. Cambridge, Mass.: Harvard University Press, 1963.

Lazarsfeld, P. F., and W. Thielens, Jr. *The Academic Mind*. Glencoe, Ill.: Free Press, 1958.

Lewis, L. S. "Institutional Inbreeding and Dissimilar Views on Faculty Autonomy," *College and University*, Vol. 42, Fall 1966, pp. 5-12.

Lowin, A., and J. Craig. "The Influence of Level of Performance on Managerial Style: An Experimental Object-Lesson in the Ambiguity of Correlational Data," *Organizational Behavior and Human Performance*, Vol. 3, 1968, pp. 440-58.

March, J. "Commitment and Competence in Educational Administration." in L. Mayhew, (ed.), *Educational Leadership and Declining Enrollments*. Berkeley, Calif.: McCutchan, 1974. pp. 131-141.

McKelvey, W. W. "Expectational Noncomplementarity and Style of Interaction Between Professional and Organization," *Administrative Science Quarterly*, Vol. 14, March 1969, pp. 21-32.

Meltzer, L. "Scientific Productivity in Organizational Settings," *Journal of Social Issues*, Vol. 12, 1956, pp. 33-40.

Miller, J. *Living Systems*. Ann Arbor, Mich.: Mental Health Research Institute, 1962 (Multilith).

Mollenberg, W. "The Hazards of Academic Administration," *Intellect*, Vol. 104, February 1976, pp. 374-378.

National Academy of Sciences, *Profiles of Ph.D.'s in the Sciences*, 1965.

Orlans, H. *The Effect of Federal Programs on Higher Education*. Washington, D.C.: Brookings Institution, 1963.

Page, H. E. "University Science Development One Hundred Million Dollars Later," *Educational Record*, Vol. 49, Summer 1968, pp. 250-256.

Parsons, T. "New Roles for Academic Faculties," in *Current Issues in Higher Education*. Washington, D.C.: Association for Higher Education, 1966. pp. 190-197.

Parsons, T. *The Social System*. Glencoe, Ill.: Free Press, 1951.

Parsons, T., and G. M. Platt. *The American University*. Cambridge, Mass.: Harvard University Press, 1973.

Peterson, M. "Organization and Administration in Higher Education: Sociological and Social-Psychological Perspectives," in T. Kerlinger and J. Carroll (eds.), *Review of Research in Education*, Vol. 2. Itasca, Ill.: F. E. Peacock, 1974. pp. 296-347.

Riesman, D. *Constraint and Variety in American Education*. Lincoln: University of Nebraska Press, 1956.

Ryan, D. W. "Administrative Control in Academic Departments and Response to Reorganization," *Administrator's Notebook*, Vol. 18, March 1970, pp. 1-4.

Ryan, D. W. "Analyzing Faculty Involvement in Academic Governance: The Usefulness of Structural and Procedural Data," *Division Generator*, Vol. 1, AERA, February 1971, pp. 4-8.

Ryan, D. W. "The Internal Organization of Academic Departments," *The Journal of Higher Education*, Vol. 43, June 1972, pp. 464-482.

Ryan, D. W. "Organizational Adaptation to Professional Differentiation in the University," *Interchange*, Vol. 5, 1974, pp. 55-66.

Ryan, D. W. "University Departments: Their Organization and Response to Reorganization." Unpublished Ph.D. dissertation, The University of Chicago, 1969.

Scott, W. R. "Professionals in Bureaucracies—Areas of Conflict," in H. M. Vollmer and D. L. Mills (eds.), *Professionalization*. Englewood Cliffs, N.J.: Prentice-Hall, 1966. pp. 265-275.

Sheehan, A. T., Sr. "Role Conflict and Value Divergence in Sister Administrators." Unpublished Ph.D. thesis, University of Toronto, 1972.

Smelser, N. J., "Epilogue," in T. Parsons and G. Platt, *The American University*. Cambridge, Mass.: Harvard University Press, 1973. pp. 389-422.

Thompson, J. D., R. W. Hawkes, and R. W. Avery. "Truth Strategies and University Organization," *Educational Administration Quarterly*, Vol. 5, Spring 1969, pp. 4-25.

Veysey, L. R. *The Emergence of The American University*. Chicago: University of Chicago Press, 1965.

Vollmer, H. M. "Entrepreneurship and Professional Productivity Among Research Scientists," in H. M. Vollmer and D. L. Mills (eds.), *Professionalization*. Englewood Cliffs, N.J.: Prentice-Hall, 1966. pp. 276-282.

Vollmer, H. M., and D. L. Mills. *Professionalization*. Englewood Cliffs, N.J.: Prentice-Hall, 1966.

Walton, R. E., and J. M. Dutton. "The Management of Interdepartmental Conflict: A Model and Review," *Administrative Science Quarterly*, Vol. 14, March 1969, pp. 73-84.

Weber, M. *The Theory of Social and Economic Organization* (A. M. Henderson and T. Parsons eds. and trans.). New York: Free Press, 1947.

Williams, R. L. *The Administration of Academic Affairs in Higher Education.* Ann Arbor: University of Michigan Press, 1965.

Wilson, L. "Academic Administration: Its Abuses and Uses," *American Association of University Professors Bulletin*, Winter 1955, pp. 684-692.

CHAPTER 8

Schools of Education as Complex Organizations[1]

by
DAVID D. DILL
The University of North Carolina at Chapel Hill

> When I think back
> on all the crap I learned in high school
> It's a wonder
> I can think at all.
> — Paul Simon

> . . . tell me I beseech you,
> Needs there a school this modish art to teach you?
> No need of lessons now, the knowing think;
> We might as well be taught to eat and drink.
> — R. B. Sheridan

> Over the last two decades, schools of education have been the
> target of steady criticism, some highly pertinent, some less
> so. . . . As a result of all this criticism, people associated with
> teaching and teacher training are defensive to an extent not
> found in other professions.
> — Carnegie Commission on Higher Education

INTRODUCTION

Contemporary events have led to increased interest in the education of professionals and to changes in the nature of that education.

Concern with the power and influence of professionals has resulted in changes in the curriculum of professional schools—for example, in the addition of courses in ethics for lawyers and doctors. Concern with the relationship between the number of professional school graduates and society's manpower needs has resulted in efforts to adjust the numbers of students admitted and graduated. Concern with the potential power of professional schools over entry into and recertification in a profession has resulted in efforts by minority and professional groups as well as governmental agencies to alter, often in opposing directions, the influence of the schools. The net effect of this popular interest has been not only an increasing curiosity about professional schools and how they function, but also a loss of autonomy by these schools.

But the effect on professional schools has varied. While all schools may feel the erosion of authority and independence, certain professional schools—most notably education—face these pressures in a period of no-growth or curtailment. Furthermore, public discontent with the quality of our public school system has led to dramatic criticism of the schools of education which produce the teachers, administrators, and counselors who staff that system. The professionals themselves, in the form of teacher unions or organizations, have raised the possibility of establishing alternative means of certification to the schools of education, a threat to the survival of the majority of these schools.

Professional schools, then, and particularly schools of education, are receiving dramatic pressures for change from their environment. The leadership or management function of these schools appears to be becoming unpredictable and uncharted, a situation which has fostered this paper on schools of education as complex organizations.[2] But, it is suggested here, there are reasons other than contemporary external pressures for the study of professional schools, reasons of particular interest to those whose field of study is educational organizations.

Ben-David has indicated that professional education in the United States represents both a structural and a functional innovation.[3] Structurally, it is almost impossible today to find a distinguished school of professional training in this country which does not have university connections. In contrast, outside the United States, many professional fields are taught in specialized non-university institutions which grant their own diplomas. For example, the Soviet Union has professional schools, both in medicine and in law, wholly disassociated from the universities. Functionally, the United States

developed professional schools without parallel in other societies—
education and business representing two prominent examples.
Perhaps most significant, however, was the orientation of all American professional schools toward the concept of clinical practice within
the boundaries of the professional school itself. This resulted in the
use of clinical research and clinical experience to improve the training
of professionals.[4] This innovation was introduced in the School of
Medicine at Johns Hopkins but also characterized Teachers College,
Columbia University. Parsons and Platt have highlighted this innovation by distinguishing between the "core of cognitive primacy"—
research and graduate training in the arts and sciences—and training
for the applied professions:

> There is . . . a basic pattern of organization common to all the
> applied professions. Their paramount feature is the orientation
> of each to a clinical focus. The level of rationalization of the
> knowledge and competence which can be applied in each field is
> a matter of the development of bodies of knowledge comparable
> to the science of medicine. There are points beyond which in-
> creasing the level of this rationalization, through bringing more
> advanced knowledge to bear, involves articulation with the
> basic-science disciplines that root organizationally in faculties of
> arts and sciences and in the intellectual disciplines which have
> their home there.[5]

While this analysis helps to suggest a rationale for the continuing
structural linkages between American professional schools and the
university, there is a clear functional distinction between professional
schools and the arts and sciences disciplines, the distinction between
"knowledge for its own sake" and the "utilization of knowledge for
problem-solving." As a result, there are parallel differences between
the role of academics in the arts and sciences and academics in the
applied professions. Parsons and Platt point out that:

> . . . For the academic the cognitive stress is on learning with
> cognitive primacy, even where the learning is not his own but
> that of students and others, such as lay audiences or
> readerships. His fiduciary responsibility is to the cognitive en-
> terprise. For the applied professional, the fiduciary responsibil-
> ity is to the utilization of cognitive resources for practical
> goals. . . . The responsibility (of the applied professional) for
> the utilization of knowledge thus implies, on the cognitive side,
> that *selection* within the available corpus of knowledge by
> criteria of *relevance* for the interests of clients must play a major
> part.[6]

The fiduciary responsibility of the applied professional also results in a more direct and influential linkage between professional schools and the "real" world than exists between the core university and society. Engineering and medicine, for example, "have institutionalized a massive involvement of science with the practical concerns of the everyday world," and have thereby created a symbiosis between the professional schools and other parts of society. [7]

The current concern with the leadership and management of professional schools which has resulted from external pressure for reform more than warrants their study. [8] But their distinctive structure, function, and influence in our society also justify the need for analysis and descriptive research by those whose interest is educational organizations.

The focus of this paper is on schools of education. The purpose of the paper is to suggest means of conceptualizing and studying these schools which will help to foster research. Because the holistic study of any organization is a hopelessly broad charge, two general strategies will be used to bring the problem under control. First, the level of discussion will be largely conceptual, based on literature in organizational theory, aided by citations from empirical research on organizations, and illustrated by examples from the writer's experience and perceptions of schools of education. Because of this orientation, no attempt has been made to review systematically the existing literature for research on professional schools or schools of education, though clearly this should be the first step in any specific research effort. The second strategy is to focus the analysis by outlining a classification of dimensions whereby schools of education can be analyzed and relevant concepts brought to bear.

In the following section a typology for analyzing a school of education as a complex organization will be presented. In subsequent sections of the paper each piece of the typology will be discussed at length, and specific concepts and questions relevant for studying a school of education will be introduced. The paper will conclude with a brief section on research problems and methods as a suggested guide to those who would like to apply these concepts in research.

Schools of education are the focus of this paper, but as this introduction has stressed, it is believed that all professional schools share common pressures as well as organizational traits. Although there is extensive discussion of examples from the field of education in what follows, the concepts and research problems outlined are assumed to be applicable to any professional school. Consequently, comparative illustrations will be made throughout.

A CLASSIFICATION OF SCHOOLS OF EDUCATION

A major assumption underlies what will follow. It is that schools of education may be conceived of as open systems. There are several implications to this assumption:[9]

1. Schools of education can be conceived of as systems within systems; therefore, the appropriate focus is on the interactions of relevant systems.
2. Schools of education are dependent on transactions with other systems for survival.
3. There is no *one* appropriate form for a school of education; for example, variation in the environment requires variation in the form of the school.
4. Schools of education have the capacity for adaptation to a changing environment.
5. Schools of education are characterized by differing layers of control and autonomy; for example, activities of various critical sub-systems must be coordinated.

In the present discussion, a school of education is defined as "the system." The environment in this context consists of organizations which have consistent transactions with the school such as arts and sciences and professional schools on the same campus, the public schools, federal research agencies, and others. For the purpose of analysis, and consistent with an open-systems perspective, the school (the system) can be further subdivided into an interrelated set of sub-systems. There have been several attempts to develop a classification or typology which could be applied to organizational sub-systems.[10]

Sub-systems

The discussion which follows utilizes a sub-system classification advanced by Kast and Rosenzweig.[11] As Figure 8.1[12] illustrates, the organization receives inputs of energy, information, and materials from its environment, transforms these, and returns outputs to the environment. The organization itself (the system) is composed of the

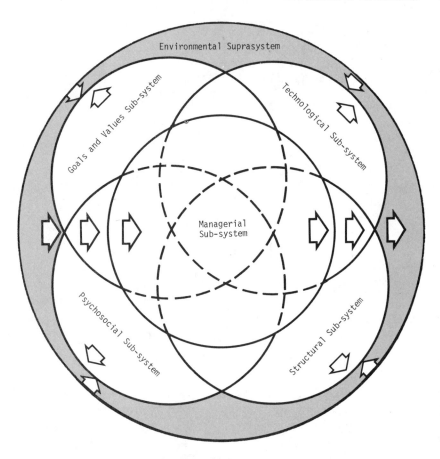

Figure 8.1. Input-output flows of materials, energy, and information.

following sub-systems: goals and values, technological, structural, psychosocial, and managerial.

There are strengths and weaknesses to any sort of classificatory scheme. The strengths of this scheme are as follows: First, the scheme is concise and simple, which in this field is not to be taken lightly. Second, the classification also connects readily to the major organizing concepts in the field. In fact, the figure is an aid to understanding the evolution of organizational theory, each historical approach tending to emphasize a particular sub-system.[13] Third, the scheme stresses the implications of an open-systems perspective: it emphasizes the importance of the relations between sub-systems and between the organization and its environment, it focuses on management as a coordinative mechanism of the various sub-systems, and it stresses that each sub-system is interdependent with the others.

There are also weaknesses, characteristic of any such classification scheme. It is a classification, not a theoretical model or conceptual scheme. Though it can be used to suggest key variables within each sub-system, it suggests no mechanism by which these sub-systems are related, no directionality to the relationships which can guide analysis. For example, if we were to change a school of education from a centralized to a decentralized structure, what would be the degree of change in the other sub-systems, indeed what would be the direction of the change? A second weakness, characteristic of the open-systems perspective, is its scope—everything is related to everything else.To the educational professional this is an advantage—its myriad patterns create remarkable insights; to the academic researcher it is a block—its very complexity creates a "chilling effect" on research. If the variables are so numerous and interdependent, then research becomes so hopelessly broad scale and expensive that it is not carried out. This matter, not easily reconciled, will be discussed in more detail in the section on research methods and problems.

System and Environment

Before proceeding to the more extensive discussion of each sub-system, several points need to be made about the relationship of the system to its environment. In accordance with an open-systems perspective, the classification scheme used here presumes interdependence between the organization and the environment. The organization is considered open to environmental influences and partially determined by them. This generalization has been persistent since the earliest writings of an open-systems perspective:

> The basic hypothesis is that organizations and other social structures are open systems which attain stability through their authority structures, reward mechanisms, and value systems, and which are changed primarily from without by means of some significant change in input. Some organizations, less open than most, may resist new inputs indefinitely and may perish rather than change. We would predict, however, that in the absence of external changes, organizations are likely to be reformed from within in limited ways. More drastic or revolutionary changes are initiated by external forces.[14]

Consonant with this point of view, Doi has suggested in correspondence that the major problems facing a dean of education reside in the relationships between the school and components of its environmental suprasystem.

This paper focuses on the sub-systems of a school of education and the interaction between them, but it assumes that the relationships between a school and its environment may be critical to an understanding of some of the contemporary pressures on these schools. (For a more explicit treatment of these relationships see McCarty's associated paper.) Since analysis of the sub-systems of a system is simply a substitution for the analysis of the system as a whole, organization-environment relationships can also be examined in terms of environmental influences on a particular sub-system. Lawrence and Lorsch, for example, found that effective organizations that function in dynamic and diverse environments were highly differentiated structurally.[15] In contrast, an equally effective organization in a more stable environment was less differentiated. They generalized that variation in environment requires variation in organizational structure. Therefore, where research or theory has suggested such relationships, the interaction between the organizational environment and a particular sub-system will be discussed in the analysis of each sub-system.

In the sections that follow, the goals and values and technological, structural, psychosocial, and managerial sub-systems of a school of education will be discussed. Each section will follow a similar outline. The nature of the sub-system will be defined and concepts characterizing that sub-system will be described. The concepts selected have been those which the organizational literature suggests as most valuable for understanding the nature and interactions of the sub-systems, and which have been operationalized and empirically tested. Each section will conclude with a set of illustrative propositions which apply the concepts in a researchable form. These propositions have been adapted from hypotheses developed in research on other organizations.

GOALS AND VALUES SUB-SYSTEM

An organization such as a school of education can be conceived of as having organizational goals and values which are distinguishable from the other sub-systems but related to them. To say that a school of education can have goals and values is to suggest certain specific things: (1) we can speak of such goals on the school or organizational level in addition to individual or group levels; (2) we can speak of an organization embodying certain values into an institutional identity; and (3) we can speak of an organization's pattern of specified ends, outputs, or priorities.

A school of education can be viewed as a contrived social system designed to accomplish specific goals. The school, for example, can offer a degree in education which, given constraints from the environment, faculty members as individuals or as small groups cannot offer independently. The goals that exist or that may be arrived at within the organization are affected by the norms held by individuals of that which is good and desirable. For example, a faculty member in education may be drawn to the academic profession because of a genuine enjoyment of knowledge for its own sake; therefore, this personal value may strongly influence his attitude toward the relative merits of a professional (Ed.D.) versus a scholarly (Ph.D.) degree. Or, certain formal or informal groups, such as ethnic minorities, may share norms which will affect the behavior of individuals and also the actions of organizations. However, the organization itself may embody certain values in the thought and life styles of an evolving group. These norms or values are developed over time and influence the values and behavior of students, faculty members, and staff.

Organizational Sagas

In case histories of three notable liberal arts colleges, Clark employed this latter orientation toward organizational values and denoted the concept "organizational saga."[16] An organizational saga refers to a coherent set of openly expressed convictions about the formal group. These convictions assume unique achievement by the organization, are grounded in its history, and are held with feeling by the group members. Nationally one could identify Teachers College, Columbia University, or the Department of Education, University of Chicago, as schools of education where this concept would have particular power for explaining organizational behavior. The personal impact of John Dewey on both institutions shaped for several generations the concept of what was important and appropriate for a school of education. But the potential for analysis may be no less great at more locally oriented schools which have developed strong traditions. Clark distinguishes two stages in the development of a saga, "initiation" and "fulfillment." The saga initially is a mission, developed and stated by one man or a small nucleus who must discover an institutional setting which is prepared or can be prepared for change. Based on his research, Clark distinguishes three types of settings where a strong saga may develop: (1) an autonomous, new organization lacking established structure or rigid custom and initially afforded some autonomy and protection from bordering outsiders; (2) an established organization in crisis or decay, whose desire for survival creates a caesura with the past, thus attracting the attention of a reformer; and (3) an established organization ready for evolutionary change, with a tradition of executive power and a self-defined need for educational leadership. While the conditions of initiation may vary, the means of fulfillment according to Clark are more predictable. There are five components at the center of the development of a saga: (1) the personnel, (2) the program, (3) the external social base, (4) the student sub-culture, and (5) the imagery of the saga. While an individual may initiate a change, the change must be embodied in a cadre of faculty members to be sustained; it must result in visible practices of distinctive accomplishment; it must become rooted in the belief system of external observers—notably alumni; it must be integrated over time with the ideology of the student sub-culture; and it must be expressed as a generalized tradition in ceremonies, in written histories, and in the various means of sharing memory and symbolizing the institution.

The concept of organizational saga is of particular value in understanding, for example, the conditions under which a new dean may carry out innovation and change in a school of education. It also suggests the potential interrelationship between the organizational goals and values sub-system and the psychosocial sub-system and the impact of this relationship on a school of education's efficiency and effectiveness:

> An organizational saga is thus a valuable resource, created over a number of years out of the social components of the formal enterprise. As participants become ideologues, their common definition becomes a foundation for trust and for extreme loyalty. Such bonds give the organization a competitive edge in recruiting and maintaining personnel and help it avoid the vicious circle in which some actual or anticipated erosion of organizational strength leads to the loss of some personnel, which leads to further decline and loss. Loyalty causes individuals to stay with a system, to save and improve it rather than to leave to serve their self-interest elsewhere. The genesis and persistence of loyalty is a key organizational and analytical problem. Enduring loyalty follows from a collective belief of participants that

their organization is distinctive. Such a belief comes from a credible story of uncommon effort, achievement, and form.[17]

Finally, the organizational saga or values significantly affect the internal operations and actions of the organization, particularly decision-making and the setting of organizational goals.

Organizational Goals

To a dean of a school of education the concept of organizational goals may be immediately comprehensible, since administrators will frequently identify organization-level goals with their own. To students, faculty members, staff, and those interacting with schools of education, and particularly to those attempting to operationalize the concept for research, it has been less clear. Organizations may not have a single goal, or set of goals, but may have multiple goals. A dean, for example, may conceive of the goals as teaching, research, and service—what has come to be termed *output goals*—a reference to the consumers toward which products are directed. Perrow has suggested that there are actually five categories or levels of goals: (1) societal goals, (2) output goals, (3) system goals, (4) product goals, and (5) derived goals, each level recognizing a different point of view—society, the customers, managers,[18] etc. Furthermore, Perrow suggests that output goals are of limited value in organizational analysis because they rarely change. In a report on an empirical study of the goals of colleges and universities, Gross makes a similar distinction between "output goals" and "support goals,"[19] the latter representing a rough approximation of Perrow's last three levels. In their survey of faculty members' and administrators' *perceptions* of institutional goals at 68 universities conducted in 1964, and repeated in 1971, Gross and Grambsch[20] reported that the four top-ranked goals were not output goals but were support goals: to protect academic freedom, ensure confidence of contributors, maintain top quality in important programs, and increase or maintain prestige.

The goals of a complex organization like a university or even a school of education not only are apt to be multiple but also may be conflicting. The degree of goal consensus among organizational members therefore becomes a potential question for investigation. In their study of colleges and universities Gross and Grambsch examined two concepts related to consensus: goal congruence and goal variability. Congruence described the relationship between what the university's goals were perceived to be and what the respondent preferred them to be. Variation referred to the relationship between faculty members' and administrators' perceived and preferred goals. In the initial study in 1964, measurements of both concepts indicated high consensus on goals for the university and the degree of consensus *increased* between 1964 and 1971, leading the authors to suggest that during this tumultuous period in American higher education, greater consensus on university goals was achieved.

In addition to distinctions between the types and numbers of goals pursued by a school of education, the degree of goal specificity can also be analyzed. A dean of a school of education may publicly state that the training of future educators, research on educational process, and field consultation with local school districts are all important goals of the school. However, a survey of how faculty members spend their non-classroom time and an analysis of budgetary expenditures other than staff salaries may suggest that 90 percent of faculty discretionary time and 90 percent of discretionary resources are directed in the pursuit of teaching and training programs. There appears to be a difference between the organization's "official" goals and its "operative" goals. Perrow has suggested that operative goals are analytically more useful for telling us what an organization is trying to do:

> The type of goals most relevant to understanding organizational behavior are not the official goals, but those that are embedded in major operating policies and the daily decisions of the personnel. . . . These goals will be shaped by the particular problems or tasks an organization must emphasize, since these tasks determine the characteristics of those who will dominate the organization.[21]

A major focus of an open-systems perspective is the interrelationship between an organization (conceptualized here by subsystems) and its environment. Gross and Grambsch, for example, found strong differences in the ranking of goals between public and private universities and traced this difference to the amount of power over the organization perceived to be held by external actors such as legislators and state agencies. These studies would suggest that the goals pursued by a school of education, and conceivably the way that it is structured as well, may vary substantially according to the environmental context, according, for example, to its degree of autonomy within the university. One might expect to find, therefore, measurable differences in both the goals and values sub-system and the structural sub-system of schools of education, particularly in public and private institutions.

Illustrative Propositions

Utilizing the research and writing on organizational goals and values, some propositions can be stated which might be tested empirically in research on schools of education. Many others than the five that follow could be stated, but these help to illustrate some of the major points concerning the goals and values sub-system.[22]

1. Schools of education characterized by definable organizational values (or organizational saga) will also be characterized by a greater degree of participant loyalty.
2. Schools of education which have a single goal are more likely to have a high degree of effectiveness than schools which have multiple goals.[23]
3. Schools of education which have a high degree of goal consensus are more likely to have a high degree of effectiveness than schools which have a low degree of goal consensus.
4. Schools of education which have a high degree of goal specificity are more likely to have a high degree of effectiveness than schools which have a low degree of goal specificity.[24]
5. The goals and value sub-system of a school of education will be systematically related to the structural sub-system and to the environmental circumstances in which the school operates.[25]

TECHNOLOGICAL SUB-SYSTEM

A general open-system model of organizations presumes that the organization receives inputs from the environment, transforms them into outputs, and releases these outputs back to the environment. The techniques or tasks effecting this transformation have come to be termed *technology*, and the system of tasks or techniques of any organization may be termed its *technological sub-system*. Students, for example, enter a school of education and commence interactions designed by faculty members to train them; at the end of some specified period they depart with a degree or certificate. The tasks or techniques utilized by the school of education could be described as its technology. Simple as this point may appear, it could have substantial value in studying professional schools. For example, the tasks and techniques utilized in comparable training processes in schools of business or medicine seem on the surface quite disparate from those traditionally used in schools of education.

The popular conception of technology has been machine technology, the mechanical means of production. But machines are only the physical artifacts of technology. What lies behind the machine is the deliberate and rational behavior—the information—of which the machine is only the manifestation. Ellul has broadened our conception of technology by using the term *technique:*

> In our technological society, *technique* is the *totality of methods rationally arrived at and having absolute efficiency* (for a given stage of development) in *every* field of human activity.[26]

Hickson, *et al.*, have defined three facets of meaning to the concept of organizational technology which, taken together, encompass the range of meanings developed: (1) knowledge technology— characteristics of the knowledge used in the transformation process, (2) materials technology—characteristics of the materials used in the transformation process, and (3) operations technology—the equipping and sequencing of activities in the transformation process.[27] Past attempts to operationalize the concept of technology and to test the concept empirically have focused on the "operations" aspect. The full span of meanings has potential significance in examining schools of education; therefore, all three meanings will be briefly discussed.

Knowledge Technology

Parsons and Platt have suggested that all professional schools possess bodies of knowledge which serve as the basis for their training function; for example, they cite the "science of engineering," the "science of medicine," the "discipline of law."[28] The more prestigious professional schools of law, medicine, and engineering are distinguishable from the less prestigious (e.g., business, education, and social work) not only on the basis of age and status but also because their "clinical sciences"—that is, the bodies of knowledge relating to their practice—are more highly rationalized and systematized. A good lawyer must achieve a modicum of cognitive mastery of "the law" and its related methods of analysis:

> Although not an intellectual discipline in the sense of the basic sciences or the specific humanities, but rather an eclectic mobilization of knowledge relative to legal processes and thus predominantly empirical, the law is not without structural conceptualization on highly general levels.[29]

Most simply stated, we may talk of the knowledge in the clinical sciences of any professional school as a knowledge technology. Potentially we could construct a continuum for ranking the degree of complexity of the knowledge technology of different types of professional schools.[30] Development of valid scales of this type would open up opportunities for studies relating the basic transformation process of a professional school to its organizational structure. Indeed, Kast and Rosenzweig have suggested that knowledge and materials technology may be the most "powerful" components of technology and therefore have impact on the structure of an organization at all levels.[31] While this proposition has thus far not been tested empirically, it suggests some interesting speculations regarding the structural implications of major changes in professional school curricula.

Parsons and Platt have pointed out the relative weakness of the cognitive base for professional competence in education and have suggested this is characteristic of emerging professions.[32] Changing from a simple to a more complex technology will entail, in their view, grounding this competence in bodies of theoretical knowledge by closer articulation with the basic disciplines.[33] In other words, the knowledge technology in education must undergo a similar evolution to that experienced by medicine in the eighteenth century. But this change in knowledge technology, which is already underway, may also create certain structural tensions.

The various programs offered by a school of education are often not related to a consistent body of knowledge. Similar to other professional schools, a school of education can be seen as a "holding company" for programs tangentially related to the core-transformation process, in this case the training of teachers. For example, the development of professional competence in therapeutic roles (i.e., the adjustment of an individual to his environment) in such areas as counseling, special education, and school psychology, and in administrative roles (i.e., achieving organizational effectiveness) in such areas as primary and secondary schools, community colleges, and higher and adult education is not potentially dependent on the same theoretical knowledge as teaching. As each of these areas in a school of education moves from more simple to more complex forms of knowledge technology, it is reasonable to project increasing differentiation between the training processes for each role, with implications for the overall structure of the school. Increasing conflict and strains on integration might be expected—goal consensus may suffer as well. If one moves from the intra-organizational level to the interorganizational level, this structural problem becomes even more apparent. The development of a more complex knowledge technology in areas such as counseling in schools of education is apt to parallel rather heavily the evolution of knowledge in schools of social work, nursing, psychiatry, and counseling psychology—all will be drawing on similar bases of knowledge from the basic disciplines. This increasing convergence is even more marked when one turns to administrative training, since schools of business administration and public administration already have a well-focused clinical content in this area based increasingly on knowledge in the basic disciplines. As the knowledge technology becomes more complex for fields such as counseling and administration in education, the redundancy and overlap of these programs with the core-training program of other professional schools may become more obvious. This may lead to increased conflict, negotiation, and compromise on the structure of programs not central to the core-transformation process of the respective professional school. Changes in knowledge technology, therefore, may result in adjustments in organizational structure both within and across professional schools.

Materials Technology

Perrow has conceived of technology as "The actions . . . an individual performs upon an object . . . in order to make some change in that object."[34] Implicit in this conception are the perceived characteristics of the object (or raw material as Perrow calls it) being changed. Perrow suggests that the degree to which raw material is perceived to be sufficiently stable to be treated in a standardized fashion is of importance, particularly in "people-changing" organizations. For example, the faculty of a school of business may perceive the students as uniform or stable, that is, not varying in their learning styles. This in turn leads to a "technology" featuring a lock-step process for all M.B.A. students, with common large lecture classes and extensive utilization of one type of instructional approach—case studies. By contrast, members of an education faculty may perceive their students as non-uniform and unstable, that is, variable in their learning styles. This in turn leads to a technology in which learning is individualized and various instructional approaches are offered. The application of Perrow's concept in this manner is highly inferential— actually there may be relatively little variability in perceptions of "raw" material in professional schools. Faculty members in schools of education may, in fact, perceive their students to be as uniform or stable as do other professional school faculties. Some additional means of operationalizing this concept are suggested by researchers who have tried to distinguish between "instructor centered" versus "student centered" instruction or to distinguish between the teacher as "expert" versus the teacher as "facilitator." The major value of "materials technology" would appear to be in understanding the relationship between the existing "knowledge technology" of a school and the "operations technology" being utilized. As those in the field of instructional development have discovered, the faculty member's perceptions of students can be an important variable in explaining the type of instructional format being employed.

Operations Technology

The vast majority of research on technology, primarily in industrial organizations, has utilized this definition, and has thereby focused on the tasks, techniques, or activities which together transform input into output.[35] There has been a variety of typologies of technology advanced including that already described by Perrow. Woodward proposes three basic types of technology which she calls the unit or small-batch process, large-batch process, and mass or assembly process.[36] Thompson also identifies three types—"long-linked," "mediating," and "intensive" technology.[37] Each of these typologies might be related to operations technology in professional schools, for example, mass or assembly process and long-linked technology might characterize an interrelated series of large lecture courses (e.g., undergraduate programs), and the unit or small-batch process and intensive technology might characterize individualized programs with high feedback (e.g., doctoral-level programs). Again a continuum might be sketched from simple or primitive operations technologies to those that are complex or advanced. Utilized in this fashion, the research efforts in operations technology parallel to an extent efforts to differentiate between various instructional formats. Friedman[38] has suggested that there are essentially nine formats of instruction (he distinguishes between instructional formats and media), and that these formats are separable from each other along a series of continuous variables characteristic of organizational aspects of the instructional process, for example, pacing, specificity of subject matter, group size, and types of interactions. Potentially these variables could also be categorized from simple to complex. Davies has synthesized the research on instructional formats and suggests that they can be differentiated according to their effectiveness in achieving various types of instructional objectives, which he classifies according to type and level (i.e., psychomotor/affective/cognitive, high/low).[39] These types of distinctions may be of particular utility in comparing the operations technology of various professional schools. For example, schools of medicine consistently use a laboratory or a clinical-instructional format, schools of business and law use a case-study format, and schools of education use a mixed or inconsistent format. Focusing on the instructional format at the school-wide level poses problems, however, because at this level of analysis there may be no consistent utilization of a particular mode or format. An alternative technique is that suggested by Hage and Aiken[40] who follow Perrow's conceptualization and attempt to operationalize the "routineness of work." Whether an organization ranks high or low on this single dimension seems to be an effective measure of operations technology.

Several researchers have assumed that technology is an independent variable which exerts causal influence on various aspects of the structural sub-systems.[41] Perrow emphasizes this point:

> To call for decentralization, representative bureaucracies, collegial authority, or employee-centered, innovative or organic organizations—to mention only a few of the highly normative prescriptions that are being offered by social scientists today—is to call for a type of structure that can be realized only with a certain type of technology, unless we are willing to pay a high cost in terms of output.[42]

Woodward suggests that change from unit to large-batch production causes changes in major characteristics of organizational structure ranging from the span of control of the chief executive to the ratios of managers to total personnel.[43] Hickson, et al., have suggested, on the basis of additional research, that technology should not be conceived as a variable independent of organizational size and environmental context, and that "variables of operations technology will be related only to those structural variables that are centered on the work flow.[44] An analogous argument might be that changes from a simple to a more complex instructional technology are apt to relate to structural characteristics such as class or teaching-group size, office hours, etc., but are not apt to relate to size of the dean's office or overall student-faculty ratios. However, as stated earlier, these latter structural variables may be systematically related to variables of knowledge technology. But by including technology as a sub-system of the organization, which is interdependent with the other sub-systems, there is an implicit assumption that it is an important, but not independent, variable.

The technological sub-system has been extensively discussed, because these conceptions appear to offer great potential for research on educational organizations.[45] There has been a significant amount of research on educational organizations utilizing concepts from organization theory, but inevitably this research has focused on what has been termed here the management and structural sub-system. The relationships between these latter sub-systems and the core processes of educational organizations—for example, teaching, research, and service in universities—have been insufficiently studied because they have not been directly researchable with the traditional concepts from organizational theory.[46] As a result, we know a great deal about the goals, organizational climate, governance patterns, innovation, and conflict of colleges and universities as organizations[47] but relatively little about the basic transformation processes of these institutions. The concept of technology, despite the obvious need for operational specification of variables, appears to offer an opportunity for spanning this gap and making organizational research a more useful method for understanding the nature of educational organizations.

Illustrative Propositions

1. As schools of education move from a simple to a more complex knowledge technology there will be changes in structure at all levels.
2. Variables in operations (e.g., instruction) technology will be related only to those structural variables that are centered on the transformation process.[48]
3. Schools of education with predictable patterns of work are

more likely to be characterized by centralization of organization power. [49]

4. Schools of education with predictable patterns of work are more likely to have greater formalization of organizational roles. [50]

5. Schools of education with predictable patterns of work are more likely to have an emphasis on efficiency as a system goal. [51]

STRUCTURAL SUB-SYSTEM

The structural sub-system refers to "the established pattern of relationships among the components or parts of the organization." [52] By structure then is meant the formal, rather than the informal, system of organizational relationships which changes slowly over time. While the study of structure inevitably involves the study of organizational patterns of behavior, it is assumed that these patterns reflect to some extent deliberate attempts at organizational design and are therefore relatively stable. Katz and Kahn have suggested that this view of structure is too static: "A social system is a structuring of events or happenings rather than of physical parts and it therefore has no structure apart from its functioning." [53] It should be feasible, however, to conceive of structure and process as two separate but interrelated phenomena—the static and dynamic features of the organization. The structural sub-system therefore focuses on the static pattern of relationships among the components of the organization. The dynamic aspects such as the processes of communication and decision-making will be discussed under the managerial sub-system.

Traditional management theorists have developed a series of principles about organizational structure which have often been utilized as the basis for research. These include: (1) organizational specialization and the division of labor, (2) the scalar principle, (3) span of control, and (4) line and staff. These principles all deal with two fundamentals of organizing—differentiation and integration of activities. Differentiation, itself, can be of two kinds, the vertical differentiation of activities as characterized, for example, by the number of hierarchical levels between the dean and the faculty, and horizontal differentiation of activities as characterized by the number of divisions, departments, or programs in the school. The traditional manner for integrating this two-directional differentiation tends to be similar in all professional schools: school-wide faculty meetings, a committee system, and a modest concern for administrative span of control.

Hall has reviewed the various writings and research on organizational structure and has suggested that the various elements identified are essentially refinements of the concept of bureaucracy.[54] Hall's use of the concept of bureaucracy is similar to Weber's—a continuous variable, the attributes of which are a set of dimensions. The attributes of bureaucracy that Weber and others have proposed are variable components of actual organizations, according to Hall, and these components appear to be central for the analysis of organizational structures:

> Thus while there is general consensus regarding the major structural components (the definitions of the components are only minimally different), the terminology is not yet common. The consensus is sufficient to permit some confidence that the major structural components have been identified. They have also been investigated empirically.[55]

The three basic components appear to be applicable to any type of organization, and have been extensively used in research on organizational structure: centralization of authority, complexity, and formalization.[56]

Centralization

A traditional distinction in organizational theory is that between bureaucratic and professional authority:

> Bureaucratic authority has its source in a superior official position, which bestows upon incumbents the power of command and puts at their disposal sanctions to enforce their commands. Professional authority has its source in expert knowledge, usually gained through prolonged training, which enables those possessing it to direct the endeavors of others to achieve certain ends.[57]

The distinction between bureaucratic and professional authority can also be thought of in terms of the centralization and decentralization of decision-making. If decision-making on educational policies and faculty appointments, for example, is centralized in the dean's office, then bureaucratic authority predominates; if it is decentralized to the faculty, then professional authority predominates. Colleges and universities have generally been considered to have a decentralized or professional authority structure in that the decisions affecting a faculty member's job are controlled mainly by himself and by his faculty colleagues at the departmental level. Blau, however, has indicated in a study of centralization of authority in colleges and universities that this dimension is indeed variable and highly related to organizational size and academic standing of the faculty.[58] It may be hypothesized that similar variations in this dimension would be found within professional schools.

Complexity

A second dimension of structure is that of organizational complexity. This can be conceptualized according to vertical and horizontal differentiation of an organization as outlined earlier.[59] Universities and colleges have generally been characterized as highly differentiated, particularly in the horizontal dimension, because the addition of any new academic field invariably leads to a new program, a new division, or a new department. The number of programs, departments, or divisions in a school of education, therefore, provides a measure of its complexity. Hage and Aiken, however, have suggested a definition of complexity in which one focuses on the varieties of skill in the organization, that is, the number of different occupational specialties and the degree of professional activity within each specialty.[60] If we were to apply this definition to a school of education we might conceive a more complex structure as one in which the faculty members come from a large number of different educational specialties or fields and demonstrate high activity in their professional organizations.

Formalization

A final dimension is that of formalization.[61] The extent to which an organization is characterized by rules and the observation of those rules is the conception of bureaucracy most prevalent in the popular mind. All organizations need to develop some predictability in behavior, however, and this predictability is generally achieved by guidelines or rules. Rules may be unwritten customs that are institutionalized to the extent that they regulate behavior, but the most important rules are generally codified and written, such as "Faculty members are permitted one day of consulting per week." If an organization is perceived by its members to have a large number of rules or regulations, it is considered highly formalized; if only a few are perceived, it is considered not highly formalized. The rules, however, must be enforced for the organization to be formalized. Therefore, measuring formalization entails attention both to the codification of rules *and* to the observation of rules. Since faculty members are in jobs where direct supervision is impractical, it is reasonable to assume that all colleges and universities are low in formalization compared to other organizations. But within colleges and universities there is apt to be variation in formalization, particularly between schools of education and other professional schools. Schools of education are frequently permeated with norms of behavior influenced by elementary and secondary education.

These three dimensions—centralization, complexity, and formalization—can be utilized to characterize the structural subsystem of a school of education. Hage[62] has argued that these dimensions are systematically interrelated, and his position has been borne out by some empirical research. For example, we would expect that a school of education characterized by centralized authority would also be high on formalization and low on complexity. In keeping with an open-systems model, however, the more interesting questions may be answered by exploring the relationship between the structural subsystem and other sub-systems. As already mentioned, there is an assumed strong relationship between variables of technology and variables of structure, in which the former limits the degrees of freedom of the latter. Certain of the operationalizations of technology and structures appear superficially to be measuring similar things, therefore strong relationships should be examined carefully. But conceptually they appear sufficiently distinct to warrant careful pursuit in studying schools of education. Another, more traditional, line of research in management and organizational theory has been the relationship of the informal (psychosocial) structure—the unofficial system of individual and group relationships within organizations—to the formal structure. Baldridge [63] and Platt and Parsons,[64] for example, have demonstrated that the distribution of formal authority in colleges and universities—the degree of centralization—explains only a part of the distribution of power in a college or university. They have illustrated in differing research studies that colleges and universities can be conceived as influence systems, in which influence is highly diffused. The amount of personal influence a faculty member might have in decision-making on his campus, for example, is related, according to Baldridge, to such factors as disciplinary achievement, scholarly productivity, and commitment to the university; in the Platt and Parsons study his influence is related to factors such as the nature of his discipline, his job satisfaction, his religious preference, and his ethnic origin.[65] The inference here would be that an understanding of the distribution of power in an institution of higher education—or a school of education—can only be achieved by an analysis of the relationship between the structural and psychosocial sub-systems.

Illustrative Propositions

1. The higher the centralization of authority in a school of education, the lower the innovation in the school.
2. The higher the centralization of authority in a school of education, the higher the formalization.
3. The higher the complexity in a school of education, the lower the centralization.
4. The higher the formalization in a school of education, the lower the job satisfaction of the faculty members.
5. The higher the formalization of a school of education, the higher the efficiency of the school.

PSYCHOSOCIAL SUB-SYSTEM

The psychosocial sub-system focuses on those organizational characteristics which intervene between the formal or recognized aspects of an organization and human behavior. This informal organization, the unofficial system of individual and group relationships within organizations, has been the particular interest of those researchers on organization from the human-relations tradition. They have consistently focused on social-psychological levels of analysis, the individual in social relationships. What is the relationship between individual motivation and organizational productivity? What is the relationship between group behavior and organizational effectiveness? What is the relationship between personality traits and effective leadership?

The characteristics of the psychosocial sub-system are extremely varied and can be explored at multiple levels of analysis using a wide array of conceptual frameworks: (1) the individual level, using theories of personality and motivation as well as role theory; (2) the group level, using small group theory; and (3) the organizational level, using influence theory and analysis of organizational climate. The variety of approaches and the multiple levels of analysis preclude application to schools of education in the format utilized for the other sub-systems. However, suggested questions for study can be articulated. For example, Culbertson (see associated paper) has defined as a domain for research, "Deans as individuals-in-organizations." The questions and conceptual framework he utilizes to illustrate this domain are conceived in the present context as characteristics of the psychosocial sub-system of the school: (1) Do deans differ in role orientations (role theory)? (2) Do deans differ in perceived leadership styles (leader-behavior frameworks)? (3) Are there differences in group characteristics among administrative groups with which deans work (leadership-contingency theory)? and (4) Do deans differ in patterns of interaction with their immediate subordinates (small-group frameworks)? These psychosocial characteristics of schools of education—attitudes and values, role orientations, group behavior, and patterns of interaction—might also be studied in relation to members of the organization other than deans such as faculty members and students. Psychosocial functions may also be analyzed for the school as a whole in comparison to other professional schools.

In addition to charting the characteristics of the psychosocial sub-system of schools of education, analysis can be made of the relationship between the psychosocial and other sub-systems. Focusing for a moment on a group thus far neglected—the students—one might seek to understand the relationship between personality characteristics of students in schools of education and the goals, technological, and structural sub-systems. Graduate students in education are often as "practice"-oriented as are students of law, medicine, and business. Yet the operational goals of the latter schools emphasize practice much more than those of schools of education. The majority of their advanced degree output, for example, is clearly applied (M.B.A., LL.B., M.D.), while schools of education often award much larger proportions of research degrees (Ph.D.). The potential conflict within a school of education may therefore be magnified by the lack of fit between the psychosocial and goals sub-systems. Recent research by Friedman and Stritter[66] has also suggested that the cognitive orientations of students toward learning—"learning styles"—may vary across professional schools, a discovery which may have some bearing on the type of instructional technology employed in a school. Finally, variation in structure, such as the centralization of authority, may be systematically related to student attitudes and values. If students in schools of education tend to be passive or have a high tolerance for authority, then one might expect relatively little student participation in decision-making compared to other professional schools where tolerance of authority may be low.

The work of writers such as McGregor, Argyris, and Likert has essentially been to reconcile or integrate the psychosocial and other organizational sub-systems in an effort to increase productivity and effectiveness.[67] Briefly stated, all three of these writers have reconceptualized motivational forces to include the need for achievement, curiosity, creativity, and affiliation. This has led to structural and managerial innovations, such as Likert's "System 4,"[68] which facilitate group emergence, increase interaction and interdependence among organizational groups, and maximize communication (e.g., lateral as well as vertical) and participation in decision-making. These highly normative models offer a basis for investigation and analysis of schools of education at the group and organizational level.

Illustrative Propositions

1. Schools of education in which deans have a high degree of interaction with the staff (in which, e.g., deans know and understand the problems faced by faculty members) will be more productive than schools in which deans have less interaction.

2. Schools of education that have high student and faculty participation and involvement in setting goals will have higher productivity than schools that do not.

3. Schools of education which take into account both cognitive and affective behavior in the design of instructional technology will have higher productivity than schools which rely exclusively on cognitive behavior.

4. Schools of education with patterns of frequent upward, downward, and lateral communication will be more productive than schools with predominantly downward communication patterns.

5. Schools of education in which decision-making is shared widely throughout the structure with well-integrated linking processes provided by overlapping groups will be more productive than organizations in which most decisions are made at upper levels.

MANAGERIAL SUB-SYSTEM

Management is conceived of as the process of coordinating organizational behavior to maximize effectiveness. The process itself is characterized by the way we speak about management—the management of change, conflict, communications, and decision-making. Each of these processes can be understood in terms of the sub-systems already analyzed—conflict, for example, might be studied by examining the strains between sub-systems. The various sub-systems of the organization, therefore, provide the constraints which constitute the complex context of the management system. Having suggested means to describe this context, we will now turn to means of characterizing the management system. This will be done through the analysis of the decision-making process.

In his lucid examination of the Cuban missile crisis, Allison outlines three primary models for analyzing the decision-making process: (1) the rational-actor model, (2) the organizational-process model, and (3) the governmental-politics model.[69] There are many variations on these three models in the literature, but Allison's categorizations include the dimensions most often used to analyze decision-making, particularly in institutions of higher education.[70]

Rational-Actor Model

The rational-actor model is derivative of Weber's conception of bureaucracy as an organization rationally designed to pursue a given goal. Underlying bureaucracy, according to Weber, is the assumption of rationality:

> What gives the life of "civilized" man . . . as opposed to the savage, its specifically "rational" flavor is . . . (1) his general tendency to believe that the phenomena of his everyday life—a bus or an elevator, money, a court of law, military affairs, medicine—are in principle rational, i.e., that they are human artifacts accessible to rational knowledge, creation, and control . . . ; and (2) his confidence that these phenomena function rationally, i.e., according to familiar rules, and not irrationally, like the powers that the savage seeks to influence with his magic, so that at least in principle one can reckon with them, calculate their effects, and base one's actions confidently on the exceptions they arouse.[71]

Rationality is an assumption, therefore, about the relationship between cause and effect, means and ends. The rational-actor model represents that individuals, groups, or organizations can make choices between means to a given end because it *assumes* the relationships between the means and ends are predictable, or rational.

Given this critical assumption, decision-making can be analyzed as a systematic process: (1) forming objectives or ends, (2) searching for alternatives (i.e., courses of action by which a decision-maker hopes to achieve the objectives), (3) comparing the consequences of those actions, (4) ranking the alternatives by order of desirability, and (5) verifying the consequences which flow from a given alternative.[72] This type of model is most often considered normative—a detailing of the way decisions should be made—rather than descriptive of how they are made. Its application in colleges and universities has been most heavily associated with various systems of planning. As a consequence, the rational-actor model serves to buttress those individuals who argue for a more systematic management component in professional schools. If we assume the decision-making process operates, or should operate, in this manner, then the office of a dean of education requires skills and competencies in planning, policy analysis, evaluation, and more carefully articulated procedures for controlling the activities of the school.

As a paradigm for research in schools of education, the model is apt to be most illuminating if used to analyze a decision-making process which has been self-consciously designed according to a similar analytic scheme—for example, the process for planning a new doctoral program. The analysis could then focus on the "goodness of fit" between the ideal and real and the possible cause of any discovered variation.

Organizational-Process Model

The organizational-process model assumes that organizational characteristics impact on the decision-making process to an extent that the rational-actor model is seriously circumscribed. Because the behavior of organizations is characterized by uncertainty, pressing problems take priority over long-range objectives, search for alternatives is limited and hasty, and the relationships between means and ends is insufficiently predictable. Consequently organizations do not optimize, they "satisfice"—they find a course of action that is good enough, that satisfies.[73]

Cohen and March have applied this type of model in a study of 42 colleges and universities.[74] In keeping with the organizational-process model, they first describe the organization of American colleges and universities as institutions with problematic goals, an ineffective formal authority system, unclear technologies, and fluid participation:

> The American college or university is a prototypic organized anarchy. It does not know what it is doing. Its goals are either vague or in dispute. Its technology is familiar but not understood. Its major participants wander in and out of the organization. These factors do not make a university a bad organization or a disorganized one; but they do make it a problem to describe, understand, and lead.[75]

Given this view of the organizational characteristics of colleges and universities, Cohen and March conceive of the decision-making process as highly ambiguous. A specific decision is an outcome, or an interpretation, of the relationships between four relatively independent streams: (1) problems, (2) solutions, (3) participants, and (4) choice opportunities. The key to comprehending this process is the concept "choice opportunity"—an occasion on which an organization is expected to produce a decision."[76] These choice opportunities are metaphorically conceived as garbage cans into which participants dump various problems and solutions.

> The garbage can process, as it has been observed, is one in which problems, solutions, and participants move from one choice opportunity to another in such a way that the nature of the choice, the time it takes, and the problems it solves all depend on a relatively complicated intermeshing of the mix of choices available at any one time, the mix of problems that have access to the organization, the mix of solutions looking for problems, and the outside demands on the decision makers.[77]

It should be noted that the structure of organized anarchy and the garbage-can decision-making process represent extreme results from the application of the organizational-process model. As analyzed by Cohen and March, the relationship between means and ends, actions and outcomes, not only is of limited rationality and predictability but also approaches irrationality and unpredictability.[78] If we adopt the garbage-can view of the decision-making process in colleges and universities, then we arrive at a view of management almost counter to that of the rational-actor model. Planning is illusory and inappropriate, the inferences to be made from past administrative experience are largely in error, and the dimensions of an administrator's personal success are unclear:

The result is that the president is a bit like the driver of a skid-ding automobile. The marginal judgments he makes, his skill, and his luck may possibly make some difference to the survival prospects for his riders. As a result his responsibilities are heavy. But whether he is convicted of manslaughter or receives a medal for heroism is largely outside his control.[79]

As a result, Cohen and March counsel "Elementary tactics of administrative action" in organized anarchies which include: (1) spending time in the decision-making process to co-opt others by your energy; (2) persisting with an issue once engaged, since most issues have low salience for most people; (3) overloading the system with information, crises, and projects; (4) openly creating garbage cans in order to siphon off "garbage"; and (5) managing unobtrusively.[80]

The analysis of the decision-making process by Cohen and March is at the institutional—college or university—level. It is reasonable to presume that application of the organizational-process model at the level of a school of education may describe a decision-making process less pathological in tendency. Organized anarchy and the garbage-can model help to illustrate, however, the relationship between goals, structure, and conventional practices on the decision-making process.

Governmental-Politics Model

The governmental-politics model assumes that the outcome of the decision-making process is not a product of an analytical procedure, not dependent upon organizational characteristics, but is the result of the political forces that have been brought to bear. As Allison points out:

The organizing concepts of this paradigm can be arranged as strands in the answer to four interrelated questions: Who plays? What determines each player's stand? What determines each player's relative influence? How does the game combine players' stands, influence, and moves to yield governmental decisions and actions?[81]

The basic concepts of the model have evolved out of theoretical work on interest-group articulation, coalition formation, and the process of conflict. Baldridge has adapted this material to develop a five-stage model of decision-making in the university.[82] In the first stage, the social context of the university promotes social groups of differing values and political interests which lead to conflict. In stage two, the groups attempt to articulate their special interests by influencing others through promises of support, threats, outside funding, and other means. In stage three, these political influences are transformed by a legislative process including negotiation and compromise. Stage four represents the formulation of policy and the articulation and commitment of the institution to a set of goals and values. In stage five, the resulting policy is executed through the existing organizational structure. The model also assumes a feedback cycle with the policy generating new tensions, vested interests, and a cycle of political conflict.

Baldridge's application of the political model is unusual in that he gives significant weight to an analysis of the social structure or organizational characteristics of the system. There is, therefore, much similarity to the conception advanced by Cohen and March of "organized anarchy." As Baldridge points out,

> Rather than a holistic enterprise, the university is a pluralistic system, often fractured by conflicts along lines of disciplines, faculty subgroups, student subculture, splits between administrators and faculties, and rifts between professional schools. The academic kingdom is torn apart in many ways, and there are few kings of the system who can enforce cooperation and unity. There is little peace in academia; warfare is common and no less deadly because it is polite. *The critical point is this: because the social structure of the university is loose, ambiguous, shifting, and poorly defined, the power structure of the university is also loose, ambiguous, shifting and poorly defined.*[83]

The distinctive features in the political model are the conceptual bases used to analyze the decision-making process and the assumption that interest group values predominate in that process.

The implications of Baldridge's political model for management are correspondingly different. Baldridge assumes that the relationship between means and ends and between political action and decision outcome is somewhat more predictable than Cohen and March suggest. An individual's decision to participate in a group and a group's decision to participate in an issue is assumed to be based on recognizable values. Furthermore, the resolution of conflict is the result of the application of differential political forces, the most critical of which is the manipulation of power. If we view the decision-making process in a school of education in this manner, we would emphasize the ability to manage conflict, negotiate skillfully, and persuade others, for example, in the selection of a dean.

The application of the rational-actor, organizational process, and governmental-politics models to the decision-making process of schools of education and other professional schools could represent an important contribution to the management of these schools. It could aid our understanding of this process, suggest the relationship between organizational characteristic and decision-making, and begin to outline the skills or competencies appropriate to management in academic settings. The systematic testing of these models will also help to sharpen our understanding of the overlaps, convergence, and possible syntheses of these and other decision-making paradigms.[84]

Illustrative Propositions

1. Faced with a strategic decision (e.g., development of a new doctoral program), a school of education will select that alternative which best achieves its goals.
2. Faced with a strategic decision, a school of education will select the first alternative that organizational expectations identify as acceptable in terms of existing goals.
3. Faced with a strategic decision, a school of education will select the alternative which results from the bargaining of interest groups.

RESEARCH PROBLEMS AND METHODS

This analysis of schools of education has suggested a scheme for characterizing the various sub-systems of these complex organizations. Relevant concepts and variables for research have been presented, and suggested questions to guide investigation have been scattered along the way. Others would undoubtedly choose to cut the pie in a different fashion, by organizing concepts according to a different scheme or by stressing different models and variables. But the focus of this paper has not been on advocating a particular conceptual framework but rather on systematically presenting concepts from the social sciences which could help stimulate research on schools of education and other professional schools. This research can be of two kinds: (1) descriptive research which attempts to describe the organizational characteristics of professional schools (e.g., the characteristic of the technological sub-system of schools of education) and (2) analytic research, which attempts to discover the systematic relationships between organizational variables in these schools. Both types of research are needed, and both types of researchers will encounter certain problems of research and certain difficulties of method which will be briefly discussed.

Problems

The current paper has attempted to provide an overview for inquiry into professional schools and has thus relied heavily on conceptual writings and empirical research in organizational theory. A needed first step in casting specific research questions would be a systematic review of the literature on academic organizations. Such a review could be organized by the sub-systems outlined in this paper, going in turn from goals, to technological, to structural, to psychosocial, and to managerial variables. The general tendency has been to argue that there is little literature in the field. Since the campus convulsions in the 1960s, however, increasing numbers of doctoral students in the field of education and in the basic arts and sciences disciplines have carried out research on academic organizations, much of which deals with variables discussed in this paper. Because it is "unpublished" in the conventional sense it has been largely ignored, but Peterson has illustrated the scope and variation of this literature as it applies to the organization and administration of higher education.[85] Similarly, there has been a steady, if not increasing, body of literature relating to variables of academic organization in the professional journals of sociology, political science, economics, psychology, management, and education. Analyses and syntheses of this literature are needed to guide the direction of empirical research efforts.

A more serious problem, already alluded to, is the difficulty of focusing on research questions utilizing an open-systems perspective. Systems theory stresses the interrelated nature of the various components—thus to study something is to study everything. This problem is exacerbated in the study of organizations because it has become inherently interdisciplinary, employing concepts from sociology, psychology, social psychology, and political science. Traditionally this dilemma has been resolved by focusing on the relationship between pairs of sub-systems or their derivative variables—such as technology/structure, goals/structure, or psychosocial/technology—and systematically exploring the nature of these relationships, considering the other variables as undetermined "disturbance" factors. The most important variable to account for in any study would appear to be the environment. While empirical research is thus far limited, there appears to be an emerging theoretical consensus that environmental factors account for a significant amount of the variance among organizational characteristics. Research studies on the organization and management of schools of education, therefore, should regularly attempt to account for environmental variance by including attributes of the environment in the analysis. Inclusion of the degree of perceived uncertainty of the environment in a research model, for example, can greatly enhance explanatory power.

An additional problem is the relevance of these studies to individuals responsible for administering organizations. Administrators have frequently been impatient with research on organizational characteristics because of its predilection for description and prediction and its lack of concern for prescription—empirical results which administrators can apply. This problem in organization theory has generally fallen under the elusive concept of organizational effectiveness. Price has surveyed 50 different studies of organizational behavior which included some consideration of organizational effectiveness and developed a series of propositions about determinants of effectiveness.[86] Price's dependent variable was the degree to which an organization achieves its goal, a problematic variable since complex organizations may have multiple and unspecified goals. Yuchtman and Seashore, applying an open-systems perspective to the definition of organizational effectiveness, have emphasized the survival of an organization over time as the most valid indicator of effectiveness.[87] As a useful measure of survival at any one time, they suggest the "Ability of the organization, in either absolute or relative terms, to exploit its environment in the acquisition of scarce and valued resources."[88] Pfeffer and Salancik have utilized a similar measure in a recent study of academic departments within a major university.[89] They demonstrated that the proportional shares of the general funds budget received by the academic departments are significantly related to measures of departmental power, even after controlling for universalistic bases of allocation such as work load of the department, national ranking of the academic program, and number of faculty. The inclusion of such dependent variables as organizational power and proportional shares of financial resources in studies of professional schools could make an important contribution toward an understanding of factors affecting organizational effectiveness.

Method

The majority of empirical research studies on organizations has utilized the survey-research method for the collection of data. This method poses certain difficulties for research on professional schools, since any enthusiasm faculty members feel toward administering questionnaires is rarely exhibited when they are asked to supply information themselves. Many faculty members have standing orders with their secretaries to permanently file all research questionnaires. The one-shot survey offers even more profound problems. Rogers has suggested that the tendency to ignore the relationship between organizational characteristics and innovation is partially a result of the predilection of cross-sectional data gathered in one-shot surveys.[90] He strongly advocates the use of over-time research designs and collection of time-series data as keys to understanding diffusion processes. Similar arguments could be made regarding conflict, communication, and decision-making. The study of professional schools may be particularly amenable, therefore, to intensive case studies such as those conducted by Baldridge and Clark which are informed by conceptual frameworks derived from organizational theory.[91]

An alternative to survey data might be information which can be collected by employing unobtrusive measures. Pfeffer and Salancik, for example, demonstrated that measures of departmental power constructed from analysis of committee memberships in the university archives significantly replicated the ratings of departmental power reported by various department heads.[92] Studies of the structural subsystem of professional schools, therefore, might make more effective use of university records as well as existing data banks such as that maintained by the federal government as part of the HEGIS survey. If there is a lesson to be learned from previous research on organizations it is the utility of multiple measures of variables and multiple sources of data as a means of achieving reliability and validity.

CONCLUSION

This paper has attempted to stimulate research on schools of education and other professional schools as complex organizations. To that end a scheme of organizational characteristics has been described and utilized in applying concepts from organizational theory to the study of schools of education. An open-systems perspective on complex organizations has been stressed throughout, and the implications of that perspective for defining and conducting research have been touched on at various points. Finally, several personal observations have been made on research problems and methods, particularly as they relate to the study of academic organizations.

The general point is that descriptive and analytical studies of professional schools as complex organizations are of importance not only to those who manage these schools but also to the faculty members and students who work within them.

NOTES

1. *Acknowledgement*: The author wishes to thank James I. Doi, Charles Friedman, and Charles Witten for their valuable critiques of this paper. Responsibility for the arguments advanced, however, remains the author's.

2. The organizational units within institutions of higher education which are directly concerned with the field of education may be schools, colleges, or departments. The analysis presented here assumes that the unit has responsibilities for teaching, research, and service and measurable influence over personnel decisions, curriculum, and budget; therefore, the term *school* will be used throughout. These assumptions, however, are as apt to be applicable to many large departments of education as to some separate schools or colleges.

3. Joseph Ben-David, *American Higher Education: Directions Old and New* (New York: McGraw-Hill, 1972).

4. *Ibid.*, pp. 92-93.

5. Talcott Parsons and Gerald M. Platt, *The American University* (Cambridge, Mass.: Harvard University, 1973), pp. 256-257.

6. *Ibid.*, p. 230.

7. *Ibid.*, p. 236.

8. See, for example, the numerous publications concerning professional education commissioned by the Carnegie Commission on Higher Education. For some more recent arguments advocating reform of professional education see, Chris Argyris and Donald A. Schon, *Theory in Practice: Increasing Professional Effectiveness* (San Francisco: Jossey-Bass, 1974); Edgar H. Schein, *Professional Education: Some New Directions* (New York: McGraw-Hill, 1972).

9. These implications follow the analysis of an open systems perspective offered in J. Eugene Haas and Thomas E. Drabek, *Complex Organizations: A Sociological Perspective* (New York: MacMillan, 1973), pp. 85-92.

10. See, for example, Daniel Katz and Robert L. Kahn, *The Social Psychology of Organizations* (New York: John Wiley, 1966), pp. 71-148; Stanley H. Udy, Jr., "The Comparative Analysis of Organizations," in James G. March (ed.), *Handbook of Organizations* (Chicago: Rand McNally, 1965), pp. 678-709.

11. Fremont E. Kast and James E. Rosenzweig, *Organization and Management: A Systems Approach* (New York: McGraw-Hill, 1974).

12. Adapted from Kast and Rosenzweig, *ibid.*, p. 112.

13. *Ibid.*, p. 113.

14. Katz and Kahn, *op. cit.*, pp. 448-449.

15. Paul R. Lawrence and Jay W. Lorsch, *Organization and Environment* (Homewood, Ill.: Richard D. Irwin, 1969), pp. 151-152.

16. Burton R. Clark, "The Organizational Saga in Higher Education," *Administrative Science Quarterly* (Vol. 17, No. 2, June 1972), pp. 178-184.

17. *Ibid.*, p. 183.

18. Charles Perrow, *Organizational Analysis: A Sociological View* (London: Tavistock, 1970), pp. 133-174.

19. Edward Gross, "Universities as Organizations: A Study of Goals," *American Sociological Review* (Vol. 33, No. 4, August 1968), pp. 518-544.

20. Edward Gross and Paul V. Grambsch, *Changes in University Organization, 1964-1971* (New York: McGraw-Hill, 1974).

21. Charles Perrow, "The Analysis of Goals in Complex Organizations," *American Sociological Review* (Vol. 26, No. 6, December 1961), p. 854.

22. The format of using illustrative propositions, and many of the propositions themselves, has been drawn from Haas and Drabek, *op. cit.*, pp. 23-93.

23. James L. Price, *Organizational Effectiveness: An Inventory of Propositions* (Homewood, Ill.: Richard D. Irwin, 1968), p. 44.

24. *Ibid.*

25. Richard L. Simpson and William H. Gulley, "Goals, Environmental Pressures, and Organizational Characteristics," *American Sociological Review* (Vol. 27, No. 3, June 1962), p. 350.

26. Jacques Ellul, *The Technological Society* (John Wilkinson, trans.) (New York: Alfred A. Knopf, 1964), p. 25.

27. David J. Hickson, D. S. Pugh, and Diana G. Pheysey, "Operations Technology and Organization Structure: An Empirical Reappraisal," *Administrative Science Quarterly* (Vol. 14, No. 3, September 1969), pp. 378-397.

28. Parsons and Platt, *op. cit*, pp. 232-238.

29. *Ibid.*, p. 238.

30. There are serious difficulties of operationalizing technology if used in this manner. One potentially fruitful measure of complexity of knowledge might be to look at the length of formal and informal training of faculty members. See Michael Aiken and Jerald Hage, "Organizational Interdependence and Intraorganizational Structure," *American Sociological Review* (Vol. 33, No. 6, December 1968), pp. 912-930.

31. Kast and Rosenzweig, *op. cit.*, p. 191.

32. Parsons and Platt, *op. cit.*, p. 247.

33. *Ibid.*, pp. 256-257.

34. Charles Perrow, "A Framework for the Comparative Analysis of Organizations," *American Sociological Review* (Vol. 32, No. 2, April 1967), p. 195.

35. Jerald Hage and Michael Aiken, "Routine Technology, Social Structure, and Organization Goals," *Administrative Science Quarterly* (Vol. 14, No. 3, September 1969), pp. 366-376; Edward Harvey, "Technology and the Structure of Organizations," *American Sociological Review* (Vol. 33, No. 2, April 1968), pp. 247-259; Hickson *et al.*, *op. cit.*; Joan Woodward, *Industrial Organization: Theory and Practice* (London: Oxford University, 1965); William L. Zwerman, *New Perspectives on Organization* (Westport, Conn.: Greenwood, 1970).

36. Woodward, *ibid.*

37. James D. Thompson, *Organizations in Action* (New York: McGraw-Hill, 1967).

38. Charles D. Friedman, *Instructional Formats* (Chapel Hill, N.C.: Office of Medical Studies, 1975), mimeographed.

39. Ivor K. Davies, *Competency Based Learning* (New York: McGraw-Hill, 1973), p. 175.

40. Hage and Aiken, "Routine Technology, Social Structure, and Organizations Goals," *op. cit.*

41. See, for example, Perrow, "A Framework for the Comparative Analysis of Organizations," *op. cit.*; and Woodward, *op. cit.*

42. Perrow, "A Framework for the Comparative Analysis of Organizations," *ibid.*, p. 204.

43. Woodward, *op. cit.*, p. 51.

44. Hickson *et al.*, *op. cit.*, p. 395.

45. For similar arguments concerning the possible importance of technology as a variable in the study of educational organizations, see Ronald G. Corwin, "Models of Educational Organizations," in Fred N. Kerlinger and John B. Carroll (eds.), *Review of Research in Education*, Vol. 2 (Itasca, Ill.: F. E. Peacock, 1974), pp. 282-285; Philip G. Schlechty, *Teaching and Social Behavior: Toward an Organizational Theory of Instruction* (Boston: Allyn and Bacon, 1976), pp. 261-265.

46. For an excellent discussion of this same point, but applied to the absence of structural variables in research on the educational process, see Schlechty, *ibid.*

47. For an effective summary of this research see, Marvin W. Peterson, "Organization and Administration in Higher Education: Sociological and Socio-Psychological Perspectives," in Kerlinger and Carroll (eds.), *Review of Research in Education*, pp. 296-347.

48. Adapted from Hickson *et al.*, *op. cit.*, p. 395.

49. Adapted from Hage and Aiken, "Routine Technology, Social Structure, and Organization," *op. cit.*, p. 370.

50. *Ibid.*, p. 371.

51. *Ibid.*, p. 374.

52. Kast and Rosenzweig, *op. cit.*, p. 207. This section closely follows Kast and Rosenzweig's discussion of structure.

53. Katz and Kahn, *op. cit.*, p. 31.

54. Richard H. Hall, *Organizational Structure and Process* (Englewood Cliffs, N. J.: Prentice-Hall, 1972), pp. 66-72.

55. *Ibid.*, p. 72.

56. For an example of operationalization of these dimensions, see Jerald Hage and Robert Dewar, "Elite Values Versus Organizational Structure in Predicting Innovation," *Administrative Science Quarterly* (Vol. 18, No. 3, September 1973), p. 290; for their application to colleges and universities, see Peter M. Blau, *The Organization of Academic Work* (New York: John Wiley, 1973).

57. Blau, *ibid.*, p. 158.

58. *Ibid.*, p. 188.

59. For example, Blau has utilized measures of vertical and horizontal differentiation as a measure of complexity. See, Blau, *The Organization of Academic Work.*

60. Jerald Hage and Michael Aiken, *Social Change in Complex Organizations* (New York: Random House, 1970), pp. 15-18.

61. *Ibid.*, pp. 21-23.

62. Jerald Hage, "An Axiomatic Theory of Organizations," *Administrative Science Quarterly* (Vol. 10, No. 3, December 1965), pp. 289-320.

63. J. Victor Baldridge, *Power and Conflict in the University* (New York: John Wiley, 1971), p. 65; Gerald M. Platt and Talcott Parsons, "Decision-Making in the Academic System: Influence and Power Exchange," in Carlos E. Kruytbosch and Sheldon Messinger (eds.), *The State of the University: Authority and Change* (Beverly Hills, Calif.: Sage, 1970), pp. 133-180.

64. Baldridge, *ibid.*, pp. 180-181; Platt and Parsons, "Decision-Making in the Academic System," *ibid.*, p. 151.
65. These propositions have been adapted from Hage, *op. cit.*, p. 300.
66. Charles P. Friedman and Frank T. Stritter, *An Empirical Inventory Comparing Instructional Preference of Medical and Other Professional Students* (Technical Report No. 3). (Chapel Hill, N.C.: Office of Medical Studies, 1976), pp. 76-78.
67. Chris Argyris, *Integrating the Individual and the Organization* (New York: John Wiley, 1964); Rensis Likert, *The Human Organization* (New York: McGraw-Hill, 1967); Douglas McGregor, *The Human Side of Enterprise* (New York: McGraw-Hill, 1960).
68. Likert, *ibid.*
69. Graham T. Allison, *Essence of Decision: Explaining the Cuban Missile Crisis* (Boston: Little, Brown, 1971).
70. For an excellent analysis of decision-making models relevant to higher education, see George B. Weathersby, "Decision Paradigms and Models for Higher Education." Paper presented at the National Meeting of the Institute for Management Sciences and the Operations Research Society of America, November 17, 1975. The discussion which follows closely parallels Weathersby's analysis.
71. Cited in Weathersby, "Decision Paradigms and Models for Higher Education." Original quotation appears in Ralf Dahrendorf, *Essays in the Theory of Society* (Stanford, Calif.: Stanford University, 1968), p. 215.
72. Weathersby, *ibid.*, pp. 28-29.
73. Allison, *op. cit.*, pp. 71-77.
74. Michael D. Cohen and James G. March, *Leadership and Ambiguity: The American College President* (New York: McGraw-Hill, 1974).
75. *Ibid.*, p. 3.
76. *Ibid.*, p. 81.
77. *Ibid.*, p. 90.
78. Cohen and March have argued elsewhere that organizations other than colleges and universities may have characteristics of organized anarchies, but they still represent an extreme form of organization. See Michael D. Cohen, James G. March, and Johan P. Olsen, "A Garbage Can Model of Organizational Choice," *Administrative Science Quarterly* (Vol. 17, No. 1, March 1972), pp. 1-25.
79. Cohen and March, *op. cit.*, p. 203.
80. *Ibid.*, pp. 205-215.
81. Allison, *op. cit.*, p. 164.
82. Baldridge, *op. cit.*
83. *Ibid.*, p. 107.
84. For an interesting attempt at a synthesis of these and other models at the individual level of decision-making, see Weathersby, *op. cit.*, pp. 33-43.
85. Peterson, *op. cit.*
86. Price, *op. cit.*
87. Ephraim Yuchtman and Stanley E. Seashore, "A System Resource Approach to Organizational Effectiveness," *American Sociological Review* (Vol. 32, No. 6, December 1967), pp. 891-903.
88. *Ibid.*, p. 898.
89. Jeffrey Pfeffer and Gerald R. Salancik, "Organizational Decision Making as a Political Process: The Case of a University Budget," *Administrative Science Quarterly* (Vol. 19, No. 2, June 1974), pp. 135-151.

90. Everett M. Rogers, "Innovation in Organization: New Research Approaches." Paper presented at the American Political Science Association, September 2-5, 1975, pp. 9-10.
91. Baldridge, *op. cit*.
92. Pfeffer and Salancik, *op. cit*.

CHAPTER 9

Schools of Education as
Organizations-in-Environments

by
DONALD J. McCARTY
The University of Wisconsin–Madison

The link between schools, colleges, and departments of education and the environment is at once both obvious and obscure. It is obvious in the sense that no matter what conceptual framework is employed, there are direct, observable, and necessary interactions and transactions between these units and their own college or university central administration, their own state department of education, and cooperating public and private school systems, to mention only a few of the most obvious links. It is obscure in that knowledge about the nature, intensity, and salience of these transactions and interactions is almost totally based on anecdotal reveries, common-sense speculations, and descriptive accounts. As researchable units of analysis, schools of education have been virtually ignored by the scholarly community; however, this lack of knowledge has not prevented popular critics from producing a spate of negative and sometimes virulent appraisals of their ultimate value to society, a small reminder that schools of education are vulnerable open systems and responsive to their environment.[1]

The prevailing tendency is to relegate internal governing mechanisms within colleges and universities to the "garbage can."[2] According to this model, the goals of higher education are inchoate, and the institution is ungovernable internally. The upshot is that both the

familiar Weberian management principles and the hallowed concept of
a community of scholars governing themselves are viewed as irrelevant if not dangerous propositions. The eminent Talcott Parsons has
questioned whether individual faculty members are at all concerned
about organizational goals.

> The most important things a typical individual member does . . .
> concern his teaching relations with a small minority of the total
> student body, the pursuit of his own research interests, which
> are inevitably in only one of the many fields of knowledge in-
> volved in the university, and his active collaboration with a
> small circle of colleagues.[3]

The conclusion to be drawn from all of this is not sanguine. If our
colleges and universities have an internal structure which encourages
the development of self-interested factional groups, generates no
overall sense of unity or cohesion, and does not seek or want leadership from deans, chancellors, and presidents, little can be done about
internal governance mechanisms.

My purpose at this time, however, is not to debate whether the
organized anarchy thesis is correct, but rather to point up that schools
of education as sub-units within colleges and universities are subject
to all the viruses in that setting, and to stress that their relationships
to the external environment outside the territorial boundaries of the
school itself are subject to a different set of contingencies and constraints. In organization-environment relationships it does not matter
so much that the faculty is ungovernable. Instead, faculty members
may find themselves firmly allied with deans when it comes to external transactions aimed at enhancing or protecting the life chances of
the school.

Support for this contention comes from Udy who noted that external pressures result in increased communications and interactions
among members, a higher level of commitment to the organization,
more authority exercised at all levels, and a greater cohesiveness on
the part of members.[4]

Most research efforts on the effect of environment on an organization have emphasized these dimensions. This theoretical perspective predicts that the internal structure of a school of education would
be molded to some degree by external forces.

At this point, it is important to discuss what is meant by the environment. Mohr and his colleagues have stated that the relevant environment may be separated from the irrelevant in terms of a threshold

of (1) dependence of the organization upon something outside of itself or (2) impact of outside forces upon the structure and activities of the organization.[5]

Schools of education are immediately dependent on the parent institution and its resources. The dean's most salient and continuing transactions are held with academic officers of superior rank who articulate the institution's administrative posture. These latter individuals approve budgetary requests, review program proposals, and evaluate the school's performance. The situation described is not unlike the familiar Weberian bureaucratic paradigm with all its trappings of a formal hierarchy, proper channels of communication, and a well-established locus of responsibility for decision-making. A dean is not likely to tilt many windmills successfully or for long if there are breakdowns in these formal administrative relationships. The magnitude of the interactions is too great.

Compounding the vulnerability for a dean of a school of education within the parent institution is the fact that deans of comparable units such as agriculture, medicine, and law have access to powerful and organized outside constituents who may be mobilized in their behalf. Education graduates may even identify more with the parent institution than their own school—a few hours of professional courses is not enough to develop the requisite loyalty.

Within the home institution, then, schools of education have a high dependency relationship with superior executives and a low prestige relationship with peer deans. These forces should affect internal structures.

Until recently, schools of education were able to compensate for their managerial status within the parent organization because they occupied the premier leadership role in the education profession itself. For years, they effectively controlled preparation programs, certification, and in-service activities. Teachers and other practitioners were seldom consulted. Now, under pressure from teacher unions, schools of education are losing their hegemony over these matters.

Major societal changes have increased the uncertainty of the environment for schools of education. Teachers are no longer in short supply, the value for formal education is being challenged, pressures for reduced costs are increasing, and accountability mechanisms are gaining popularity.

Teacher unions are in the forefront of the action; their assertiveness is in stark contrast to the developmental stance toward change practiced by most schools of education. Licensing and accreditation are two key areas where the National Education Association is attempting to secure gains by political power. Since it is the professoriate who is being excluded from the deliberations of the organized teaching profession, the view from outside may seem more problematic to schools of education than their position within the parent organization. When we discuss organization-environment interrelationships we are dealing with the survival of the organization.

SYNTHESES OF CONCEPTUAL FRAMEWORKS FOR ANALYSIS OF ORGANIZATION-ENVIRONMENT INTERACTION

The current literature readily points up the importance of the environment to the organization, but there is considerable debate about what the environment of an organization consists of, how it impacts on the organization, what processes are involved, and how the relationship between the two may be studied.[6]

Hall has proposed that in order to examine the topic systematically, it is necessary to divide environmental conditions into two categories, general and specific.[7] The general category refers to those conditions that must be of concern to all organizations such as the state of the economy, the nature of the political system, and the like. While schools of education may respond only to those conditions most relevant to them, the conditions themselves are the same for all types of organizations.

The second category contains specific environmental influences on the particular organization. In the case of schools of education, a change in teacher certification requirements by the state legislature or the decision by a college or university to phase out its special education program are examples. The interactions in these instances are direct and have the potential of being critical.

Emphasis on the general category has been championed by Emery and Trist in a brief but seminal article.[8] They see the environment as an independent variable and are concerned with its "causal texture." Four types of causal textures are identified: placid, randomized environment; placid, clustered environment; disturbed-reactive environment; and turbulent fields. It is the turbulent environment which interests them the most because it maximizes uncertainty; even large organizations have trouble adapting to an environment which is full of interdependencies.

Terreberry, building on the work of Emery and Trist, sees organizational change being undertaken not so much for internal as for external reasons—in her terms, "Survival of the fittest is a function of the fitness of the environment."[9] She argues that the fate of like but competitive organizations in a stable environment tends to be inversely correlated, that is, if one organization gains, the other loses. In a more turbulent environment, dissimilar organizations have independent fates which may even be positively correlated. In other words, cross pressures and competition among external pressure groups may increase the decision alternative available to an organization. Organizational adaptability, therefore, is related to its "ability to learn and to perform according to changing environmental contingencies."

Building on the concepts of Emery and Trist and others, Jurkovich has designed a descriptive model to describe the relationship between a particular type of environment and possible decision-making strategies.[10]

Table 9.1. Jurkovich's Model

Environmental Movement	Design of Strategies, Operations, and Tactics
Low-change rate/stable	Easily accomplished
Low-change rate/unstable	More complex
High-change rate/stable	Very complex—characterized by muddling through
High-change rate/unstable	Most difficult—problem-coping in the place of problem-solving

In sum, as the environment becomes more complex, the organization must adjust its internal decision-making processes. This representation of the environment does not vary greatly from Thompson's homogeneous-stable, homogeneous-shifting, heterogeneous-stable, and heterogeneous-shifting four-cell typology although the implications for the organization are more carefully spelled out.[11]

Lawrence and Lorsch are among the few researchers who have conducted significant research in this domain.[12] They see differentiation and integration as the distinguishing characteristics of organizations. Differentiation refers not only to the division of parts that perform different functions such as sales, research, and production but also to the differences in attitudes and behavior on the part of the members of the differentiated departments. Integration refers to the quality of the state of collaboration which exists among departments that are required to achieve unity of effort because of environmental demands. The authors note that their two major concepts—

differentiation and integration—are basically antagonistic to each other. The more differentiated an organization, the more difficult it is to achieve integration.

According to Lawrence and Lorsch, the environment refers to the demands placed upon differing segments of the organization from outside the organization. In sampling 10 industrial organizations through the use of questionnaire and interview data, they found that departments within organizations are differentiated from each other according to the environmental pressures faced, and they suggest that the environment itself will probably shift toward less certainty and more complexity, implying that conflict resolution will become more difficult in the future. Therefore, the more turbulent the environment is, the more complex the organizational structure will become in order to make adaptations to all parts of the environment.

Lawrence and Lorsch's study occupies a prominent place in the literature of organization-environment relations, but the authors do not make the distinction between the organization and environment clear; the upshot has been a number of criticisms of their methodology.[13] Still, their research is without question the most impressive empirical work yet conducted in this complex domain.

Simpson and Gulley reported that voluntary organizations with diffuse environmental pressures had more decentralized structure and higher internal communication; those with specific and restricted pressures had the opposite characteristics.[14] Their study provides additional evidence that the internal structures of organizations are related to characteristics of their social environment.

Corwin has attempted to examine the larger and more general environmental framework in which schools of education have had to function by focusing on the Teacher Corps.[15] The Teacher Corps was developed at the federal level by individuals who believed that educationists were incapable of training the kind of creative teachers needed for today's complex society. They launched a natural-field experiment where students with unconventional backgrounds, usually college graduates in the liberal arts and/or members of minority groups, were placed in public school settings for the purpose of performing as change agents. Colleges and universities who participated were expected to adopt innovative training methodologies.

Corwin's study, supported by the Ford Foundation and the National Education Association, describes the impact of Teacher Corps programs on participating colleges and on cooperating public schools.

Ten separate Teacher Corps programs and 42 cooperating

schools were studied intensively over a two-year period. Large-scale survey-analysis techniques were combined with case-study analyses.

Corwin's well-measured analysis points out that the structural features in the organizational life of the public schools are deeply rooted and difficult to alter. The public schools saw the Teacher Corps personnel not as change agents but as student teachers who could help out with the daily routines. Many of the interns became disenchanted when their leadership attempts were rejected and they became radicalized, socialized to the system, or defeated. The colleges had neither the financial nor the intellectual resources to overcome the powerful influence of the local schools which, in the final analysis, controlled activities in the supposedly experimental schools. The investigation is a fascinating case study of the influence of the external environment on schools of education. Exogenous forces do make a difference.

Since the general environment of an organization is conceivably composed of an infinite set of elements, Dill has suggested that we become more specific and focus our attention on the task environment, defined as that portion of the total setting which is relevant for goal setting and goal attainment.[16] This approach enables the researcher to place an emphasis on the organizations with which the system under analysis interacts.

Clark has stressed the value of inter-organizational patterns in education using the Physical Science Study Committee as an example.[17] Not unlike the Teacher Corps, the original impetus came from the national level. A federal agency provided the funds while a private nonprofit group developed the new course of study. Commercial organizations disseminated the new materials to all units of the educational system, and universities and colleges used the new materials to train teachers. Local school systems then adopted the materials. By focusing on a particular enterprise, Clark was able to show how these linkages occur.

The term *organization set* was invented by Evan to describe those organizations which impact directly on the organization under analysis.[18] An organization set is the complex of organizations with which another focal organization interacts, or it may be defined as the complex of organizations with which a class of organizations interacts.

Schools of education are, by definition, organizations encased within another organization. Thompson has indicated that dependency may be viewed in terms of both contingencies and constraints and has implied that as the level of dependency and risk increases, the management of the organization becomes more difficult.[19]

For example, a school of education in the most prestigious public university in the state is probably in a favored position. Its resource base is reasonably secure since it benefits from its affiliation with its powerful parent institution. It may, also, be able to moderate risk by seeking funds from outside grants and from entreprenurial field-service activities.

On the other hand, schools of education in marginal private institutions facing budget deficits may find the dependency relationship threatening. Their ability to attract outside funds is limited, and the surplus of teachers weakens their case for more local funding. There is no escape either—the unit must remain where it is and fight the battle on that terrain.

Another pioneer paper from Thompson and McEwen links the environment with goal setting of organizations.[20] Their analysis centers around transactions with other organizations; moreover, they suggest that organizations operate in a field of other organizations and that these affect what the focal organization does.

Accordingly, organizational goals are far from being static and are controlled by the environment. Goal setting is essentially a problem of defining desired relationships with the environment, and any change in either the organization or the environment demands a modification of goals. They also classified the organizational strategies for coping with the environment into two broad types: competitive and cooperative, the latter of which is divided into bargaining, cooperation, and coalition.

In this regard, interactions between the organization and the task environment are usually conducted by leaders themselves. It is the dean who must decide whether to use a particular strategy. Power plays, co-optation, and coalitional arrangements have to be engineered by leaders who occupy boundary-spanning roles.

To review the themes presented in this section, it is apparent that the effort to develop more adequate theory dealing with organization-environment interaction is hampered by the lack of careful research into the various processes of such interaction. Although there is no shortage of speculative treatises on what organizations do in relation to their environments, there is a lack of studies that document what organizations actually do, and predictive models are nonexistent.

Useful concepts that capture the essence of significant

organization-environment issues are still in the developmental stage; moreover, there is an inadequate data base to which conceptual frameworks and tentative hypotheses may be compared. Suffice it to say that we are dealing with a research field in its infancy.[21]

SUGGESTED RESEARCH QUESTIONS

It is abundantly clear that educationists have not been very active in generating research in this area. The reason for the neglect is only too well understood. It is more common for professors of educational administration to become involved in selecting a school superintendent, participating in an accreditation visit, or directing a field-service activity. These missions are both challenging and remunerative. It is also more risky to put time and resources into fundamental investigations which at best may result in a journal article. To be perfectly fair, the organization-environment domain is a messy one to research.

The environments of schools of education, even of a given type, can differ markedly. This variation provides a fertile basis for research on the relationship between environment and internal administrative structure.[22]

We have already noted that schools of education are sub-units within another system and do not interact as directly with the general environment as public school systems do. Hence, the host institution acts as a filter through which some inputs from the general environment are treated. How are these transactions handled?

It would be instructive to develop typologies of the particularistic environments found. As parent institutions assume different postures toward their schools of education (i.e., supportive, neutral, or antagonistic) how differentiated are the response patterns?

Schools of education engage in many transactions with other schools and colleges within their institution. Are these sub-units all treated alike or are there observable differences? Medical schools receive substantial outside funds, usually maintain a hospital, permit professors to practice medicine for extra income, and provide advantageous research opportunities. A study of how the environmental climate of various schools and colleges within a host institution varies and what effect these differences have on internal decision-making practices would be very informative.

How do schools of education respond to environmental inputs from outside the host institution? With what policies, strategies, or tactics do they respond to these environmental inputs?

For example, schools of education are not totally dependent on their parent institution. To the degree that they are preparing certificated personnel for the public schools, one of their main reference groups is the state department of education. It is the state department which decides whether a particular professional program is acceptable or not. This fact may even provide a bit of leverage for a school of education with its host institution, if preparing teachers and other school personnel is seen as a legitimate and necessary mission.

State legislatures also impose regulations directly on schools of education. Requirements for performance-based teacher education, courses in state history, and the like cannot be ignored. The federal government and foundations circularize requests for proposals and an enterprising school of education may feel compelled to compete for these grants. Is there a level at which the school of education is dependent and is influenced by these outside forces?

Are there relationships between the administrative behaviors of deans of education and the mode of interaction with the environment? At least two styles are probable. Either a dean will take a reactive approach and wait for things to happen or he will engage in proactive maneuvers designed to influence targets in the environment. Take the current pressure from teacher unions to champion legislation in each state with the intent of fostering teacher control over program accreditation. A dean might sense a threat to the future of the organization and engage in a number of strategic moves to resist the movement or he could let the issue pass. Do these different approaches result in different internal organizational structures and decision-making processes?

√ What are the key environmental characteristics for schools of education? Such indices as geographical location, type of client served, source of resource support (public or private), prestige ranking, size, and type of technology are all variables which could be salient. A survey of these dimensions should result in an environmental characteristics instrument which could be used in further research.

Much of the literature reviewed has concentrated on defining environments along a continuum from placid to turbulent with the implication that the kind of environment has a direct impact on the organization. Direct experience with a great variety of schools of education leads me to suggest that this framework could be used to develop a descriptive model. There are many departments of education of one or two persons opting to prepare a few teachers a year where the environment might easily be classified as placid or even inert. On the other hand, many schools of education are engaged in multiple interactions with a whole host of professional organizations, federal and state suprastructures, and public school systems resulting in a turbulent environment. In classifying these environments, additional types are likely to be identified.

LIKELY METHODOLOGIES

Theory in the organization-environment field is hardly sufficient to permit immediate testing of directional hypotheses. This suggests that a logical start is to undertake a number of in-depth case studies of a selected sample of markedly different types of schools of education in order to determine the quantity and nature of environmental inputs and to begin simple classifications.

If these exploratory studies are undertaken by investigators who have made a thorough review of the literature, it is highly probable that initial findings will generate a number of subsequent studies. Certainly, it is presently possible for researchers to design survey questionnaires to be given to the professional staff members of a broad stratified sample of schools of education for the purpose of determining their perceptions of environmental inputs. This effort would yield useful comparative data across a number of units and should provide interesting leads to follow.

The ultimate objective is to move from the early-abstract formulations which will emerge from these data, proceed as quickly as possible into testable hypotheses, and, finally, arrive at theory development.

NOTES

1. The author's particular favorite in this genre is James D. Koerner, *The Miseducation of American Teachers* (Boston: Houghton Mifflin, 1963).
2. Michael D. Cohen, James G. March, and Johan P. Olsen, "A Garbage Can Model of Organizational Choice," *Administrative Science Quarterly* (March 1972), pp. 1-25.
3. Talcott Parsons, "The Strange Case of Academic Organization," *Journal of Higher Education* (June 1971), p. 489.
4. Stanley H. Udy, Jr., "The Comparative Analysis of Organizations," in *Handbook of Organizations*, James March (ed.) (Chicago: Rand McNally, 1965), p. 692.
5. Lawrence B. Mohr, "Report of the Study Group on Administrative Structure, Effectiveness, and Efficiency, to the National Institute of Education," *Institute of Public Policy Studies* (Ann Arbor: The University of Michigan, 1975).
6. Koya Azumi and Jerald Hage, *Organizational Systems* (Lexington, Mass.: D.C. Heath, 1972).

7. Richard H. Hall, *Organizations: Structure and Process* (Englewood Cliffs, N.J.: Prentice-Hall, 1972).

8. Fred E. Emery and Eric L. Trist, "The Causal Texture of Organizational Environments," *Human Relations* (August 1963), pp. 20-26.

9. Shirley Terreberry, "The Evolution of Organizational Environments," *Administrative Science Quarterly* (March 1968), pp. 590-613.

10. Ray Jurkovich, "A Core Typology of Organizational Environments," *Administrative Science Quarterly* (September 1974), pp. 380-394.

11. James D. Thompson, *Organizations in Action.* (New York: McGraw-Hill, 1967).

12. Paul R. Lawrence and Jay W. Lorsch, *Organization and Environment: Managing Differentiation and Integration* (Homewood, Ill.: Richard D. Irwin, 1967).

13. Henry Tosi, Ramon Aldag, and Ronald Storey, "On the Measurement of the Environment: An Assessment of the Lawrence and Lorsch Environmental Uncertainty Scale," *Administrative Science Quarterly* (March 1973), pp. 27-36.

14. Richard L. Simpson and William H. Gulley, "Goals, Environmental Pressures, and Organizational Characteristics," *American Sociological Review* (June 1962), pp. 344-351.

15. Ronald G. Corwin, *Reform and Organizational Survival: The Teacher Corps as an Instrument of Educational Change* (New York: John Wiley, 1973).

16. William R. Dill, "Environment as an Influence on Managerial Autonomy," *Administrative Science Quarterly* (March 1958), pp. 409-443.

17. Burton R. Clark, "Interorganizational Patterns in Education," *Administrative Science Quarterly* (September 1965), pp. 224-237.

18. William M. Evan, "The Organization Set: Toward a Theory of Interorganizational Relations," in James D. Thompson (ed.), *Approaches to Organizational Design.* (Pittsburgh: University of Pittsburgh Press, 1966).

19. Thompson, *op. cit.*, p. 30.

20. James D. Thompson and William J. McEwen, "Organizational Goals and Environment: Goal Setting as an Interaction Process," *American Sociological Review* (February 1958), pp. 23-31.

21. An excellent review of most of the key issues is found in Richard N. Osborn and James G. Hunt, "Environment and Organizational Effectiveness," *Administrative Science Quarterly* (June 1974), pp. 231-246.

22. The author is indebted to Dr. Paula Silver, for many of the ideas which appear in this section.

CHAPTER 10

Organizational Change in Schools of Education: A Review of Several Models and an Agenda of Research

by
JOSEPH GIACQUINTA
New York University

The early concern for maintaining control and stability in large-scale work organizations has been replaced during the past 50 years by a strong interest in the complementary problem of inducing change. Theorists and managers are trying more and more to understand how and why change occurs in such settings and to encourage such change for either theoretical or practical reasons. With regard to colleges and universities, a literature tracing their evolution has grown over the years. But, most of these studies have not defined colleges and universities as formal work organizations in the midst of change; neither have these studies been proffered as organizational change analyses. Moreover, when the social science literature is examined, little empirical study is found on universities as complex organizations undergoing structural change.[1] So, it follows that there is a natural absence of systematic investigation of the processes of organizational change taking place within their schools of education.[2]

A formal organization[3] for the purposes of this paper will be defined as a particular kind of societal sub-system, deliberately structured to accomplish officially stated goals. In such a system, there are designated statuses (positions) which have sets of expectations (roles) attached to them. These expectations for behavior are in the form of rights and obligations and link the positions to one another. These positions and roles make up the organization's structure, the basis of its systems of authority and communication, and its division of labor.[4]

An organizational analysis would involve the use of structural concepts and typically would focus on their empirical interrelationships, their determinants, and/or their consequences for the organization or for the environment in which the organization is embedded. Schools of education can be treated as formal settings in their own right since among the other qualities mentioned, they do have deliberately and officially stated goals, and since the activities of their members are consciously coordinated in the effort to accomplish these goals.[5] Their most obvious purposes are the training of educational practitioners and the development of educationally related theory and knowledge.

Organizational change refers to *actual alterations* in structural components such as statuses and roles or to the *process* whereby these structural changes take place: their initiation, implementation, or incorporation.[6] The phrase "organizational innovation" is used most often to refer to preconceived *ideas* about how the statuses and roles making up the core of an organization's structure would be modified. For example, instructional television, student involvement in governance, and faculty unionization can be considered organizational innovations because they require by definition various alterations in the prevailing roles of students, faculty, or administrators. Taken macroscopically, these innovations are organizational because they necessitate changing the authority structure, the division of labor, the system of communication, or, perhaps in some way, even the mission of a school. Some innovations also require the addition of new and/or the abolishment of existing positions.

The general literature on the process of organizational change is voluminous,[7] even though there has been little description of the kinds and the extent of change occurring in schools of education and little clarity about how such change takes place. The fact that they can be thought of as formal settings, however, makes conceptions of the change process derived from other work settings such as factories, hospitals, and public schools useful in their study.

The purpose of this chapter will be to discuss three conceptions or models of the organizational change process depicted in the general literature. The analysis will be made to provide a backdrop for proposing future empirical work. It is not meant as a comprehensive review of the studies or concepts found in the literature on each model. Tentative application of this analysis will then be made to schools of education with special focus on the role of dean. In this context, several lines of research on schools of education will be proposed. How such research might benefit organizational change theory will be considered as well as how it might provide useful suggestions for improving change efforts. Important differences between schools of education and other types of formal work settings will also be raised during the research discussion in order to highlight the value of using schools of education to investigate dynamics of change.

THREE CONCEPTIONS OF THE ORGANIZATIONAL CHANGE PROCESS

Although there appear to be many models or descriptions of how change occurs in formal work settings, the three to be discussed in this chapter, I believe, succinctly take into account most of the current thinking. Two of these conceptions are derived from observations of deliberate or conscious efforts to produce change. For these planned conceptions of change, I will use the terms *Research, Development, and Diffusion of Innovations (RD and D)* and *Organizational Self-renewal*. The third conception describes a process of change that is essentially unplanned. It will be called the *Organizational Drift* model of change. While the three models will be discussed separately, for the most part, they will be compared at several points in the discussion. Actually, as processes of change, they may occur simultaneously in a given situation and may influence each other in various ways.

RESEARCH, DEVELOPMENT, AND DIFFUSION OF INNOVATIONS

The RD and D model, unlike the drift and renewal conceptions, begins with the assumption that difficulties of organizational effectiveness and efficiency[8] are resolvable through the deliberate but organizationally removed efforts of people who specialize in research and development into such problems. More specifically, those working within this framework believe that needs for change can be isolated and defined for types of organizations such as public schools, since public schools tend to experience the same kinds of difficulties. They also believe that appropriate solutions can be created and field tested by these specialists and that such solutions can be packaged in the form of *innovations* and diffused among organizations in need of them. Agricultural extension bureaus and regional educational laboratories are but two of many types of enterprises created with the RD and D approach to change in mind.[9]

The enormous numbers of change articles, research and evaluation studies, and reports of change attempts found in the literature and related to this purposeful model of change are in no small measure due to the prevailing wishes of people to bring about or induce change, rather than to merely study its underlying dynamics.[10] Persons using this model in their work typically talk about "target or client systems," "communication linkages," and "change agents." Of central concern to them is making the targets of change aware of innovations out there in the environment and overcoming or avoiding their resistances to these new ideas in order to assure that, once cooperation is secured, implementation takes place.

Communicating Information about Innovations

The RD and D version with the longest history relies heavily on effecting change through the creation of new channels of communication or effective use of existing organizational linkages to transmit new information to client groups, be they doctors and nurses in hospitals, teachers and administrators in schools, or tribesmen in primitive societies.[11] The major element of this early strategy is the use of an outside change agent who is knowledgeable about new ideas and presumably about the steps necessary for their effective communication to clients. E. Katz and his associates define diffusion as:

> . . . The acceptance over time of some specific item—an idea or practice, by individuals, groups, or other adopting units, linked to specific channels of communication, to a social structure, and to a given system of values or culture.[12]

Often change agents distribute various kinds of publications, set up demonstration sites, and directly engage clients in discussion groups. Creators or proponents of innovations use specific tactics such as discussions, newsletters, demonstrations, and other forms of communication to *tell* clients about new ideas or practices, to *show* them what they look like in operation, and to *elicit* their positive reactions.

Promoting Receptivity to Innovations

The difficulty with much of the work emanating from this approach is that change agents who rely primarily on the announcement, communication, or demonstration of new ways often fail to elicit a positive response from clients. Often the targets of change are not as readily accepting of an innovation as are its advocates. More frequently than not, clients may demonstrate apathy or outright hostility to proposals of change. To put it another way, neither the desire for change nor an effective installation seems to come about very easily by simply making people aware of particular innovations and by demonstrating their "advantages."

As some agents of change have maintained, receptivity to change is especially missing when innovations are imposed by the top people of organizations. It was in this context that a second key tactic, that of power equalization, eventually emerged.[13] Power equalization or the participation of subordinates in change-related decisions, it is argued, leads to the reduction or avoidance of resistance to change and concomitantly to increased receptivity to innovations which are adopted.[14] Change agents also believe that participation produces greater understanding of the need for change, greater clarity about the specific problems and possible alternative solutions, as well as greater commitment to the adopted innovation.[15]

The meaning of participation varies by author. Some authors use the term to mean simply that people are present when decisions are made, while others use it to refer to situations in which subordinates are asked their opinions or advice. Others use it to show that subordinates actively take part in carrying out the innovation. Still others use the term to signify that the decision-making has been shared, and fairly equally so, by superordinates and subordinates.[16]

In spite of one's usage of "participation" and the rationale given for its value, resistance to change remains the bane of many a change agent, that is, a complex matter not clearly understood. Some students of resistance argue that lack of receptivity is just the natural state of man. Others seem to think of it as a consequence of the aforementioned way innovations are introduced; still others believe it is a function of personality.[17]

While these views of resistance or receptivity all have merit in their own right, there is another largely unexplored perspective which is decidedly more sociological in its basic assumptions about resistance. This more sociologically oriented conception has been labeled by J. Giacquinta[18] as the status-risk explanation of resistance and receptivity. This perspective views receptivity as connected, though not exclusively, to a member's organizational statuses.[19] It postulates that people, especially at work, vary in their receptivity to innovations on the basis of how much risk there would be to their status perquisites—prestige, money, job security, work hours, power—were a particular innovation to be introduced.[20]

I believe that this status-risk orientation has a great deal of potential value in explaining, for instance, why the *same people* vary in their receptivity to *different innovations*, why people grouped into *different statuses* respond differently to the *same innovation*, why people who change their organizational statuses then alter their earlier orientations to an innovation, or why the same people over time might change in their degree of acceptance of an innovation.

An important activity for change agents emerges from this status-risk perspective. If receptivity is largely a consequence of whether an innovation, when put into place, promotes or threatens one's status benefits, then one key change-agent activity would be the development of risk profiles for each status of a given organization where an innovation is being introduced or considered.[21] The tactic of creating risk profiles would make clearer just what actual risks there would be for the incumbents of each status. To the extent that there are real losses, high risks, or serious ambiguities, resistance will remain high. Indeed, where there are real and important losses, resistance will be a constant unless incumbents can be persuaded to reduce their perquisite demands or unless they are replaced with people who have perquisite expectations and desires in line with those that can be met once the innovation is put into place.

A second and equally important part of this risk delineation would be the determination of people's *perceived* risks and/or benefits. Are they realistic? Using the profiles (assuming they are accurate) as a guide, the discrepancies between member perceptions and the profiles would provide change agents with concrete areas in which efforts to reduce unnecessary ambiguities and misconceptions can be made.

Assuring Implementation of Innovations

Although the step from creating awareness and understanding to increasing member receptivity to innovations seems important, in most cases it may not be enough to gain the desired changes. Considerable experience with and study of what happens in organizations after innovations have been adopted suggests that the introduction of innovations, even when there is member support, often leads to undesired change or to no change at all.[22] So, while receptivity or member willingness to go along with new ideas and practices seems to be an important condition, it represents only one of many general conditions that are required if actual and appropriate implementation is to occur.

The empirical study of public schools and a critical appraisal of existing literature on the implementation process in organizational settings has led Neal Gross and his associates[23] to conclude that there are five important conditions which must be developed and maintained during an implementation effort. If a successfully *initiated* change is to be carried out accurately within an organizational setting, the following conditions must exist: (1) that an innovation's goals and new role expectations be clearly understood by members, (2) that the members remain willing to make the efforts necessary in carrying out these new role prescriptions, (3) that members possess or develop the appropriate skills and abilities for enacting new role behaviors and for supporting the new underlying values and attitudes, (4) that the resources necessary for their new role enactment be available and adequate, and (5) that the remaining organizational structure be compatible (or made so) with the new role structure to be carried out.

In line with the conception presented above, Gross maintains that the administration would be responsible for providing adequate rewards and support for members who must carry out the innovation. It is also responsible for creating feedback and problem-solving mechanisms whereby difficulties often unanticipated can be effectively expressed and properly resolved. A change agent in such a setting, were the agent not actually the administrator in charge, would have the job of facilitating the administration's achievement of these conditions.[24]

The weight of the discussion makes clear that the RD and D model views the impetus for change as originating largely outside a given organization in the form of prepackaged innovations and sees the major organizational task as one of changing people, that is, preparing organizational members to properly receive the new idea or practice by making sure that certain conditions prevail. A summarization of this RD and D literature in the form of a series of postulates is provided by Giacquinta:

... Organizational change, when successfully completed, proceeds in three distinct stages: initiation, implementation, and incorporation.

Successful completion of one stage, however, does not guarantee successful completion of the next.

... These stages are influenced by attributes of the innovations that are introduced, the manner of their introduction, characteristics of the . . . personnel who must make the changes, and structural properties of the . . . settings.

... These factors do not influence initiation completely in the same way they influence implementation or incorporation.[25]

ORGANIZATIONAL SELF-RENEWAL

The diffusion model stresses the value of generating outside solutions to problems—innovations—and then spreading the word about them to organizations in need. The planned self-renewal conception places importance for successful organizational change elsewhere. Rather than looking to the outside for specific, prepackaged innovations on a one-at-a-time basis, this model begins with the postulate that organizations contain the seeds within themselves for continued growth and development. As one recent organization development publication notes:

> We recognize that change is inevitable and think that by planning, we can influence the direction of change and help maximize the benefits for all concerned.[26]

For the resolution of difficulties related to organizational effectiveness and efficiency and also those related to member satisfaction and productivity, members in concert with management must develop an awareness and understanding of how they interact, communicate, make decisions, and distribute power and influence. Successful change comes about as such organizational processes as communication, maintenance, problem-solving, decision-making, and task accomplishment are perfected. Change is a natural and ongoing outgrowth of this organizational fine-tuning by its members. Richard Beckhard describes the model as well as anyone:

> Organization development is an effort (1) planned, (2) organization-wide, and (3) managed from the top, to (4) increase organization effectiveness and health through (5) planned inter-

ventions in the organization's "processes," using behavioral-science knowledge.[27]

In short, this model emphasizes improving the ways in which organizations generally operate instead of the search for adoptable, outside innovations.

Present in the execution of most self-renewal interventions are the participation of organizational members, management, and an external organization-development consultant. At the outset, a contract or mutually agreed upon set of obligations between these parties is created. Once set into motion, a healthy structure becomes self-renewing, still with the help of the OD expert, though such expertise may be most needed in getting the renewal processes started. Planned self-renewal does not deny the value from time to time of using RD and D ideas as alternative solutions to local problems.

This model received its impetus from the group dynamics work conducted at the National Training Laboratory founded at Bethel, Maine, in the late 1940s.[28] So far, it has gained greatest acceptance as an approach to organizational change in business.[29] Presently, school reformers at all levels are giving it close scrutiny.[30] Concepts assuming a central place in this approach to change include "sensitivity training," "power equalization," and "team building." The basis of this model is summarized in the work of Schmuck and Miles, especially their OD cube.[31] Other seminal work which contributes to this formulation includes McGregor's theory X and theory Y notions,[32] Maslow's ideas of a needs' hierarchy and self-actualization of organizational members,[33] and Blake and Mouton's managerial grid.[34] Among the many activities which comprise this model, three stand out in my mind as central: organization diagnosis, team building, and rational problem-solving, which includes priority setting and conflict resolution.

Organization Diagnosis

Organization diagnosis includes gathering information about the current state of an organization—goals and priorities of members, functional and dysfunctional elements of a structure, member morale and cohesiveness, productivity, and the like—and about the effectiveness of the OD intervention once it has begun. More generally, the survey-feedback techniques of questionnairing and interviewing, T groups, and group conferences are often employed to collect information necessary for diagnosing the present state of an organization or for assessing the effects of an intervention strategy. These techniques are often supplemented by the OD consultant's informal interviewing of management and workers and his direct observations.

Once gathered, information is used to uncover or refine problems such as organization-environment effectiveness, intra-organization conflict, and member dissatisfaction. Typically, these problems are given a priority, and work devoted to resolving them begins. Usually, members must go through a process whereby they take responsibility for the task of solving difficulties and in many cases must assume ownership for at least part of the reason why a particular problem exists.

Team Building

More often than not, OD specialists see team building as being the heart of any serious self-renewal effort. Jim Shonk[35] describes team building as "A process a group goes through to examine and improve its working effectiveness. . . . Usually done with the help of a third party consultant who helps the group collect the data and keeps them on the track . . . " According to Shonk, a group examines its functioning in four general areas: goals and priorities, allocation of work, internal processes such as decision-making and conflict resolution and communication, and role relations between workers and management and among workers.

Teams may, for purposes of self-renewal, consist of intact work groups, for instance, an academic department in a school of education might be defined as a team for carrying out an OD intervention. On the other hand, more loosely formed work groups such as the dean and his staff might be so designated as a team for a particular building effort. An entire school staff might be the focus of still another team-building effort, though the larger the number of people or unit involved, the more difficult it is to engage in just one such effort.

Schmuck and Miles give us the flavor of what one team-building attempt, which took place in a summer laboratory setting, was like:

> The objectives of the first week were to help participants learn more about (1) the value of joint inquiry (to promote cooperative inquiry and to minimize competitive arguments), (2) ways in which to be helpful in interpersonal relations, (3) group problem-solving methods, (4) ways in which to give and receive constructive feedback, (5) group processes in general, and (6)

the participants themselves in interaction with others. More generally, the objective was to build *interpersonal trust*. A variety of techniques were employed, including unstructured inquiry groups, "fishbowl" arrangements with observers providing feedback to participants, various systematic data-gathering procedures and feedback of results . . .

They go on to say that during the second week:

> . . . The transformation of the lab participants into a "work group" in a "natural setting" was begun. The focus of the intervention was shifted from assessment and training in basic interpersonal skills to a focus on the "real life" problems of a newly formed work group: e.g., decision-making, agenda-setting, and conflict management.[36]

It is important to note that this was a laboratory designed to get organizational members started on the road to installing a long-term intervention in their real work setting; otherwise, OD may appear to some to be just another organizational innovation which is being diffused according to the RD and D model, early vintage.

If team building is treated as the basis of the renewal process, then such activities as conflict resolution and priority setting are usually depicted as natural outcomes of this process. It is true, however, that priority setting and the resolving of conflicts can be carried out in the absence of team building per se; though, I suspect that such activities, were they to be long-term and continuing objectives, would require effective team building to begin with.

Rational Problem-Solving

Many of the techniques used in organization diagnosis and team building are also employed in this general area of self-renewal. Often the distinction between this area and general OD activities is not made. To my mind, however, there is a strong emphasis placed here on figuring out how to better structure behavior in order to carry out the necessary tasks of the group. So, the division of labor and its effectiveness takes center stage. It appears to me that less emphasis is given to the importance of sensitivity training, building interpersonal trust, designing work so that it will lead as much to member satisfaction and personal growth as it will to productivity, and matters generally that pertain to organizational maintenance. This is not to say that matters such as these are completely ignored, rather that they are given a lower priority in an OD intervention that stresses rational problem-solving.[37]

ORGANIZATIONAL DRIFT

The organizational drift model, proceeding from a very different set of assumptions than either the diffusion or renewal models, pictures change as the result of impersonal, non-deliberate change forces or conditions located in the environment of an organization.[38] These conditions impinge on an organization in such a way that alterations in organizational goals and structure happen, for the most part, haphazardly. In other words, this conception portrays an organization's structure, at any point in time, as a function of pressing environmental forces.[39] For instance, the confluence of such environmental factors as inflation, the demand for greater social egalitarianism, and the need for more schooling if acceptable occupations are to be reached might be used to account for why many colleges and universities are moving toward open-admissions policies.

Those who write with this model in mind generally view organizations as open systems[40] and frequently are concerned with uncovering the specific pressures embedded in the larger social system to which particular types of organizations are vulnerable. Another of their interests is figuring out just how these pressures come to influence what goes on within the settings, that is, the process whereby conditions are translated into influence and power and manifested structural change.

Since the drift conception as discussed so far does not represent a deliberately induced model of change, discussion of purposeful tactics associated with it may not appear sensible. However, there are essentially two versions of this drift model. Change tactics are very real and important to one of them.

The Natural-Selection Version

A recent article by Howard Aldrich and Jeffrey Pfeffer argues that both the natural-selection and the resource-dependence versions of open-systems analysis agree on the importance of organizational environments for understanding organizational decisions and structures. The article also outlines in a clear fashion major differences between them:

> The natural selection model, developing the strongest argument for an environmental perspective, posits that environmental factors select those organizational characteristics that best fit the environment. . . . A complementary model . . . a resource dependence model . . . argues for greater attention to internal organizational political decision-making processes and also for the perspective that organizations seek to manage or strategically adapt to their environments. . . .[41]

Aldrich and Pfeffer go on to say that in the natural-selection model, as in its biological counterpart, the environment is seen as selecting the fittest or optimal organizations for that environment. Moreover, the model views the organizations in question as being essentially powerless to affect this selection process.

From the perspective of organizational members in settings where this model applies, modifications due to these kinds of forces may often be seen merely as disturbances to policy and procedures rather than as clear-cut organizational changes. Conversely, organizational members may often respond to other more obvious changes caused by such pressures with resignation, for example, the growth of union-like behavior among educators. Perhaps of even more import, because they are the slowly formed results of indirect, often unobservable pressures, many changes may go *unperceived* as such by substantial numbers of personnel affected by them. The movement toward no-fail school structures may be viewed as an example of this kind of change.

The Resource-Dependence Version

The resource-dependence model begins, according to Aldrich and Pfeffer, with the assumption that formal organizations cannot generate from within themselves the resources and functions required if they are to continue as viable entities. They *must* strike up relationships or engage in transactions with segments of the environment that can supply the needed goods and services (resources) for survival. Moreover, this conception portrays the organization as active, capable of changing, and able to respond to the environment in a purposeful way. It calls attention not only to the importance of environmental contingencies and constraints, but also to the possibility of strategic choice by an organization's members.

It seems most appropriate to discuss tactics of change in the context of the resource-dependence version. What are the primary responses organizational personnel can exhibit to environmental forces of change? At one extreme there are tactics designed to protect an organization's boundaries and the existing social structure within it, that is, to resist changing. Externally, a manager's effort to control or manage influential environmental conditions may be the main way change is resisted. Internally, the application of sanctions according to prevailing rules or norms in order to stabilize the behavior of members who might be sympathetic or especially sensitive to environmental pressures may be the most important way.

A second reaction might be labeled "reluctant compromising." This might be defined as trying to maintain organizational structure by facilitating change only to the extent that it is necessary to keep intact as much of the structure as possible. A third response, creative accommodation, might be defined as taking the opportunity caused by external pressures to alter parts of the structure which were undermining organizational efficiency or effectiveness.

At the other extreme, management and workers might respond to change pressures with indifference, allowing the organization's fate to take whatever directions the environment pushed in. I doubt that any organization can survive such a situation for more than brief periods, especially since outside pressures usually seem to be many, strong, and frequently contradictory.

Organization drift according to this resource-dependent model might appear to some to come very close to the self-renewal model, in so far as both acknowledge the organizational need to respond or adjust to the environment and to renew on a frequent basis its relationships with segments of the environment. Except, the OD model reflects a deliberate, long-term effort to alter the organization's internal structure and processes in ways that would assure its self-renewing capacity. The drift model contains no long-term, internal plan to deal with change. Instead, it views, when it does so at all, organizational change as a more or less *ad hoc* necessity—resisting change pressures when possible, trying to control the surrounding environment in order to allow it to operate as is, or changing internally only in so far as is necessary for survival.[42] In short, the stress is placed on maintaining a kind of dynamic balance, not on inducing change. Change is a necessary, and often bitter, pill taken for the sake of survival.

As a way of providing a summary of the discussion presented so far in this chapter, the three models—RD and D, self-renewal, and drift—will be contrasted. The first comparison employs two criteria: whether the organizational change that occurred in a given setting was deliberately proposed in advance of its occurrence and whether the process whereby the structural change took place was intentionally created for the purpose of bringing about change. Where neither end nor process are planned in advance, it was argued that the most appropriate characterization of it would be according to the organizational drift model. Where a change effort is deliberately initiated with a specific end (innovation) in mind and some plans for carrying out that specific innovation, the RD and D model probably best depicts the process. Where the focus is on improving essential organizational processes, with structural change seen as a natural and open-ended outcome, the self-renewal conception would best describe the change dynamics involved.

A second way of comparing these models would be to ask the following question: Does the conception focus on organizations internally or on the external environments in which they are embedded? With the environmentally oriented model of organizational drift, the explanation of change focuses on conditions external to organizations, to those external conditions that produce or evoke organizational adjustments or modifications. The interest, at the other extreme, for organizational renewal is on internal structure and on the activities of members within the organizational settings; these activities, to be sure, are often due to externally originating factors, but nevertheless, the explanatory spotlight for change is on what happens internally. The diffusion model in its original form stresses the problem of articulation, linking certain environmental forces with the target organizations; its basic concern is with communicating about particular environmental elements—innovations—, with alerting the organizations for which the innovations are intended. The second version stresses an internal organizational condition, that is, the receptivity of organizational members to ideas from the outside. The third version, like the second, takes the external situation as a given: an innovation is being diffused. What happens within organizations to their structures when an innovation which is being diffused is introduced, and why it happens, become paramount matters.

SOME SPECULATIONS ABOUT THE PROCESS OF CHANGE IN SCHOOLS OF EDUCATION

Several papers in this volume attest to the fact that it is hazardous to discuss schools of education as if they were of one common cut.[43] Still, there is the need to provide some picture of what I have in mind when talking about the three models of the change process as they apply to schools of education. Moreover, some aspects are common to most schools. On the one hand, it is clear that some schools, given their larger university settings, are more autonomous than are others. Some stress pre-service training, while others focus on graduate training and academic studies. Within some schools, deans are treated as little more than administrators who have few real decision-making prerogatives. In others, deans are viewed as institutional leaders who set school direction and structure. Some schools have large administrative staffs with a variety of assisting deans, office directors, and department and program heads. Some schools have faculties that are more research-oriented than training- or service-oriented. Some faculties are housed in departments and have strong identifications with outside disciplines; others are not so oriented. Faculties differ in their size: some place emphasis on small-group learning and field experiences, and some stress lecturing and the accumulation of course credits. Some student bodies are small, professionally oriented, and concerned with the advancement of educationally related knowledge; others are large, training-oriented, and interested in perfecting their teaching skills. In sum, schools do differ in their purposes, their technologies, their degree of bureaucratization (centralization of decision-making, formalization of roles, and stratification of positions), and their student bodies and faculties.

On the other hand, most, if not all, schools have research, teaching, and service components. Schools are embedded in larger university settings so that immediate and strong environmental pressures come from the larger university itself. They do have full-time administrative staffs headed by a dean who oversees the internal activities of the school and who acts as chief articulator of the school with its environment. There is a faculty, which actually carries out the work of the school: instruction, scholarship, and service. Faculties typically have a governance body called a faculty council. Finally, there are students, who are seen as members, clients, or products of the school depending upon the organizational perspective taken and the level of student being considered. So, there are obvious aspects which most schools hold in common. Moreover, the differences mentioned above as well as many not touched upon may be related to the dynamics of change which schools manifest or fail to manifest. The fact that schools hold certain common characteristics makes their comparison possible. Their differences also can be used advantageously by the student of organizational change in his comparative research designs.

The Harvards and Stanfords may exhibit patterns of change very different from the Columbias and New York Universities or the Ohio States and Michigans. Solid empirical research could uncover the actual facts and provide valuable insights as a result. For now, I will make some general speculations about how schools have responded and are now responding and leave for research their eventual rejection, confirmation, or qualification.

There are a number of conditions which provide strong reason for studying schools of education in order to advance our understanding of the organizational change process. First, and perhaps foremost, is that they are currently under attack. Serious professionals and public officials both within and outside the educational enterprise are questioning their effectiveness, efficiency, and missions. These questions are more critical now because of (1) the future need for fewer pre-service-trained teachers; (2) the generally poor showing of public schools and their college-trained teachers to increase the cognitive and affective achievements of large numbers of children, especially in urban areas; and (3) the difficulty education schools seem to be having in making clear advances in their understanding of the educative process and in effectively training teachers and other educational practitioners, such as guidance counselors and school administrators. Since the existing structures of schools of education are being examined, the pressure is on for organizational change which might resolve many of these pressing issues.

A second condition involves the composition of the typical school-of-education faculty. Many, if not most, schools contain large numbers of tenured faculty whose original and preferred professional and organizational roles are being challenged. This is due in great part because of the changing needs and conditions of public school systems alluded to under the first condition. If organizational change is to take place at all, these relatively stable staffs will need to change their behavior, their attitudes, and their values. Put another way, many faculty members will have to undergo some process of resocialization. Schools of education, therefore, make excellent settings in which to study such topics as resistance to change, the resocialization of organizational members, and the implementation of organizational innovations. They also provide fertile situations for the comparative study of the three models of change: To what extent does each exist within and across a given setting? and, To what extent does each provide an accurate picture of how change in schools of education proceeds?

The third condition is related to the fact that schools of education manifest two major principles of organization: bureaucratization (especially of that part of the structure created to meet the school's training and advisement obligations) and collegiality (particularly of that part of the structure devoted to the production of scholarship and research). Schools of education in their collegially organized activities exhibit far greater participation of organizational members in decision-making than do most other work settings. This permits the study of the strengths and the weaknesses of power equalization as a tactic of change and allows the whole issue of the effects of participation in decision-making on the quantity and quality of organizational change to be examined naturally. The dual structure also allows for the comparison of rates of change of particular parts of a school's structure: that which is bureaucratically organized as compared with that which is collegially constructed. In short, these conditions associated with schools of education permit valuable evidence to be collected on the processes of initiation, implementation, and incorporation of change.

It is my guess that the vast preponderance of organizational change in schools of education has occurred according to the organizational drift model: haphazardly, by accretion, due to the pressures located in the environment rather than according to planned diffusion of innovation efforts by R and D change agents or according to the self-renewal efforts of organizational members guided by an outside OD specialist. There are few, if any, organizations that publicly announce themselves as having as their purpose the development of innovative practices for schools of education. From time to time, federal and state agencies have insisted or imposed this or that change, for instance, affirmative-action hiring practices and competency-based teacher education. Moreover, a variety of innovations have been diffused nondeliberately across many schools, for example, student evaluation of faculty instructional procedures and the Keller plan for individualizing college instruction. However, neither state or federally demanded change nor unarticulated diffusion constitutes evidence for the RD and D model of change. With regard to self-renewal, a few recent starts within several schools, largely at the departmental level, have been reported. But while these would be of value for empirical research, there has been only a modicum of activity according to this model which attests to the paucity of change occurring according to this model in schools of education. So, important questions linger: How much change is taking place in schools of education? and,

At what rate and according to which of the models is it taking place? Both of these questions await empirical research to answer.

In my estimation the deans of schools of education play key roles in each of the three conceptions of change. Their involvement in the RD and D model might be depicted as "directive." As important inside change agents in their own right, deans could actively and purposefully search out new ideas or practices being generated elsewhere or find qualified outside change agents, expose faculty to them, and, when appropriate, seek to introduce promising innovations into their schools. The role could include not only the active selection and introduction of innovations or change promoters but also the overcoming or avoiding of resistance to change including: actively encouraging members to adopt changes; reducing, when possible, the faculty and staff's misperceptions about the risks and uncertainties associated with particular innovations; and assuring that the proper conditions prevail for the implementation and incorporation of any particular innovations which are initiated.

According to the renewal model, the dean's role in change attempts has a somewhat different image, one which might be considered primarily, but not solely, supportive. The dean would still be interested in promoting change, but in this case, his major task would be to support and encourage the staff members and the OD consultant in their efforts to alter ongoing organizational processes. In addition, the dean, to the extent necessary for the particular OD intervention underway, would be expected to take part in actual organizational diagnosis, team building, and problem-solving.

The dean's role in the organizational drift conception might be best depicted as reactive: defending the organization from an overload of change pressures and engaging in necessary or creative compromises to assure the survival of the school. The dean, here, is more of a defender of the *status quo* than a promoter of change and is a key to maintaining a balance *between* the forces of change and the forces of stability.

Deans with certain change orientations or personalities might be more effective in change situations involving one model rather than another. For example, deans with local orientations might find self-renewal attempts more attractive, while cosmopolitans might be more drawn to the diffusion of innovations. On the other hand, deans with a leadership conception of their role might be more active as agents of diffusion, while those with an administrative conception might find the compromise activities depicted as part of the organizational drift model more amenable. Those with egalitarian personalities might discover that the organizational self-renewal model and strategies, which in general involve participation of subordinates, more to their liking than would deans who exhibit authoritarian characteristics.

Since there might be a better fit between the deanship and the various modes of organizational change depending upon the characteristics of the man or woman who occupies the position, a dean might demonstrate more "effective" performance according to one model but not another model. Research into the personalities and professional characteristics of deans could help advance our understanding of how key organizational members hinder or promote the change process according to each of the three models of change. Though this discussion has focused on deans, it could be extended to other administrative positions and to the faculties of schools of education as well.

THE STUDY OF ORGANIZATIONAL CHANGE OF SCHOOLS OF EDUCATION: SOME SUGGESTED DIRECTIONS

Comprehensive research into the dynamics of organizational change in schools of education would include longitudinal as well as cross-sectional investigations within and across school settings. To what extent *have* schools changed over time? How adequately does each of the three models describe what has happened? What part have deans played in blocking or facilitating the various change processes and how? Put another way, central to any systematic analysis will be the determination of how deliberate the process of change in schools of education has been. To the extent that change has been demonstrated, another important area of inquiry would involve uncovering the frequency with which particular aspects of school life have changed and specifying, to the extent possible, exactly what those structural changes have been, that is, the creation of a laundry list of sorts of changes. In what follows, I will emphasize areas of investigation that in my estimation are of value to both practitioners and theorists and that often cut across the three models.

Research into the Diffusion of Innovations and the Use of Change Agents

To the extent that there have been similar changes in schools of which some were intentionally created and introduced, a series of questions about diffusion and the use of outside change agents is in order. While it is obvious that various journals and professional associations (especially those involving deans) may act informally or inadvertently as mechanisms of diffusion, schools of education have no direct, purposefully designed and coordinated mechanisms of inter-communication for the sharing of change proposals. Studies into the conditions that promote or perpetuate this isolation would contribute to our understanding of why the RD and D approach may describe so little of the change manifested in schools of education at this time.

To the degree that innovations *are* diffused among schools of education, however, there are important questions to be answered by research. They include the following. What are the specific changes which have been or are presently being diffused? What are the rates at which they have been or now are being diffused? Who are the diffusion agents and what are their channels of communication? Have certain innovations been diffused at faster rates and more pervasively than others? If so, what kinds are they and why have they enjoyed more success? In-depth case studies and survey analyses could help uncover and describe not only the existing channels, agents, and common patterns of diffusion but also the gaps between the sources of new ideas and the channels for communicating these ideas to the targets, the schools of education.

Since there appears to be, to date, little deliberate planning of the diffusion of specific innovations or use of self-renewal strategies of regeneration, the prevalence of outside-change agents, specialists of diffusion, and/or OD has naturally been minimal as well. Still, valuable research questions would be: To what extent are outside-change agents used by schools of education, and in what capacities? To what degree are they welcomed as third parties by deans and their faculties and staffs? When employed, do they make a difference say in improving the adequacy of organizational diagnoses conducted to uncover environmental pressures and organizational needs, in raising the rate and quality of change that is initiated and implemented, or in increasing the level of superordinate-subordinate participation—deans, administrative staffs, and faculties—in the decision-making process? What general conditions block or facilitate the success of their performances in school-of-education settings? Do the findings about such conditions match those based on the investigation of other types of organizational settings?

Investigation of these kinds would add to our clarity about the value of these change mechanisms. Furthermore, designs in which schools employing change agents are examined and compared to those without change specialists would facilitate our understanding of some of the road blocks to the efficient use of outsiders in the planning of organizational changes for schools of education.

Research on the Implementation of Organizational Innovations

A self-renewal effort may create the need for the introduction of a specific change; an innovation created elsewhere may be introduced by a change specialist; environmental pressures may force a change proposal onto a school. Regardless of how an organizational change arrives at the doorstep of a school of education, the fundamental issue around which others revolve is the implementation of that change. If a proposed change is to have its espoused or expected effects, then implementation must become paramount in one's thinking, even though it is true that many related and important phenomena such as diffusion channels, member receptivity, and resocialization deserve study as dependent variables in their own right.

The investigation of implementation can take the form of case studies of individual institutions in which relatively unique proposals for change are adopted, say, for example, one in which a new way of assessing yearly faculty performance is initiated. Implementation can also be examined across schools in which the same innovation is adopted, for instance, the competency-based teacher-education curriculum. A third type of study would compare the quasi-experimental schools in which a particular innovation is introduced for degree of implementation or for effects with those that do not adopt the innovation, for example, open admissions.

Several major questions should guide implementation research. One is: How do people define particular innovations? One of the most perplexing matters is that often the same term is used to refer to very different structural changes, for example, team teaching. The meanings faculty members and administrators give to various terms differ so greatly that before implementation and effects research can be carried out, clear definitions are required. A second question is: To what extent are changes as defined on paper actually carried out? This question deals directly with the need to describe exactly what is put into place—the actual structural changes that are installed. A third question concerns the reasons why some schools carry out innovations more quickly or thoroughly than others. Why some innovations are installed with greater fidelity than other innovations is a fourth important matter for empirical research to determine.

In any explanatory analysis of the implementation of innovations, there are five factors to consider: the clarity among the members of the organization, the willingness and the capabilities of the members, and the resources and compatability of the organization. More generally, when thinking about the classes of conditions that may affect implementation and, therefore, be used in directing research, one class deals with the characteristics of innovations themselves, for example, their ease of explanation and communication, their potential trial on a partial or limited basis, their complexity, their congruence with existing values and behavior patterns, and their superiority over what already exists. Another more basic way of classifying them is according to their technological or social focus.

A second class of potentially influential variables relates to characteristics of faculty and administrative personnel, for example, their willingness, capabilities, and understanding. A third set of factors involves the tactics or manner whereby innovations are introduced: by imposition or through participation, with or without the aid of change specialists. The fourth set of factors concerns properties of schools of education as organizations, for example, their degree of centralization, formalization, or stratification. There is great need for research into these conditions and for the testing of directional hypotheses. Suffice it to say that at this time the links between these conditions and implementation are often based on speculation and contradictory evidence.[44]

Although implementation is the crux of the change process, it can never start without successful initiation. Important research questions here include: To what degree are changes successfully initiated in schools of education? Are they initiated through deliberately planned efforts or non-deliberate environmental forces? If they are deliberate, are they initiated by superordinate imposition or subordinate participation? If they are not deliberate, are there conditions which are generally more forceful than others, namely, economic, political, or moral pressures?

At the other end of the change process is incorporation—making innovations standard operating procedures within a school. Clearly, unless implemented innovations *are* incorporated, the hoped-for effects will either not occur or not last. The same sets of factors that influence implementation may affect both initiation and incorporation, though they may have different effects. A highly authoritarian faculty and staff, for instance, may take an order from the dean to carry out a reorganization of administrative and advisement services, and yet this very characteristic may make the members so rigid that it blocks the change from being effectively put into operation; so while initiation was successful, implementation failed. In short, studies devoted to the initiation, implementation, and incorporation of changes in schools of education will help advance our rather minimal understanding of this fundamental process of change. Such work would also sensitize faculties and their administrators, especially deans, to the underlying dynamics and conditions affecting this process.

Receptivity-to-Change Investigations

As in the case of implementation, receptivity of faculty and administrators to change touches all three models. Pressures to innovate whether deliberate or inadvertent may be openly supported or vehemently fought. Often, faculties are characterized as openly or surreptitiously resistant to change. Still, research suggests that lack of receptivity to the extent that it does exist (and we are not yet clear about its degree) may be a function of the degree to which their perquisites are threatened or enhanced.[45] Hence, unionism for instance may be supported by some faculties and not by others, with support being a function of such status characteristics as tenure, rank, and administrative obligations.[46]

The status-risk perspective could be used in survey-research designs to explore responses of school personnel to changes under consideration or already adopted in schools of education. The value of developing risk profiles and actively seeking to reduce unwarranted perceptions of risk and uncertainty with them as a guide could be one way of determining the value of this perspective. Moreover, competing explanations such as those employing personality factors could also be tested. Eventually, a better grasp of why faculty and administration support or reject change initiatives could be developed. It is important to note that receptivity to the entire notion of self-renewal could also be studied this way. Since self-renewal involves the permanent alteration of the distribution of power and, thus, qualifies as a meta-level organizational change in its own right, exploration of faculty and administrative responses to proposals of OD interventions would benefit those who advocate this model of change as well as students of receptivity and resistance.

Participation of Subordinates in Decision-Making

Closely related to implementation and receptivity is the issue of member participation in key decision-making. It has become a shibboleth of organizational life, a part of the democratization of work. Without doubt, success of the complete self-renewal model, the initiation phase of the RD and D model, and the organizational environment needs assessment in the resource-dependence version of drift appear to depend on participation. Yet, in spite of various ideological stances on this matter, we have precious little direct study of participatory tactics of change as compared to others. Studies of schools of education (where participation is far more pervasive than in public schools, hospitals, and factories) could prove to be very illuminating.

Logically, participation might lead to as much harm as benefit. Often, serious conflict among faculty may, and to my mind in fact does, arise when participation is encouraged. Not only could participation lead to the exasperbation of conflict, but also it might lead to the kind of group consensus wherein watered-down decisions and subsequent innovations are produced. The watering-down, in turn, reduces the chances of the desired improvement to occur. Everybody may be happy and satisfied, but nothing solid may be invoked; there might be a lot of commotion, but no real motion.

Some deans appear to be most comfortable with the top-down approach to change, whereas others value the participatory approach more. It would be of value to conduct careful case and survey analyses of the decision-making that results from these two approaches and of the quality and quantity of changes occurring within and across schools where deans try one or both of these gross strategies.

Research on the Resocialization of Organizational Members

While many people in educational circles talk about participation, far fewer seem to understand that in order for members to participate effectively, they must possess a number of important skills: listening skills, communication skills, skills of compromising and negotiation, and the like. The simple putting of one's two cents worth into the pot or the proliferation of faculty and administrative committees and meetings probably leads to little more than the lowest level of participation (shows of power, influence, antagonism, and clique affiliation) without such skills. The self-renewal model recognizes the need for member resocialization and theoretically makes more of resocialization in the form of developing human interaction skills than either RD and D or drift conceptions. One serious kind of research would shed light on how viable, given the need for resocialization, is the renewal model for changing schools of education. This is especially serious since faculties are notorious in their quest for autonomy[47] and for their minimal efforts to express their positions openly and honestly, particularly about how they feel towards others. Can deans and faculty be made to see the need for greater openness of communication and can they be taught the skills of promoting greater trust among themselves and the building of teams? Can faculty and administrators come to value the process whereby they conduct business as much as the desired goals of their interaction? It would be beneficial to research into the kinds of conditions that promote the development of trust and openness of communication within some schools and block achievement in others.

The resocialization of faculty and administrators for better performance as participants in decision-making and process analysis is one level at which this change topic can be discussed. It can be discussed at another level. Adult resocialization—the changing of values, attitudes, and behavior patterns—is required to varying degrees *anytime* a specific innovation is introduced or a change occurs.[48] For an innovation such as individualized college instruction to be installed, faculty would, at a minimum, need to relate to students differently; their work tempo would need to alter as would their attitudes toward group instruction and the ways young adults learn most efficiently. For another—collective bargaining—many faculties would need to redefine their expectations for the administration and the images they have of themselves as an occupational group.

Since changes *are* occurring, knowledge of how resocialization takes place and of the factors that block or facilitate this process would be of considerable value. What kinds of mechanisms of resocialization are employed that do work, for example, when schools of education successfully alter their missions from pre-service to graduate-level institutions or from a training to a research and service emphasis. Indeed, to what extent can faculty and administrators be successfully resocialized at all, is a central question to be addressed and uncovered by comparative and accumulative resocialization research. It may very well be that the reason so many changes are watered-down, resisted, or not adequately implemented, in the last analysis, resides in the lack of necessary mechanisms or the weakness of those that do exist to overcome the earlier socialization of organizational members. Given the large number of tenured faculty, this is a critical issue of change.

This final section has pointed to a number of areas worthy of empirical study and of import to both change theorists and school-of-education personnel. No one research approach—experimental, survey research, or case study—has been championed over another. Furthermore, given the uneven quantity and quality of existing change studies, both explanatory and exploratory studies are justified. Descriptive as well as hypothesis generating and testing work is justified on similar grounds. In addition, studies of the *content* of change as well as the dynamics or *process* whereby they occur are needed. In combination, this research would give us greater insights into what and why changes are occurring within the walls of schools of education organizationally at this time. The above research agenda could be used ultimately to improve the operation of schools of education, give guidance as to when and how to plan change efforts, and contribute to our understanding generally of organizational change in formal work settings.

NOTES

1. Three excellent volumes that summarize existing work on universities as complex organizations are J. V. Baldridge (ed.), *Academic Governance* (Berkeley, Calif.: McCutchan, 1971); E. Gross and P. V. Grambsch, *Changes in University Organization, 1964-71* (New York: McGraw-Hill, 1974); and J. B. Lon Hefferlin, *Dynamics of Academic Reform* (San Francisco: Jossey-Bass, 1971). Several authors have discussed models of decision-making and organizational change within universities. Two outstanding articles are T. N. Clark, "Institutionalization of Innovations in Higher Education: Four Models," *Administrative Science Quarterly* (Vol. 13, No. 1, June 1968), pp. 1-25; and M. Cohen, J. March, and J. Olsen, "A Garbage Can Model of Organizational Choice," *Administrative Science Quarterly* (Vol. 17, No. 1, March 1972), pp. 1-25.

2. The author is indebted to his colleagues Floyd Hammack and Carl Steinhoff with whom he discussed various parts of this manuscript. They helped to avoid several embarrassing errors. Throughout this chapter the term, *school of education*, to include colleges of education is used. To the extent that large departments of education approximate the structural properties of schools and colleges of education, this

discussion is applicable to them as well. For a recent study of school of education faculty and their responses to a wide variety of organizational changes, see C. Kazlow, "Resistance to Innovations in Complex Organizations: A Test of Two Models of Resistance in a Higher Education Setting." Unpublished doctoral dissertation, New York University, 1974.

3. A number of terms will be used as rough equivalents for the purposes of this paper: *complex organization, formal organization, formal work setting, organization, and work setting.*

4. For several definitional statements cf. P. M. Blau and W. R. Scott, *Formal Organizations* (San Francisco: Chandler, 1962), pp. 2-8; and A. Stinchcombe, "Social Structure and Organizations," in J. March (ed.), *Handbook of Organizations* (Chicago: Rand McNally, 1965), p. 142.

5. The classical piece remains C. I. Barnard, *The Functions of the Executive* (Cambridge, Mass.: Harvard University Press, 1938), pp. 56-81.

6. This paper is based on the conception of the process presented by N. Gross, J. Giacquinta, and M. Bernstein, *Implementing Organizational Innovations* (New York: Basic Books, 1971), pp. 16-17. For other, similar formulations using somewhat different terminology see J. Hage and M. Aiken, *Social Change in Complex Organizations* (New York: Random House, 1970); and K. Lewin, "Frontiers in Group Dynamics," *Human Relations* (Vol. 1, No. 1, 1948), pp. 5-41.

7. Two recent reviews of this material as it relates to education are M. Fullan, "Overview of the Innovative Process and the User," *Interchange*. (Vol. 3, No. 2, 1972), pp. 1-43; and J. Giacquinta, "The Process of Organizational Change in Schools," in F. N. Kerlinger (ed.), *Review of Research in Education: I* (Itasca, Ill.: F. E. Peacock, 1973), pp. 178-208. An earlier but still valuable collection of papers is M. Miles (ed.), *Innovation in Education* (New York: Teachers College Press, 1964).

8. Effectiveness means how well organizational goals or social functions are carried out; efficiency means the costs (money, time, and energy) required to carry out the goals or functions at the levels they are being accomplished. One useful critical appraisal of the RD and D approach to organizational change is contained in J. I. Goodlad, *The Dynamics of Educational Change* (New York: McGraw-Hill, 1975), pp. 13-20.

9. The outstanding review of the diffusion process and the studies devoted to this topic is E. Rogers and F. Shoemaker, *Communication of Innovations* (New York: Free Press, 1971).

10. Giacquinta, *op. cit.*, p. 178.

11. A forceful proponent of this approach is Ronald Havelock. His thorough review of this topic is presented in a monograph entitled, *Planning for Innovation* (Washington, D.C.: U.S. Department of Health, Education, and Welfare, 1969).

12. E. Katz, J. L. Levin, and H. Hamilton, "Research on the Diffusion of Innovation," *American Sociological Review* (Vol. 28, No. 2, April 1963), p. 237.

13. A seminal article on this topic is that of H. Leavitt, "Applied Organizational Change in Industry: Structural, Technological and Humanistic Approaches," in J. March, *op. cit.*, pp. 1153-1167.

14. Giacquinta, *op. cit.*, pp. 183-189.

15. *Ibid.*

16. *Ibid.*

17. *Ibid.*, pp. 191-193. The term *receptivity* is used to refer to the internal orientations of organizational members toward various innovations; the term *resistance* is used to refer to behaviors that members exhibit prior to or during the occurrence of structural change. For the purposes of this chapter they can be discussed together. See also Kazlow, *op. cit.*

18. J. Giacquinta, "Status, Risk, and Receptivity to Innovations in Complex Organizations: A Study of the Responses of Four Groups of Educators to the Proposed Introduction of Sex Education in Elementary School," *Sociology of Education* (Vol. 48, Winter 1975), pp. 38-58. Also, J. Giacquinta, "Status Risk-Taking: A Central Issue in the Initiation and Implementation of Public School Innovations," *Journal of Research and Development in Education* (Vol. 9, No. 1, Fall 1975), pp. 102-114.

19. *Ibid.*

20. *Ibid.* For a similar treatment more macroscopic in level, see the work of F. Cancian, especially, *Change and Uncertainty in a Peasant Economy* (Stanford, Calif.: Stanford University Press, 1972).

21. Giacquinta, *op. cit.*, Fall 1975, pp. 111-112. It is important to note that obviously there are informal organizational statuses as well as formalized statuses. Here the discussion is taken generally; in any given situation informal organizational statuses such as those of sex and age might be critical. Two recent papers examine data in light of both informal and formal statuses: C. Kazlow and J. Giacquinta, "Faculty Receptivity to Organizational Change." Paper presented at the American Educational Research Association Meeting, Chicago, April 1974; and J. Giacquinta and C. Kazlow, "Support of Unionism Within the Education Faculty of a Large Private University: Some Unexpected Findings." Paper presented at the American Educational Research Association Meeting, San Francisco, April 1976.

22. For example, see R. Carlson, *Adoption of Educational Innovations* (Eugene: Center for the Advanced Study of Educational Administration, University of Oregon, 1965); M. Fullan, *op. cit.*; Gross *et al.*, *op. cit.*; and the Rand Corporation's recent work on the problems of implementation of organizational innovations in public schools.

23. Gross *et al.*, *op. cit.*, pp. 202-203.

24. *Ibid.*, pp. 212-215.

25. Giacquinta, in Kerlinger (ed.), *op. cit.*, p. 200.

26. The newsletter of the New York Organization Development Network, John A. Bromer, Network Coordinator (December 1975), p. 1.

27. R. Beckhard, *Organization Development: Strategies and Models.* (Reading, Mass.: Addison-Wesley, 1969), p. 100. In this chapter, OD and organizational self-renewal are being used interchangeably, even though OD may be conceived by some as one way of bringing about self-renewal. For example, Goodlad, *op. cit.*, discusses self-renewal for public schools and describes a five-year renewal effort in southern California without the use of any of the nomenclature and expertise developed among those trained in OD intervention-strategies.

28. For an excellent description of the early Bethel days, See K. Back, *Beyond Words* (New York: Russell Sage Foundation, 1972), pp. 3-12. An early cl.ssic describing the methods and underlying tactics is E. Schein and W. Bennis, *Personal and Organizational Change Through Group Methods* (New York: John Wiley, 1965).

29. The following are examples of this work. C. Argyris, *Management and Organizational Development: The Path from Xa to Yb* (New York: McGraw-Hill, 1971); W. G. Bennis, *Organization Development: Its Nature, Origins, and Perspectives* (Reading, Mass.: Addison-Wesley, 1969); R. Blake and J. Mouton, *Corporate Excellence Through Grid Organizational Development* (Houston: Gulf Publishing, 1968); R. Blake and J. Mouton, *Building a Dynamic Organization Through Grid Organization Development* (Reading, Mass.: Addison-Wesley, 1969); the entire issue of *The Journal of Applied Behavioral Science* (Vol. 10, No. 4, October-November 1974), special issue on OD practice and theory; and E. Schein, *Process Consultation: Its role in Organization Development* (Reading, Mass.: Addison-Wesley, 1969).

30. At the public school level see R. Owens and C. Steinhoff, *Administering Change in Schools* (Englewood Cliffs, N.J.: Prentice-Hall, 1976); and R. Schmuck and M. Miles (eds.), *Organization Development in Schools* (Palo Alto, Calif.: National Press, 1971). At the higher education level, see the entire issue of the *Journal of Higher Education* (Vol. 44, No. 5, May 1973), which is a special issue devoted to organizational development in higher education.

31. Schmuck and Miles, *op. cit.*, pp. 1-23.

32. D. McGregor, *The Human Side of Enterprise* (New York: McGraw-Hill, 1960).

33. A. Maslow, *Motivation and Personality*, 2nd ed. (New York: Harper & Row, 1970).

34. Blake and Mouton, *op. cit.*

35. From a four-page mimeographed handout. This was part of a team building educational module used by Shonk, a well-known OD consultant, who discussed this module at the October 1975 meeting of the New York OD Network, p. 1.

36. Schmuck and Miles, *op. cit.*, pp. 90, 92.

37. For an earlier general review of the work pertaining to decision-making and problem-solving, see D. Taylor, "Decision Making and Problem Solving," in J. March (ed.), *Handbook of Organizations* (Chicago: Rand McNally, 1965), pp. 48-86.

38. Environment is meant to be the matrix of social and technological forces in which an organization (with its boundaries maintained) is embedded. Many of these forces have the potential for directly or indirectly affecting the organization of focus. Key environmental forces for schools of education are (1) the larger university community, (2) the public schools with which it deals, (3) the federal, state, and locally elected officials or their offices, (4) the economic and political institutions which prevail, and (5) the parents, students, and other members of the community served by the school. Obviously, environment, here, refers to a social, not necessarily geographic, conception. The image of drift is comparable to Washburne's notion of "sociocultural drift," in *Interpreting Social Change in America* (New York: Random House, 1954). W. Moore calls it "evolutionary change," in *Social Change* (Englewood Cliffs, N.J.: Prentice-Hall, 1963). Both of these conceptions apply to larger social units such as societies, but the sense they convey can be applied to formal organizations as well. The two papers included in this collection and which deal directly with organizations as they are embedded in environments are those by Donald J. McCarty and David D. Dill. Both are excellent treatments of various aspects of this area and of the literature bearing on it.

39. For an excellent discussion of the topic of vulnerability as it applies to public schools, see S. Sieber, "Organizational Influences on Innovative Roles," in T. Eidel and J. Kitchel (eds.), *Knowledge Production and Utilization in Educational Administration* (Eugene: Center for the Advanced Study of Educational Administration, University of Oregon, 1968). The papers of both Dill and McCarty are also valuable for conceptualizing the problem for schools of education. A current review of this topic is to be found in H. Aldrich and J. Pfeffer, "Environments of Organizations," in A. Inkeles (ed.), *Annual Review of Sociology: Vol. 2* (Palo Alto, Calif.: Annual Reviews, 1976), pp. 79-105.

40. For both a theoretical and an empirical application to public schools, see R. Herriott and B. Hodgkins, *The Environment of Schooling: Formal Education as an Open Social System* (Englewood Cliffs, N.J.: Prentice-Hall, 1973). Dill deals with schools of education in this way (this volume), Chapter 11.

41. Aldrich and Pfeffer, *op. cit.*, p. 79.

42. D. E. Griffiths, "Administrative Theory and Change in Organizations," in M. Miles, *op. cit.*, p. 431.

43. Cf. other chapters in this volume: Griffiths, Chapter 2; Clark and Guba, Chapter 4; Cyphert and Zimpher, Chapter 5; and Coladarci, Chapter 6.

44. Giacquinta, *op. cit.*, 1973.

45. Kazlow, *op. cit.*

46. Giacquinta and Kazlow, *op. cit.*, 1976.

47. P. Blau, *The Organization of Academic Work* (New York: John Wiley, 1973); T. Parsons, "The Strange Case of Academic Organization," *Journal of Higher Education* (Vol. 42, No. 5, June 1971); and T. Parsons and G. Platt, *The American University* (Cambridge, Mass.: Harvard University Press, 1973).

48. For a basic conceptualization of the organizational and personal factors affecting adult socialization in formal settings designed to influence the attitudes, values, and behaviors of entering recruits, see O. Brim and S. Wheeler, *Socialization After Childhood* (New York: John Wiley, 1966). Their discussion can easily be generalized to settings whether or not they have socialization as a formal goal.

CHAPTER 11

The Deanship: An Unstable Craft[1]

by
WILLIAM R. DILL
New York University

Like medieval galleons, deanships come in many sizes and styles. They range widely in cost and complexity and in accommodations for crew and cannon power. Most are built without designs, improvised instead from memories of previous successes and failures and elaborated to the extent that local initiative and creativity will allow. They are often slow and clumsy craft, hard to maneuver, and not well suited for long voyages in stormy seas. Some, like the great Swedish ship *Wasa* in 1628, have been known to capsize in calm water and sink, flags flying, shortly after leaving the dock.

Snide similes aside, deanships are important and, today, almost universal elements in the organizational structures of American colleges and universities. Yet deanships as offices, deans as people, and "deaning" as the share of time a dean spends in the leadership and administrative roles a deanship calls for have received relatively little attention in studies of higher education. Just as with business and government, it has been more interesting to report on what presidents do than to study the responsibilities and performance of middle management.

Deanships, deans, and "deaning" deserve more study than they have received. Deanships are relatively new as distinct roles in American higher education. The word "dean" has ancient origins in church history, but the evolution of academic deans—unlike that of presidents and professors—is measured in decades rather than centuries. The evolution has been unplanned and shaped in specific instances by all kinds of local forces. This makes the deanship, like middle-management positions in most institutions, an amorphous, variegated, perhaps ultimately indescribable role. Deanships are ephemeral creatures of place, time, discipline, personality, and circumstance. They are not fixed points in the academic firmament.

The deanship as role and deans as personal leaders have, despite time-worn jibes and jokes, achieved remarkable power and status. Today, however, there are as many signs pointing toward an ebbing of powers as toward their further enhancement. The deanship needs help. New demands from various constituencies for miracles of performance are being added to old expectations, which were presumptuous enough! Even without the new demands, the role implies activities for which most deans are poorly prepared. We have to strike a new balance between what we expect and how we approach recruitment, training, information flows, and incentives. Ask, and ye shall receive—but only if you help to seek, find, and develop what you are asking for.

ORIGINS OF THE DEANSHIP AND ITS EVOLUTION

Deanships go back to the 1860s, when the median American college or university had only *four* administrative officers[2] and, in total, was not as large as many university departments are today. Harvard named a dean for its medical school in 1864 with the chief function of maintaining "friendly and charitable intercourse with the students," and within five years there was a dean of the college faculty and talk of a law school dean. Charles Eliot, reflecting on the first year of his long presidency, wrote:

> President Gurney had just been appointed Dean of the College Faculty; but the nature of his functions and influence was not yet visible. Whether the functions of the Dean of the Law School were to be chiefly clerical and eleemosynary or not was not clear to Professors Washburn and Holmes; but at any rate neither of them desired the office.[3]

Eliot's first annual report listed in detail functions that the dean of the faculty should perform. Most are still familiar today. As an extension of the president, the dean had power to preside at faculty meetings in the president's absence, to administer discipline of the college, to handle all petitions from undergraduates to the faculty, and in general to supervise all clerical and administrative business of the college. In later statements, Eliot put more stress on academic leadership than on student counseling or record keeping. The functions of a dean related mostly to his own school, but within that school these functions were "comprehensive." He was to be the president's chief advisor about instruction in his own school; to take responsibility for students, for planning, and for the orderly conduct of faculty business; and for younger faculty, to serve as counselor and friend.[4]

Lincoln University, Syracuse, Fisk, Howard, Pennsylvania, Nebraska, Southern California, and Marquette were among early followers of Harvard's lead. By 1900, one careful source estimates that fewer than 20 percent of colleges and universities had named deans.[5] Not all deans were given the broad responsibilities that Eliot had delegated. One observer comments:

> The deanship was born out of servile tasks which the registrar no longer had time to perform and the faculty regarded as unworthy of the time needed to assemble for deliberation.[6]

Charles Franklin Thwing, president of Western Reserve, barely mentioned deans in his 1900 treatise on academic administration. Twenty-five years later though, he described them as a very significant new feature of the academic scene.[7]

It is not easy to reconstruct how and why deans proliferated. Growth seems to have been a primary factor, but the way first appointments clustered suggests that imitation had something to do with it, too. A dean for the main college arts and sciences faculty clearly was an extension of the presidency—not like department chairmen, an extension of the faculty. Thwing, Eliot, and others all described a symbiosis between dean and president which still has a force in many settings today. A dean and his president did not need to interact a great deal, but the dean was to be someone the president could trust and be comfortable with, someone who, in phraseology from Yale, could exercise "responsibility without interference." Where that trust was broken, the president should have been able to get a new dean.

Deans as extensions of the presidency also show in modes of selection. As recently as 1947, surveys reported only a few cases in which faculty were even involved, much less influential in the selection of deans.[8] Even today, with faculty-student search committees being so common, presidents or other central officers still reserve substantial powers for the final choice.

Diversification probably counted more in the proliferation of professional school deans. Medicine, law, and, to a lesser extent, theology dealt with specialized programs and audiences separate from the mainstream of university or presidential interests. Appointing a dean in some cases gave the schools a new measure of autonomy and individuality; in other cases, substituting a dean for a president marked a step toward integration and subordination of independent fiefdoms within a university structure.

By the 1960s, deans had "arrived." There were more on some campuses than there had been faculty members a century earlier. David Riesman saw deans as the chief remaining force for innovation and constructive change in large university systems.[9] Salmen lauded them as "The most important group of administrators in the whole of higher education, for they are the officers who must translate the aspirations of teachers into an organized program which will fall within the necessities of the budget."[10] Barzun, Corson, and others described roles with substantial creative, policy-oriented, leadership content.[11]

Today, the varieties of deanships range from "A" (for agriculture, architecture, and arts and sciences) at least to "V" (for veterinary medicine). A recent survey gives an interesting, if probably understated, profile on the numbers of deanships by field. In 1,138 institutions, including 705 four-year colleges and universities, there are at least 416 which have deans or directors of arts and sciences. Business and education deanships are next most frequent, as Figure 11.1 shows, with pharmacy and dentistry deans (at 48 and 43, respectively) fewest in number among the categories surveyed. These numbers seem to be conservative; the figure of 392 for business school deans is 20 percent less than the 494 deans listed in the directory of the American Assembly of Collegiate Schools of Business, which in turn is far from a complete listing for the country as a whole.

A FRAMEWORK FOR VIEWING DEANS AND DEANSHIPS
WITHIN THE UNIVERSITY ORGANIZATION

Although deans and deanships have grown in numbers and influence they still have not been studied extensively as a general ingredient of college and university organization. Most studies have been specific to one variety and have dealt with the dean as a person rather than with the deanship as a role. Lists of functions and services read like most job descriptions. Confused by their vagueness, the reader is

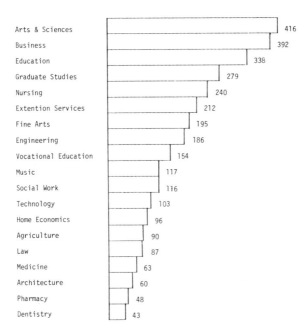

Figure 11.1. A comparative profile of numbers of deans based on numbers of responses to a salary survey conducted by the College and University Personnel Association. Of 1,138 institutions surveyed, 62 percent, or 705, were four-year institutions, and the remainder were two-year institutions. Because the survey did not distinguish deans from directors, it may overstate the numbers of real deanships. On the other hand, comparisons with other lists of deans for specific fields suggest that overall, the numbers probably understate the national totals. From *The Chronicle of Higher Education*, February 17, 1976, p. 4.

likely to view deans as Lewis Carroll regarded one member of the crew who set out to hunt the snark:

> There was also a Beaver that paced on the deck
> Or would sit making lace in the bow,
> He had often (the Bellman said) saved them from wreck,
> Though none of the sailors knew how.

If we view the deanship as a role within colleges and universities, we need a framework with which to describe these organizations. A simple and appropriate framework is the one that builds from the ideas of Chester Barnard and Herbert Simon.[12] They would see the college or university as, in fact, they saw even the more tightly structured, hierarchically defined institutions of business and government:

as assemblages of constituencies, some like faculty inside the boundaries of the institution and others like alumni or charitable foundations outside those boundaries, drawn by various kinds of inducements to affiliate with the organization. Deans, like presidents, help orchestrate the actions which attract the various constituents, hold them together, and draw from them contributions which in totality yield the output of services and products that characterize a university or school.[13]

The deanship, then, is a leadership role with much heavier political and social than hierarchical and technical overtones. Deans, following the Barnard-Simon model, have three major duties. In consultation with at least their most closely bound constituencies, they must pull together a sense of what they have come together to do and a specification of the participants and contributions from them that will enable things to get done. Formalists would talk about setting goals and making plans, but universities are only beginning to call for such levels of formalism and integration.

Second, from commitments and contributions that have already been received, deans must create incentives. These are applied, in turn, as inducements to get continued contributions from some constituents and to invite other contributions by drawing in new participants. Some transactions involve flows of money; others, allocations of human talent and energy; still others, stimulation and transfer of feelings of satisfaction, affiliation, or status. The deanship exists at least to facilitate and in many settings to lead the collection, conversion, and distribution process.

For example, the work of faculty is guided not only to provide the education and assurance of credentials that current students will pay for but also to create an overall ambience that may help attract larger numbers of applicants another year. Funds from students must be rationed not only to keep good teachers but also to hold good janitors and development officers. Deans must study prospective donors to know whether their gifts and social endorsements are most likely to be motivated by promises of recognition, tax benefits, additions to human knowledge, or simple personal satisfaction. Alumni can be challenged to help the school because, as the school gains in reputation, the status and market values of their own degrees may be enhanced.

This same framework also applies to understanding the fragile interdependence between school and society. In normal times, the community "contributes" an extraordinary grant of freedom for the university to explore, to deviate from standard social norms, and to criticize in return for the prestige, the fresh ideas, the young talent, and the independent perspective on other institutions that the university provides. But at other times, when independent university actions threaten the community (e.g., campus tolerance for marijuana or early opposition to the Vietnam War), there is less inducement. The community's grant of freedom is sometimes narrowed in reaction to what it sees as a poor return for its earlier tolerance.

All this juggling of inducements and contributions, though, has another dimension. A dean's third major duty is to help the system achieve efficiency in the transformation of participation and contributions into incentives and the school's ultimate product and services. Efficiency is important because some key contributions are difficult to generate and sustain. If their conversion into inducements and product is done casually and wastefully, there will not be enough to stimulate the same level of contributions next time around. Students, faculty, or supporters will drop away; and the school will decline. The goal of the whole process is to keep the flow of contributions and the efficiency of their conversion at levels more than sufficient to sustain the necessary flow of inducements. So long as contributions exceed inducements, according to the Barnard-Simon model, the organization can survive and grow, but when the need for inducements exceeds the organization's capacity to provide them, the organization will decline and eventually break up.

THE VARIETIES OF DEANSHIPS

Using the Barnard-Simon framework as background, we can begin to ask some useful questions about the nature and diversity of deanships across the university, among colleges and universities, and at different points in time. The framework lets us get at categories which mean more than simply talking about deans of education versus deans of law. It also helps us understand why "deaning" today is different than it was 5 to 10 years ago, and why it will change again over the next decade.

Consider first the simple question of size of the organizational system. How many different constituencies are there, and how large is each? Just within New York University, there is a 1:10 ratio between the smallest and largest deanships in numbers of students served and, roughly, a 1:100 ratio between smallest and largest in terms of budgets managed. Nationwide, the variation would be at least one order of magnitude greater: 1:100 in enrollments and 1:1,000 in budgets. Variations in size of external constituencies may be even greater. A small new school may treat alumni as hardly part of the system, but a large, established school deals with tens of thousands of them. Some schools have a single major source of funding. Others deal with supporters of many kinds from around the world. Specialized facilities and equipment bring suppliers, operators and maintenance staff, and even environmental protection groups into the picture. While an academic unit in the humanities may still need little more than a roof over the log on which Mark Hopkins and his student sit, schools of engineering or medicine have to build and keep changing very complicated assemblages of technology and staff in order that students can learn and professors can do research.

Size and diversity of constituencies help explain whether in examining a deanship one will find:

- A part-time dean, not significantly distinguished from other faculty members of his age and experience in salary or perquisites, furnished at best with a limited amount of administrative support and divided in his activities between "deaning" and significant amounts of teaching and research.

- A full-time dean with assistants and administrative support, perhaps engaged in teaching and research for personal satisfaction or symbolic effect in reinforcing academic credentials more than because there is really time for the diversion.

- An office of the dean, in which a dean and up to a dozen associates work as a team sharing leadership responsibilities over a single faculty and student population. The supporting staff to the office of the dean in a medical school and hospital complex may be larger than the entire faculty of, say, most schools of theology or social work.

We need to know, in particular, more about what goes on in situations where the deanship has evolved into an office or team form with significant amounts of supporting staff. As in businesses which have changed from simple personal chains of command to hierarchies of teams and committees, there are design problems beyond the meshing of personalities to make teams effective and to keep clear lines for communication, influence, and control with other parts of the organizational system. In universities particularly, with relatively weak central objectives and strong centrifugal pulling by diverse constituencies, the office may break down into a forum of competing constituencies rather than achieve a capacity for integration and leadership. In universities, too, movement to an office or team form with surrounding staff has to be handled carefully to avoid deterioration of relationships with constituencies like faculty and students who value personal access to leaders and "flatness" in the organizational structures.

If size and diversity affect the structure and manning of the deanship, a variety of conditions largely internal to the university affects the deanship's nature and powers as a decision center. Perhaps most important are the pressures that the school's educational and research missions and traditional forms of organization put on the deanship to manage the flow of incentives and contributions so that the school "works" from a programmatic point of view. In many small schools of all kinds but even in large schools of law and business which put most of their students through a single, multi-disciplinary-degree program, there is a base for a single faculty in which departmental divisions do not dominate and for something like an *organic* deanship. In other situations such as medicine, with a unifying teaching program on one hand but strong philosophical divisions between clinical and scientific faculty and strong departmental fragmentation in research on the other hand, the deanship operates in *mixed mode*. The dean deals with strong separatist forces on some things but still has to play an integrative role overall. In arts, sciences, and engineering where departmental lines separate faculty interests, degree programs, and research commitments, the deanship is often at best a *balancing act*, allocating resources, trying to stimulate cooperation, and adjudicating competing departmental claims.

Deanships also vary greatly in the kinds of powers their occupants are allowed to exercise. From the top, there is great variance in the willingness and ability of presidents and other central officers to delegate. Delegation is likely to be fuller in periods of enrollment and budgetary stability than in periods of uncertainty and change. Delegation is likely to be fuller when the deans rather than the presidents control major sources of funding or when the school in question is located some distance from the main campus.

From the surroundings, a great deal depends on the degree to which a school shares faculty, students, facilities, or other resources with other schools and on the degree to which a school exists to serve others, as many liberal arts units do to provide preparatory work for undergraduate professional programs. Deans of law and medicine may be at one end of a scale of horizontal independence because of the high degree of self-containment of students, faculty, and programs. Even on a matter like faculty unionization, these schools are generally not pressed by either side to join a general university bargaining unit. Deans of arts and science whose budgets depend on enrollments attracted by colleges of education and business, and conversely, deans of business whose promotion and tenure recommendations must pass review by arts and science review committees sometimes feel themselves in very dependent positions.

All deans can manipulate flows of inducements and contributions by personal intervention with faculty and students, but they vary widely in the degree to which they influence financial flows by helping to plan and administer budgets. Some deans still are only limited extensions of a president or other central officer, with access to information and powers restricted so that they have almost nothing to do with budgets. Others have little involvement in planning the budgets for their units but are expected to administer the budgets which central administration sets. Still others are well informed and actively involved in the process of setting budgets, sometimes not just for their own units but, on a consultative basis, for other parts of the university as well. Finally, some really have almost complete financial autonomy from central administration; they plan revenues and expenses and guarantee, at risk of their jobs, to keep things in balance. Since money is the form in which a major share of incoming "contributions" are represented and the medium through which, directly and indirectly, a large part of the "inducements" come, degree of involvement in the process which plans and allocates flow of funds for future periods becomes a touchstone for distinguishing strong deanships from weak ones.

Discussion of budgeting also turns our attention to constituencies outside the organization. If there are truly differences between deanships in public versus private institutions, a great deal of the difference rests on the way that budgets are put together and budgetary results assured. In the public college or university, what matter most are the central administration, state agencies, and legislature, supplemented in increasing numbers of cases by faculty and staff collective bargaining units. The dean is first and foremost a negotiator. He works within formulae and bureaucratic structures to negotiate the best allocation he can for his school and, sometimes, outside the bureaucracy to find incentives which will generate support from political forces within the state. The major effort is in securing the budgetary commitment, because once it is set, except for the extraordinary circumstances we have seen recently in a few states, it is a dependable commitment on which to run the school.

In an endowment-dependent, enrollment-secure private university, deans may engage in similar negotiations, but the parties with whom they negotiate for a budget commitment are more clearly confined to the officers of the university itself. The dean's special leverage lies in his ability to cultivate his own constituency of sources for endowment income and other sustaining gifts.

In a tuition-dependent private university, particularly during periods of uncertainty about enrollments, the negotiations are still important, but less central. They represent an important forecasting, planning, and allocation effort, but the dean's attention must also turn to the constituencies of students and prospective students whose tuition payments are needed if revenue projections are to be met.

The contrast may be greatest, say, between the dean of a public university school of education or social work which gets almost all its funding from state and federal agencies and the dean of a private university school of business whose budget comes entirely from what students pay and what corporations and individuals can be persuaded to contribute. The former might not even know what a "development officer" does; the latter is not likely to have thought about hiring an assistant for legislative relations. Deans of education or social work, in fact, can be so dependent on the same state programs that private and public schools often organize together and hire staff to represent them in the state capital. Deans of business or theology would find little reason to get together with deans of counterpart schools on a state-wide basis.

Other aspects of a school's relationships with external constituencies are also important in shaping the deanship. Some schools, particularly professional schools, have stable ties with outside groups to accomplish important teaching or research objectives. The medical school needs such close links with a hospital that it often winds up running one. Schools of education need arrangements for practice teaching. Schools of business want sites for research and case studies and reliable sources of students for part-time programs and executive seminars. Schools of engineering seek outside links both for long-term research affiliations and for providing students with internship or cooperative study experiences.

When a constituency which provides links for teaching and research is also a constituency that represents a major source of funding for the school, as happens with corporations and business schools, this even has an effect on the places a university looks for deans. Although good statistics are not at hand, it seems safe to observe that business schools are much more likely to appoint as dean someone who has spent part of his career at high levels of corporate life than schools of education, law, or medicine are to choose someome who has not been a lifetime academic. Where education and medicine reach outside, they are more likely to look for government rather than corporate service to match their chief funding sources. Liberal arts deans recruited from other than pure academic backgrounds are quite rare.

Alumni for some schools are an important external constituency well beyond their fund-giving potential. In medicine and dentistry, there may be frequent cycles of reaffiliation with the school for continuing education. For schools of business and education, alumni form an important part of the network for student placement and often come to expect the school to provide career-long help on job changes. For undergraduate colleges, the alumni may be a constructive force to mobilize in recruiting new students.

Finally, some deanships carry greater expectations than others in terms of responsibility for handling relationships with the broader public. Because of the tightly-knit nature of the professions, involving both the requirements of university training and the licensure, deans of law and medicine are more likely to be drawn in as spokesmen and defenders when the profession is under public attack than deans of business or education are when something goes wrong in the corporations or in the public schools. Schools of the performing arts make a major contribution today to the preparation of actors, dancers, and musicians, but the public is so much more conscious of individual performers than of their origins that the schools seldom get blamed for failure or credited for successes.

These suggestions for untangling the many varieties of deans and deanships are far from complete. The analysis should go ahead but should rest, as we have tried to rest it here, on some underlying concepts about the workings of colleges and universities as organizations. It should recognize, as we have tried to point out, that traditional labels, based on the names of schools, help very little and that in studying deans and deanships today, we are often looking not only at the behavior of individuals but also at the behavior of some complicated work teams.

COMING CHANGES IN THE DEANSHIP

Quotes earlier in this paper made deans sound like the most important leaders of the university. Even in the earliest days of deaning, presidents like Eliot and Thwing suggested that deans' tenure generally ought outlast the president's to provide stability for a college or university during periods of presidential transition. Clearly the prominence and power of deanships have grown. Yet today it is possible that they are reaching their peak.

As the first major subordinate position created to augment the leadership that presidents gave to faculty and students, the deanship is now just one of many. More and more, in large institutions especially, the deanship is a middle-level position, sometimes remote from all three of the major parties who want to maintain direct relations on many things without intermediaries. Above the deans, one now finds provosts, academic vice-presidents, budget and development officers, chancellors, and a host of other officials. In a multi-campus system, the dean may not even have unique responsibility within the system for a profession or range of disciplines. He may simply be one of several deans of the same kind of school contending with each other for attention and support.

The deans also become more remote from faculty and students in large systems. A job which was first created to insure guidance and counseling to young faculty and personal attention to students has now become so complex that many of these functions have been delegated again. Division heads and program directors in some settings complicate the links to faculty, and deans in large schools have to make a special effort to reserve time for meaningful involvement with students, above and beyond those who have protests to register against faculty and administration.

As deans drift more toward the ill-defined "middle" of academic administration, they and others (like division heads and vice-presidents) in that position are sometimes little more than spectators in the campus power game. Presidents and governing boards have been pressed to create tighter management of institutions to help them survive the enrollment and financial crises that lie ahead. At the same time, students and faculty—feeling these and other pressures and being part of a national restlessness toward more egalitarianism in organizations—are creating counter pressures. The students are largely seeking guarantees of participation and influence on the campus. Faculty members work sometimes for internal procedural change but also turn sometimes to unions and collective bargaining. In this interplay, the dean is more likely to be seen as a potential intermediary than as a primary contender.

The main threat, though, is that the deanship will be outflanked because deans and others who choose the deans and set the limits within which they operate will not let the job change as fast as it could to meet new needs. The deanship remains, first and foremost, an academic-management role, but to use the distinction that Selznick made,[14] there continues to be a need for more emphasis on academic leadership rather than academic administration. Today's best ways of doing education and research will not be best tomorrow. There is no field and no profession in which the rate of change in subject matter, teaching focus and technique, and interrelationships with other fields is not increasing. Yet to an increasing degree, we will have to meet new challenges for flexibility and change, not by adding to staff and resources as we have in the past but by reassigning and retraining staff and by difficult reallocation of a diminishing resource pool. Deans, if they are to survive as major figures on the academic scene, have to earn the compliment that Riesman paid them. They must become active leaders in reflection, analysis, proposal making, and action to set their schools and the university off in new directions.

Beyond traditional concepts of academic leadership, though, there are added challenges. Whether or not involved in the university's budget processes, every dean must begin learning the relationships between economics and education. At a minimum, to protect his school during a period when resources are being rationed, it is a matter of self-defense. More than self-defense, however, the deans have a stake in building systems for financial administration of universities if universities as we know them are to survive. We cannot continue with accounting systems that take no account of depreciation and replacement costs, with planning systems that view three years as long-term, with budgets so fragmented that no one has a dependable bottom-line, and with control systems whose guiding axiom is that there is no legitimate way to measure productivity. At the same time, wholesale importation of experts and methods from business and government will not provide viable solutions, either. New answers must be developed within academe, and deans must choose whether they will be part of that process.

Deans must also become better personnel managers. We in the universities have been a main force in American society for raising everyone's expectations about rationality, due process, participation, justice, and humanity in the way that the world works. Our teaching and our research have contributed considerably to the emerging respectability of unionism, the civil and human rights movement that now has spawned affirmative action regulations for us as well as for southern bus companies and lunch counters, and the growth of organizational and legal protections against arbitrary managerial action. At the same time, as our institutions have grown and become more impersonal, we face many of the same problems of delivering on those promises that corporations and government agencies do. But we were the advocates, and we have a special responsibility to learn how to deliver.

It is no longer just a task of changing a dean's personal behavior. He has to be able now to improve the tone and performance of an entire school organization: advisors dealing with students, chairmen with secretaries, tenured with probationary professors, clerks with prospective applicants. Again, he is manipulating inducements in order to upgrade the quality of contributions but doing so in ways that often may seem to violate the old atomistic traditions under which members of the faculty, in particular, have been accustomed to operate. The goal of collective civility and humaneness in a system which still must respect and protect individuals who combine talent and cantankerousness will not be easy to reach.

Deans, finally, are charged with keeping their schools socially responsive and responsible. One can argue fervently about society's need to tolerate universities as detached islands of study and contemplation, but the truth is that we have built most of the current establishment of higher education in this country on aggressive promises of relevant service. Universities, like corporations, have the right to tell society what they want to do and to remind it about what they can and cannot do well.[15] In the final analysis, though, universities and corporations exist at the sufferance of society, and today, for both, the clear message back seems to be that for what society is permitting, it wants more in return.

Forget about the difficult questions of initiatives for community outreach in programs beyond the university's normal scope. Consider only some questions about whose relevance to traditional university missions there would be wide agreement.

- We are seeing today a substantial shift of students away from liberal arts to professional curricula, a disaster for arts and sciences budgets but a boon to fields like law, business, and public administration. Language and culture programs are disappearing at a time when it is clear that more graduates than ever will travel and work overseas. Biology, literature, history, and anthropology are pinched while organizations all seem to be complaining that the primary barriers to progress are human rather than technological. Deans of thriving schools clearly have an obligation to fight for the resources needed to do their current tasks well, but what obligations do they have to volunteer subsidies to make sure that other key disciplines, currently in trouble, keep their vitality and quality for the future?

We continue to operate with crude and rather narrowly validated standards for admission. Status in academe still depends far more on the quality, in terms of tested aptitude and earlier grades, of students taken in than on any other input characteristics or than on any measure of the educational transformation accomplished with them while enrolled. Admissions criteria, at best, predict less than half the variance of students' performances while in school and have little demonstrated relationship to accomplishments or social contribution in later life. To the extent that successful completion of our programs become prerequisites for entry to certain careers, have we done enough to insure that our ways of handling applicants contributes as it should to the achievement of equal opportunity in American society?[16]

- When approached to contribute to the solution of community problems, we often seem puzzlingly unresponsive—in comparison, say, to some corporations—to those who ask. They do not grasp that there is little slack in our budgets and that there are no tax incentives for us to make "charitable contributions." Where a corporation can provide a seasoned expert and volunteer his time while paying his regular salary, we can offer seasoned experts who usually charge private consulting fees for undertaking such service. Where a corporate executive can use hierarchical authority to find volunteers, deans operate within a tradition that claims little control over the discretionary time of faculty members. How much responsibility should a dean take for organizing voluntary school or individual efforts on community problems, or how often does he undertake only those things for which support to do the work has been provided?

- If current predictions about demand and capacity are correct, the number of colleges and universities is likely to shrink over the next decade. The alternative to a "shake-out" is a massive campaign to insure levels of governmental funding that will allow us to keep idle capacity in reserve. If a shake-out comes, it can be done by planned cut-backs or as a consequence of competitive battles for survival. Society has never made it clear whether it means universities to operate as a planned, cooperative network or as a decentralized, competitive system. How hard should deans fight for public funding, given other valid demands on society's resources? What balance of planned decision and competitive happenstance should we advocate for a time of cut-backs, both to insure as low transition costs as we can and to leave in place the strongest possible structure when reductions have been completed?

- We, like the press, place high value on the university's role in housing critics. Individuals within universities comment with verve and with effect. Yet some critics of universities say we are irresponsible. We became so indignant about Vietnam, perhaps because our students faced the real threat of being drafted for service there, that we could hardly control the debate; yet we have taken very little leadership in getting the country to face up to world energy and food shortages, perhaps because for us, too, the realities of shortage still seem remote. We seem sometimes more willing to tear down than to teach how to build. We are accused of promoting theories and ideologies about how the world ought to be run with active disdain for protests from experienced practitioners that the "real world" is more complicated than our theories assume. We know that individuals or groups within the university sometimes pull their punches in what they say or write to keep favor with their colleagues or with an outside benefactor. To put it simply, how do we oversee the exercise of academic freedom and the development of self-critical faculties within the university to make sure that the public remains satisfied that academic freedom is an important privilege and that we are using it well?

SELECTION, DEVELOPMENT, AND DIRECTION OF DEANS

As this review of developments suggests, the deanship is not becoming an easier role to fill. Events and constituencies seem to be calling for stronger leadership, yet within a kind of organization that has never accepted hierarchy gladly and that is presently the place for intense debates about the locus and exercise of managerial power. Filling the deanship in many instances means naming a team rather than simply choosing an individual.

Yet how do we go about selecting deans? A recent scanning of advertisements in the *Chronicle of Higher Education* shows most listing similar criteria, and in similar order:

1. An earned doctorate.
2. Experience which demonstrates capability as a teacher and scholar.
3. Often, but not universally, commitment to particular values and philosophies important to the school seeking the candidate.
4. Evidence of administrative ability.

Schools of business and education sometimes break the pattern by moving administrative training and experience as high as second on the list of qualifications, but even these schools are vague about the kinds which they think have value

Surveys over the years confirm that previous managerial experience does rank low as a necessary credential. For various deanships, the surveys show that from one-half to two-thirds of new deans have had no previous managerial experience. With rare exception, when there is experience, it has been as a department chairman, a subordinate dean, or an administrator outside the university where the primary tasks were operational, not planning and policy-setting ones.

The general tendency to stress academic background which fits the school's disciplines and programs adds further to the problem. Deans of law, business, education, and public administration are likely to have had some relevant educational preparation even if they have not had managerial experience. Most other kinds of deans are likely to have had no managerial education whatsoever.

Some note should be taken of the committees which conduct the search. In recent years, the big fight has been over participation: to reduce the president's influence and to transfer powers to representatives of the faculty and student body. For many schools, the degree of faculty-student participation is still an issue. However, other schools now seem to be entering an era where the question is whether the president should have any voice at all. Generalizations are dangerous, but the thrust of this essay has been that in terms of both historical precedent and future need, the dean should be more president than department head. Committees which ignore the managerial dimension may get a strong academic advocate but, when financial and organizational dimensions have been brought into the debate, a weak defender of the things they want him to advocate.

Once the dean is on the job, educational development opportunities are minimal. There is rarely the kind of support at higher levels or the kind of investment in building a relationship of collegiality and trust among deans that would generate collective management development efforts within a college or university. There has been some effort by national deans' associations to fill the gap. Perhaps the best program, with the most carefully developed educational content, has been put together by deans of medicine. The American Assembly of Collegiate Schools of Business runs seminars on a regular schedule for both "new" and "old" deans, with other deans doing most of the teaching. Many schools of administration and a number of outside consultants have developed seminars to which they would like to attract deans, but acceptance and participation for most of these remain low.

Universities may be paralyzed by their own mythology that those who inhabit the halls have extraordinary skill and motivation for self-education. Not only for administrators who have to grow to handle new tasks but also for faculties who need to extend or change their discipline, universities are going to have to learn to do what they have commended to other organizations. They are going to have to develop internally planned programs to help deans, other administrators, and faculty grow to meet the demands of their jobs.

Some of the best training for a dean comes through the way information and incentive systems work on a day-to-day basis. Deanships are quite varied around the country in the degree to which they involve access to both the primary academic and the financial performance data that bear on school and university decisions. On the academic side, it is still more common to find information about faculty work assignments than about results through tracking the competition of students for places in a class, their reactions to teachers and courses, or measures of what they have learned. On the financial side, it is more common to find deans handling expense budgets for their schools than it is to find them carrying through integrated analysis of revenue and expense flows for both their schools and the university as a whole. We are still shy of concepts, technology, and experience for academic information systems that match the ones that have been built for some business organizations.

Yet even with limited access to information and limited resources for its analysis, deans learn from working with such data. Experience at New York University suggests clearly that deans become more effective leaders for their own schools and more effective advisors to central administration when presented with detailed information that helps them assemble balanced pictures of the ingredients to academic and financial performance. Simulation models, say, of the student attrition or faculty-tenure streams can help in planning. Reports that have highlighted imbalances in the use of facilities or faculty resources have led to models for more efficient allocation and scheduling at some universities. Many possibilities exist for helping deans and the faculty groups with whom they consult to develop further as managers by improving the information and models to which they have access.

Beyond the power of information lies the power of incentives. Here academic traditions pose real dilemmas. Deans are still regarded by faculty and others primarily as academic leaders. Their successes as administrators do not clearly cumulate as credentials for the next job. Such successes help little if a dean's aim is to return to research and teaching. In fact, over-devotion to managerial tasks may mean real loss of ground with respect to one's professional field. Even if the next goal is something higher in academic administration, search committees are likely to seek those candidates for provosts' or presidents' jobs who had managed, while deaning, to add to both their managerial and their professional lustre. People still apologize for being managers in the college or university in ways and for reasons that most business or government executives simply would not understand.

The dubious esteem in which academic administrators are held gets reflected, too, in salary schedules. Deans' salaries do relate to budgets, enrollments, and complexity of job and probably as well to salary levels of the faculty from which they are drawn. Medical school deans are the best paid, at an average double the average for the lowest categories of deans and well above the salaries of many college and university presidents. Dentistry, business, engineering, and law seem to come next, but well down in level from medicine. For the top 10 and the top 40 deans in different fields, the ratios of median salaries are shown in Table 11.1.

However well some deans' salaries may compare with others', or with salaries for non-academic administrators within the university, comparisons with salaries for the professoriate from which most deans come do not look as favorable. In business schools, the mean salary for deans of accredited schools is 28 percent above the mean 9-month salary for full professors of those schools, but with deaning usually a year-round activity, only 2 percent above the mean salary for professors on 12-month appointments.[17] A dean often enjoys perquisites and expense allowances that few professors get; however, on the other hand, just as his time for research and teaching is cramped, his discretionary time to add to his income by consulting and professional activity is also limited. The limits come not only from time

Table 11.1. Ratios of Median Salaries for Deans in Different Fields[1]

Field	Ratio of Median Salaries (Vocational Education =1.0)	
	10 Best-Paid Deans	40 Best-Paid Deans
Medicine	2.0+	2.0
Dentistry	1.7	
Business Law Engineering	} 1.5−	} 1.6
Arts and Sciences Graduate Studies	} 1.3	
Education Pharmacy	}	} 1.4
Extension Services[2]	1.2	
Architecture Social Work	} 1.3	
Nursing Agriculture Fine Arts Home Economics Music	} 1.2	} 1.2
Technology	1.1	
Vocational Education	1.0	1.0

[1]Derived from a salary survey of 1,138 institutions by the College and University Personnel Association. The rankings are approximate because they derive from frequency distributions rather than from specific data, but they show relative standing of different kinds of deans than the medians of the original survey, which were not adjusted for variance (43 to 416) in numbers of deans and schools reported per field (refer back to Figure 11.1).

[2]The only kind of dean with different relative standing in both the "10 best" and the "40 best" lists.

Source: *The Chronicle of Higher Education*, February 17, 1976, pp. 4-5.

pressures of his job but also from his duty to set a responsible example of full commitment to the college or university.

Salary levels by field seem generally to be set according to the principle that the dean comes from the faculty, is not to be encouraged to feel superior to the faculty, and should be able to afford to return to the faculty. The leadership differential is smaller and performance incentives that might supplement base salary are much less common than at comparable levels of management in many business settings.

Monetary incentives in universities have rarely been designed to encourage administrative commitment and excellence to the same degree that they have been focused on academic commitment and excellence. Without detracting from the primacy of the academic tasks, some greater attention to administrative inducements may be in order. There may also be room to experiment, as businesses have done, with special kinds of rewards beyond base salaries for deans and faculty to encourage changes in direction and to stimulate improvements in performance.

CONCLUSION

A hundred years ago, deans were rare, almost accidental characters on the American academic scene. Their proliferation and the growth of the functions and powers of the deanship have been major developments in the years since. They provide important kinds of personal leadership in the college or small university, and, in large university systems, they are perhaps the senior administrative officer with whom faculty and students can feel any close identification and contact. Deaning remains an attractive occupation even though the salary and perquisites that go with the job do not match the time and, in many cases, the outside income that a top professor gives up to take the job.

Yet the deanship remains an insecure job, and deans may be becoming an endangered species. The role has moved from an extension of the presidency to a more ambiguous middle-management position. Many new tasks have been added to the job description, but few have been taken away or successfully delegated to other levels. Both tempers and tenures can get short as incumbents wrestle with all the things they are expected to do.

We can help define deanships more sensibly if we begin to study the role across fields and within a framework which treats the deanship in an organizational context. We can plan for better deanships if we invest more energy into studies of ways in which the role may be changing. We can have better deans if we look more carefully at what the job involves and then revise selection practices, develop training and development programs, and modify flows of information and incentives to suit. We may not be able to find better men and women for the role, but we can certainly improve their background and preparation to enable them to handle it well.

NOTES

1. Based on a Presentation to a Research Development Seminar co-sponsored by the University Council for Educational Administration and New York University's School of Education, Health, Nursing, and Arts Professions, January 26-28 1976.

2. Earl James McGrath, *The Evaluation of Administrative Offices in Institutions of Higher Education in the United States from 1860 to 1933* (Chicago, 1938), pp. 190-193. Cited in Frederick Rudolph, *The American College and University* (New York: Vintage Books, 1965), p. 435.

3. From Charles W. Eliot, *A Late Harvest* quoted by Charles Franklin Thwing, *The College Presidency* (New York: Macmillian, 1926), p. 46.

4. Charles W. Eliot, *University Administration* (Boston: Houghton Mifflin, 1909), pp. 242-245.

5. Merle Scott Ward, *Philosophies of Administration Current in the Deanship of the Liberal Arts College* (New York: Columbia Teachers College, 1934), pp. 21-23. It should be noted that other estimates had deans in as many as two-thirds of all colleges and universities by 1900. See, for example, James A. Perkins, *The University as an Organization* (New York: McGraw-Hill, 1973).

6. J. M. Bevan, "The Deanship," *Liberal Education* (Vol. 3, No. 3, October 1967), p. 344.

7. Cf. *The College Presidency* with his earlier book, *College Administration* (New York: Century, 1900).

8. Ruth L. Higgins, "The Functions of the Academic Dean," *Association of American Colleges Bulletin* (Vol. 33, No. 2, May 1947), pp. 393-399.

9. David Riesman, *Constraint and Variety in American Education* (Lincoln: University of Nebraska Press, 1956).

10. Stanley Salmen, *Duties of Administrators in Higher Education* (New York: Macmillan, 1971).

11. Jacques Barzun, *The American University* (New York: Harper & Row, 1968); John J. Corson, *Governance of Colleges and Universities* (New York: McGraw-Hill, 1960); Frances H. Horn, "The Dean and the President," *Liberal Education* (Vol. 50, No. 4, December 1964), pp. 463-475; Victor E. Hanzeli, "The Educational Leadership of the Academic Dean," *Journal of Higher Education* (Vol. 37, No. 8, November 1966), pp. 421-428; J. W. Gould, *The Academic Deanship* (New York: Teachers College Press, 1964); John Murray, "Schizophrenia in the Front Office," *Journal of Legal Education* (Vol. 24, No. 3, 1972), pp. 358-361; Jerald C. Bachman, "Faculty Satisfaction and the Dean's Influence," *Journal of Applied Psychology* (Vol. 52, No. 1, January 1968), pp. 55-61; Miriam B. Conant, "The Academic Dean as a Subversive Bureaucrat," *Educational Record* (Vol. 48, No. 3, Summer 1967), pp. 276-284; Bernard Berelson, *Graduate Education in the United States* (New

York: McGraw-Hill, 1960); Nicholas Demarath *et al.*, *Power, Presidents, and Professors* (New York: Basic Books, 1967); J. Douglas Brown, *The Liberal University* (New York: McGraw-Hill, 1969).

12. Chester Barnard, *The Functions of the Executive* (Cambridge, Mass.: Harvard University Press, 1938); and Herbert A. Simon, *Administrative Behavior* (New York: Macmillan, 1947).

13. For other more recent efforts which try this kind of framework to describe the workings of university administration, see Michael D. Cohen and James G. March, *Leadership and Ambiguity: The American College President* (New York: McGraw-Hill, 1974); Warren Bennis, *The President's Mid-Year Report* (Cincinnati, Ohio: University of Cincinnati, March 15, 1975); and Edward Gross and Paul W. Grambsch, *Changes in University Organization: 1964-1971* (New York: McGraw-Hill, 1974). Gross and Grambsch are particularly interesting because they try to map the constituencies and rank them by relative influence.

14. Phillip Selznick, *Leadership in Administration* (Evanston, Ill.: Row, Peterson, 1957).

15. As the great debates of a few years ago about university governance demonstrated, there are pure and mixed conceptions of university mission which compare with the debates between seekers of profit and seekers of social service and responsibility in business. Some like Sidney Hook argue for a cleanly restricted role: "The university is for learning as an airplane is for flying. This is its elemental and defining purpose." Others want the university more involved with the community: "Events in recent years have shown clearly that universities constitute powerful and prestigious institutions in modern American life. Power consists not only of capital assets but of the intellect and energies of faculty and students and when effectively marshalled and sensibly used, these resources can have a forceful impact on the molding of national policy. It seems to me immoral—particularly in times of national crisis—to stand aside and fail to use that power and prestige when it can contribute to the solution of grave national problems." (Quotes from internal working papers of a New York University task force on governance in 1970.)

16. For a recent critical analysis of both the university and society on this topic, see Samuel Bowles and Herbert Gintis, *Schooling in Capitalist America* (New York: Basic Books, 1976).

17. *1975-1976 Salary Survey* (St. Louis: American Assembly of Collegiate Schools of Business, 1975).

From Here to There

by
DANIEL E. GRIFFITHS
DONALD J. McCARTY

It seems quite clear that although traditional research approaches have the potential of providing a significant amount of knowledge about the deanship, there is a great deal about the deanship that eludes conventional methodology. The book ends on a brief review of each chapter and a presentation of problems, issues, and situations not caught in the research net of the first 11 chapters.

SUMMARY

Culbertson set the tone for the book in calling for formally tested or scientific knowledge. Kuhn's, *The Structure of Scientific Revolutions*, forms the basis of Culbertson's approach to generating knowledge. He argues that the administration of higher education, as a field of study, is in a pre-paradigm state and that steps must be taken to move to the paradigmatic state. These steps include reducing the diversity of research perspectives among higher education professors; using more concepts from social science disciplines; establishing national networks of communication; building consensus on the parameters of the field; encouraging acceptance among scholars of the importance of scientific generalizations, models, and values; and fostering movement towards theory-based research in the direction of shared examples. Culbertson then delineated domains of inquiry which form most of Part III of this book:

1. *Baseline Data About the Deanship*—who deans are; their background, professional experiences, and career patterns; the settings in which they work; comparisons among various types.
2. *Deans as Individuals*—personality characteristics, needs, value orientations, motivations, and conceptual styles; personal histories; others' perceptions of their personalities.
3. *Deans as Individuals-in-Organizations*—the role of the dean, including what deans do and are expected to do; their role orientations; leader behavior; small group interaction patterns.
4. *Schools of Education as Complex Organizations*—structural characteristics of schools of education, including governance and decision-making structures, communication patterns, and organizational complexity; bureaucratization; policy implementation.
5. *Schools of Education as Organizations-in-Environments*—typologies of environments; the organizational suprastructure; policy and policy making; boundary-spanning mechanisms; system openness/closedness; influential external groups; social forces.
6. *Organizational Change and the Deanship*—diffusion of innovations in higher education; research, development, and diffusion structures in higher education; the dean as change agent; strategies and tactics for change; planning mechanisms; the implementation of innovations within schools and colleges.

In reviewing the literature on the administration of higher education, Griffiths concluded that the administrative system is, in many universities, quite advanced in its use of management science, but that the operative (academic) system lags far behind. He concluded that the study of the administration of higher education was similar to the study of educational administration in the early 1950s. He advocated the development of research which would form the basis for theorizing. Griffiths criticized the paradigm now used for the study of higher education administration, finding it inappropriate and inadequate. He reviewed the evidence and concluded that higher education is a special case and general theories have little applicability to the administration of universities. Research done on other types of institutions should be applied to higher education only when it meets a set of criteria such as that developed by Katzell. Griffiths advanced the argument that while the present theoretical base is not sufficient to allow anyone to operate on it, exclusively, theoretical knowledge should be developed using what is commonly called the scientific method. And last, Griffiths argued for what is a recurring theme in this book, that is, research should be done on what administrators actually do. This means, methodologically, that observation must replace questionnaires as the dominant research tool.

Silver's chapter is devoted to a discussion of problems and strategies of doing research on the deanship. Problems are presented under four headings: financial constraints, competition for resources, theory-practice dichotomy, and interpersonal conflict. The strategies are discussed under four patterns: high centralization, moderate centralization, moderate decentralization, and high decentralization. She concludes that moderate decentralization has the highest probability of success. She also discussed the need for coordination among domains of research and judged that the two most likely to succeed would be a steering committee composed of the domain leaders and a UCEA staff member and a steering committee made up of a UCEA staff member and leading educators not members of domain task forces.

The Clark and Guba chapter is a report of a national study of schools, colleges, and departments of education. It is the first such study and presents very useful insights into professional education. Clark and Guba present first, a set of demographic data not previously available and second, a series of generalizations based on their visits to campuses and their study of questionnaire returns. Some of the more interesting generalizations (from a research and theory perspective) are as follows: SCDEs exist in a strongly idiographic culture; SCDEs have less autonomy in operation and decision-making than most graduate and professional units at the university; national, bureaucratic decision-making models are generally not used in SCDEs and IHEs; R and D, service and change programs in schools and responsiveness to new missions are generally not integral to the SCDE; most SCDEs have minimal budgets in comparison with other units in IHEs; and while SCDE faculties feel they ought to do R and D, few do with resulting personal dissatisfaction and role dissonance. In addition, Clark and Guba offer a number of insights gained from the data.

Cyphert and Zimpher reported the results of the first national study done on education deans. Using a 20 percent stratified random sample they questioned deans on their personal characteristics, professional backgrounds, and professional activities. They also inquired into the perceptions and role expectations which superordinates have of deans. The Cyphert, Zimpher study provides baseline data which can be used in future studies of the deanship.

Although a scholar steeped in nomothetically oriented inquiry, Coladarci argues for a healthy intellectual agnosticism about a science of administrative behavior applicable to deans. He recommends that encouragement be given to case studies of deans and deanships in contexts that are maximally inclusive of the known and presumed relevant parameters of person, inter-person, institutional process, and agenda. What are the reasons for the rejection of the time-honored canons of behavioral research? According to Coladarci, there are three important considerations which call for a shift in emphasis. First, deans live and work in institutional contexts exhibiting marked differences; second, there is the multivariate reality of administrative roles; and finally, the ways in which institutional and personal characteristics bear upon the role and performance of a dean probably vary with the differing contexts for the role and performance. He, of course, is not advocating a return to the single-person case study replete with anecdotal data with limited generalizability. Instead, he is seeking a collective or research team approach where political, economic, sociological, psychological, and anthropological insights may be directed toward inductive quests for hypotheses about relationships between and interactions among performance, personal attributes, institutional characteristics, and the like. There is practically no research knowledge about the relationships between characteristics of the dean and performance in the role. Coladarci's suggestions offer hope that we may be on the threshold of a new line of revealing inquiry.

Ryan asserts that the behavior of deans as individuals-in-organizations cannot be understood without prior understanding of the nature of the organizations that they inhabit. She reinforces this starting point by demonstrating that institutions of higher education are characterized by a dual organizational structure, both arms of which have some bureaucratic and some professional attributes. Ryan illuminates her analysis by frequent references to her own considerable research in this domain. The idea that there are two separate systems (administrative and academic) operating in the university setting is an easy oversimplification which she quickly puts to rest. Both are present, but they are in constant interaction, and the distinction between them blurs. The dual organizational structure in higher education forces deans to establish different coping strategies than middle management employs in business, government, and the military. For instance, the dean's potential role stress arises primarily from tensions emanating from sub-units rather than from hierarchically derived expectations. The basic governance unit, the department, is relatively autonomous; moreover, among and within the sub-units under the dean's control great normative diversity exists. Physical education and educational administration, for example, are likely to approach issues from different contexts. Unity of purpose may be difficult if not impossible to achieve. In fact, Ryan's narrative implies that deans might well be advised not to attempt to coordinate their diverse sub-units; a better strategy, it seems, is to deal directly with one sub-unit at a time. This provocative essay closes with a remarkable series of researchable questions growing out of the well-known Katz and Kahn open-system model. Different methodologies are suggested including survey-type instrumentation and qualitative field studies. Students and scholars interested in pursuing this line of research will benefit from a careful study of Ryan's formulations.

The organizational behavior literature is vast but much of it has not been adapted very successfully to higher education. David Dill sets out to correct that failing. He systematically explores how the sub-systems of schools of education and the interaction between them might be researched. Dill explains why schools of education are complex organizations; moreover, he employs an open-system perspective to identify five critical sub-systems: goals and values, technological, structural, psychosocial, and managerial. Not only does the author present a definitive short course in organization theory, but he also illuminates his narrative by illustrative research questions. The thrust of this intriguing essay is to stress the interrelated nature of the sub-systems; a change in one sub-system generates a change in the others. Dill believes that the environmental context in which a school of education operates is unusually important, and he quotes approvingly writers who state that drastic changes are initiated by external forces. Like many of our other contributors, Dill believes that intensive and longitudinal case studies of these interrelated sub-systems are likely to be more informative than cross-sectional data gathered in one-shot surveys.

How do schools of education respond to uncertainty in their environment? McCarty reviews contemporary theory on this topic and reports that organizations respond to ambiguity in their external relationships by either attempting to gain control over the situation by co-optative or bargaining mechanisms or trying to shield the organization against these outside contingencies. He suggests that in this field of study, useful concepts that capture the significant issues in organization-environment interaction are still in the development stage and that adequate data simply do not exist against which conceptual frameworks or tentative hypotheses might be tested. McCarty further advocates that we must do more than conventional survey research. His preference is for field studies where careful observation and participant observation research may be carried out. Case studies utilizing ethnographic methods are needed to develop a substantial descriptive data base against which conceptual frameworks that exist can be tested and to develop data-linked concepts.

The literature on change has tended to emphasize normative approaches rather than theoretical constructs. Giacquinta has immersed himself in this controversial material and out of his dissection emerge three distinctive models for change which are applicable to schools of education. The first model, the RD and D model, is the most familiar. Its major thrust is making the targets of change, that is, faculty members, aware of innovations out there in the environment and overcoming or avoiding their resistances to these new ideas in order to strengthen the implementation phase. The second model, named "organizational self-renewal," emphasizes improving the ways in which organizations generally operate instead of the search for adoptable, outside innovations. Successful change comes about as organizational processes such as communication, maintenance, problem-solving, decision-making, and task accomplishment are perfected and fine-tuned by the organization's members themselves, perhaps with the aid of an organizational development specialist. The third model, entitled "organizational drift," pictures change as the result of impersonal, non-deliberate change forces or conditions located in the environment of the organization. Organizational change is not planned; it occurs more from necessity—resisting change pressures when possible, trying to control the surrounding environment in order to allow the organization to operate as is, or changing internally in so far as it is necessary for survival. Giacquinta is convinced that people vary in their receptivity to innovations on the basis of how much risk there would be to their status perquisites, such as prestige, money, job security, and power, were a particular innovation to be introduced. He concludes his seminal essay with a recommendation that no one research approach on this topic be preferred to another in view of the uneven quantity and quality of existing change studies.

William Dill, who speaks from experience, states that the deanship is a leadership role with much heavier political and social than hierarchical or technical overtones. Using the Barnard-Simon model for analytic purposes, he sees the dean as a juggler of inducements and contributions so that contributions exceed inducements in order that the organization can survive and grow. According to Dill, deans are reaching the peak of their institutional influence. Caught between a bevy of central administrators and autonomous faculty members, the deanship is drifting into an ill-defined middle of the academic firmament. Size, prestige, and diversity of a particular school affects the leverage that a dean might have to play the part of an academic leader in Selznick's terminology. The author suggests that the difference between a strong and weak deanship is likely to be the amount of discretionary budgetary power which is granted within the university setting rather than the presence of leadership skills. In concluding his chapter, Dill refers to the haphazard process commonly employed in the selection of the deans and the lack of financial and organizational incentives for role occupants. He recommends that more administrative training be provided to deans in order that they may benefit from the new management technologies.

MISSING ELEMENTS

If the reader has come to the conclusion that this book presumes to describe how answers can be found to all of the problems of deans then the reader should be quickly disabused of the idea. The authors hold no such presumptuous concept. The book falls short on two counts. First, there is much in administration that very probably lies outside the scope of theory and research. The practice of administration is largely an art and reflects the personal style of an administrator and the environment in which that person functions. Much of this lies beyond theory and research as it is now known. Second, there are topics which either have been omitted or have been treated very lightly.

The ethical issues which arise in a dean's work have been avoided like the plague in the literature and in this book. There have been some general references to ethical problems in the literature of administration and educational administration which have been discussed by Miklos.[1] He suggests that systematic research is needed to provide a knowledge base for the "moral and ethical components and dimensions of administrative action" and raises many questions of a researchable nature. Particularly significant are questions such as

"What principles do administrators use to determine and justify different courses of action? On what types of value frameworks do they rely?"[2] Since ethical or moral behavior can be judged only by reference to standards and since in the modern western world consensus is lacking on what the standards are, the establishment or identification of standards being used would be most helpful. The moral and ethical questions faced by administrators are not abstract, ethereal issues, but rather practical down-to-earth situations. For instance, should a distinguished professor be allowed to pad his expense account? Does it matter if a supervisor of student teachers is reputed to be engaging in fraternization with the students in questionable surroundings? Should a dean exaggerate needs in the budget process under the assumption that one must ask for more than one needs in order to get what is really needed? Is it ever proper to hold back information in order to attain a desired end? Needless to say, there is little or no research on which a dean can draw. While a dean might rely on his own values in resolving the issues, this would result in conflict with others' values. At any rate, research on ethical and moral aspects of the deanship is not included in this volume.

The dean's social life is another major consideration. Being sociable with everyone may be feasible, but it is more difficult to have close friends on the job. Those members of the faculty and staff who seek social contacts could be perceived by others as special advisors with access to inside data. The inevitable small talk which accompanies mass social gatherings attended by deans may generate into pointed gossip, requests for help, and unwanted information. The assumed conviviality of such affairs presents opportunities for political strategies of a different sort than is customary in the non-social setting. Recognizing this pitfall, deans may feel isolated and emotionally separated from their co-workers if they desire to leave the impression of impartiality. Of course, to align oneself with cliques deliberately is to choose partiality as a strategy, and social contacts would be used to reinforce these bonds. Comparing how various deans structure their social life, and with what consequences, might well offer useful information. The dean in the process of administering is forced to develop a way of looking at the organization and the people who inhabit it. This perception is likely to take a positive or negative flavor over time. The dean may see the faculty primarily as colleagues, as friends, as enemies, or as a large inhuman abstraction. Whatever the preference, these attitudes are worth recording if we are to understand what deans are all about.

Although William Dill discusses certain aspects of the politics of the deanship there is much more that might be investigated. The political life of the dean might be considered in three categories: external to the university, within the university, and within the school. All deans have a political life of sorts: they contact congressmen or legislators to influence the passage or defeat of bills, they provide information to legislative staff people, and they negotiate with regents or state education department officials. It may be that deans in public institutions are more politically active than those in private institutions. Or it may be that deans in schools such as agriculture and medicine are more involved with politics than those in schools of social work, liberal arts, or education. Or it may be that the level of political activity is a function of the dean's personality rather than a locus of operation. What is clear is that little is known on this topic and that it is a fertile area for research.

It is a fact of life that within the university as well as within the school, the dean must function as a political animal. In attempting to gain needed resources the dean must "wheel and deal" in the sense that alliances must be formed, cases made, and bargains struck to gain what is needed. In each case there is a price to be paid. The research literature has little advice to offer on this crucial aspect of the dean's behavior. In fact, much more could very probably be learned by reading novels such as C. P. Snow's, *The Masters*.

The last topic to be discussed here is one rarely mentioned in the literature of administration and that is the symbolic aspects of the job. The dean is called upon, particularly in large universities, to open conferences; welcome groups to the campus; and host luncheons, dinners, and other social events. How significant is this function that is often called "showing the flag"? Does it make a difference, for instance, if when the dean opens a conference a jolly welcome is offered in contrast to a well-worded statement on the goals of the conference which shows thought and attention? Do the participants feel the conference to be a better one because of the latter approach, or would they appreciate more the jolly effort? How does each affect the way the participants feel about the university? On the other hand, in a day of apparently growing equalitarianism should the dean "show the flag"? Perhaps the time for such behavior has passed. At any rate, here is an unexamined aspect of the deanship.

Some wonder about the dean as a model for others' personal behavior. Does the way the dean behaves affect others, or is it ignored by the faculty, students, and administration? Years of observation by the authors lead them to believe that the dean's personal behavior is neither ignored nor slavishly emulated, but just what is ignored, what is emulated, what is objectionable is not all that clear.

Even though a volume has been devoted to a design for research on the deanship, some aspects have been neglected. Calling attention to these topics does not mean that they are more important than those in the main sections of the book, in fact, they may be less important. But it is hoped that someone will pick up the suggested research questions to further enrich the knowledge base of the deanship.

NOTES

1. E. Miklos, "Ethical Aspects of Administrative Action: Implications for Research and Preparation," *Administrator's Notebook*, Midwest Administration Center, University of Chicago (Vol. 26, No. 5, 1977-78).
2. *Ibid.*, p.4.

Index